DRUGS

My Curse

My Savior

To Robert,

From my soul to yours.

"Anything Is Possible"

Many Blessings,

Jenny

NSN 8/13/11

My Savior

BY: JEMAL OMAR GIBSON

GW PUBLISHERS
ATLANTA, GEORGIA, USA

Drugs: My Curse, My Savior.
Copyright © 2010 Jemal Gibson
First Edition

Printed in the United States of America
ISBN: 978-0-9830808-0-0

Photography by Bettina Dennis

Cover revision and inside typography:
Toth Agency, Inc.

GW PUBLISHERS
1415 Hwy. 85 N, Suite 310-333
Fayetteville, GA 30214
404-590-4565

This book is dedicated to:

My Dad, Mommy & Ant ~ may your legacy of love live forever…

To my daughters ~ may your light shine bright in the world…

To those who have been cursed by drugs in any way ~

may this offer you inspiration…

Table of Contents

Foreword
by Les Brown

They say life is 5% of what happens to you and 95% of how you react to it. With that being said, Jemal Gibson has certainly defined and mastered the art of life! It takes a courageous person to be true to himself during the defining moments in his life. Life presents those moments when we find ourselves up close and personal with the ugliness the world sometimes dishes out, those moments when we can't see past the tip of our nose due to all the "noise" and obstacles blocking our dreams and visions, and those moments when it would be so much easier to give up than to give back. Yes, those defining moments are all about living your truth.

How is it that Gibson faced those moments, yet did not become a casualty of failure like so many others do? I believe it has everything to do with attitude. Throughout his life's journey, he has demonstrated an attitude that is fearless, resilient, and willing to go a hundred extra miles. As I reflect on my own life, where much like Gibson, my challenges began at birth, there were many opportunities where I could have asked, "Why me?" I realized then, as I do now, that asking that question serves no real purpose in overcoming the situation. Instead, I used my energy to focus on the solution, not the problem. In "Drugs: My Curse, My Savior," it's obvious that Gibson used a positive vision of himself beyond his circumstances to bring about positive results—not just for his own benefit, but for many others as well.

In chapter after chapter, Gibson shows such resolve of character in sharing his past trials with his readers. Instead of covering up the weaknesses of those loved-ones enslaved to drug addictions with lies about their lives, he has found strength in the truth. I believe his confidence that we observe throughout these pages comes from that truth, as well. When all is said and done, who can argue with the fact that the successes Jemal Gibson has achieved at such a young age are a result of the power of living his truth? And, that truth has indeed set him free!

— Les Brown

World renowned and award-winning motivational speaker, Les Brown, is also a best selling author and speaking coach. He has several more books soon to join the ranks of "Live Your Dreams," "It's Not Over Until You Win" and "Up Thoughts for Down Times. To check out his events, or book him as a keynote, visit: www.lesbrown.com.

Introduction

There are several reasons it has taken me many years to write this book. First of all, writing my story was something my dad and I spoke about doing together. Unfortunately, that never panned out, so I decided to do it alone—a much more daunting task than I ever imagined. I found out that discouragement leads to procrastination. Secondly, it took so long because of my own second-guessing. I believe *everyone* has a story to tell; therefore, I kept asking myself, "What's so special about *my* story? Who would care to read it?" Those two questions made me hesitate. Thirdly, every time I got the urge to write out my thoughts, some sudden and devastating event would occur—either in my personal life or throughout the world—causing my writings to wither into a realm of insignificance.

Some of those worldly events included... Lives and buildings shattered by our nation's 9/11 tragedy. Our country at war, with thousands of American troops being killed or seriously injured. People in Iraq and Afghanistan hit daily by stray bombs. A tsunami in the Indian Ocean washing away 250,000 people—leaving loved ones to mourn, suffer, and struggle. Tragic flooding in New Orleans, claiming the lives and homes of thousands of people as the entire nation helped them heal. Human loss beyond imagination due to the earthquake in Haiti that tugged on the heartstrings of people around the world. Not to mention numerous guests on TV talk shows with life-altering, heart-wrenching, tear-jerking experiences that make most of us as viewers thankful for how comparatively easy things are for the rest of us.

I continued to question, "Who would desire to read my story in the midst of so many world-wide stories of despair and heroism?" So, I stopped writing from time to time and then started again. Stopped; started. Aside from the reasons already given, I came to grips with perhaps the real reason it took so long to write this book: my life was too painful to relive. Some things I couldn't even write about because the memories stung; other things seemed too embarrassing. As you will notice when reading through the chapters, my tears flow pretty freely at times. I'm not ashamed about that. Those are aching tears that you'll read about; yet the tears that flowed from me while writing about these experiences and people were nothing short of cleansing tears.

Because my life has taken many twists and turns, and my path has crossed so many others, you will find a lot of names used in my book. Most are the real names of individuals; some are not. In the cases of altered names, I did so to protect those individuals from embarrassment, disappointment, or any other negative emotion that could result from me sharing about my encounter with them. I apologize in advance to anyone who feels they were negatively impacted by this memoir. My intent was not to hurt but rather to share my life experiences and lessons. While most of my experiences were extremely positive, and I am forever grateful for the life-changing opportunities bestowed upon me, I changed the name of the pharmaceutical companies I worked for and the drugs I sold to prevent any perception of damage to the companies in any way. Had I used the real names, it probably would have been great publicity, but I'd rather play it safe, just in case something is misunderstood or misconstrued.

Also, some of my life experiences may overlap from chapter to chapter. For instance, in one chapter I may talk about an event that happened when I was fifteen-years-old. Then, the next chapter may share something occurring from ages fourteen through seventeen. Hopefully that does not distract from the message being relayed.

It is important for me to ensure you that every situation or incident in this book is authentic, either as it was told to me or as I recall the experiences firsthand.

When I handed my initial four hundred page raw manuscript to my editors, it was void of exaggeration or embellishment. I then granted them the creative license to help me paint a lively picture on every page so that you could virtually join me to see what I saw and feel what I felt. That was our goal, and one that I am proud to say was accomplished to my liking. With that said, I am willing to provide social security numbers, prison records, death certificates, newspaper articles, and names of those who have been changed to any credible source that challenges anything I've written.

Most of my life's events have involved drugs in some form or fashion. As my book title implies, those drugs have played a bad role and a good role in my forty-one year journey. Sometimes, however, even within those roles, the bad became good and the good became bad. Through it all, I trust that my life's story will provide hope, encouragement, and inspiration to the many people who feel they have been cursed by drugs or any other substance, spirit, or pressure. It is my hope and prayer that they seek and find the desire, discipline, and determination to overcome any obstacle.

To those of you who are concerned about our future generation and who take to heart the problem of the prevalence of drugs in our country, I say this: All children who are affected by drugs do not end up as drug addicts, nor as dysfunctional, defiant, in jail, or dead. Many of us work, attend church, and even live in neighborhoods with you or near you. May we all be reminded of the value of empathy, compassion, and the restraint from judgment. For those of us battling through this "curse," accepting our paths and our plights instead of hiding behind them could possibly lead to more people like me opening up and being an inspiration for so many others in need. Through one story at a time, we just may be able to reduce the devastating, debilitating, and destructive consequences that illegal substances cause to many of us as individuals and to all of us as a nation.

My Curse

"You say one word, we blow his head off!"

The intensity and anger with which the stranger spat those words out left no doubt about the truth behind them. I can only imagine the terrified thoughts racing through my dad's mind, frozen in that chair like the proverbial deer caught in headlights.

A second gunman stood across the room holding me, a mere six-month-old baby, firmly in one arm while pointing a gun to my head with his other hand. What kind of maniacs would do this to a harmless baby? That may have been one of the questions going through my dad's mind; however, it was certainly not the time to question their morality. He just needed to comply.

"Sam, hurry and buzz me up!" my mother yelled a third time. "What are you waiting on?"

There sat my dad, powerless, in our upstairs, one-bedroom St. Louis Avenue apartment on Chicago's West Side. My mother, at the street level entrance to that worn-down building, repeatedly pressed the door buzzer long and hard. She knew my dad was up there, but figured he was passed out on the sofa.

This time, however, circumstances were quite the contrary, and my dad remained very much alert and sober. I would think that's to be expected from any loving parent (even a drug addict parent) who is watching a gun placed at his child's head. The mouthy head gunman violently ransacked the place and confiscated all my parents' hidden drugs and drug money while the quiet one stood glaring at my dad, waiting for an excuse to pull the trigger on me.

That was the first story my dad ever shared with me concerning his life. It was a life defined by the miserable world of drugs—a world that still envelops me in certain ways to this very day.

"I never buzzed your mother up," Dad somberly continued. "Those robbers kept making threats about killing you and your mother if she came upstairs. I gave them everything they asked for—the drugs, the money, and anything else they could stash in their pockets. They tossed you down on the sofa and ran out of that apartment." He paused, shifting his eyes from his clasped hands to the ceiling in an unsuccessful attempt to choke back some uninvited tears.

"My crazy, uncontrollable hunger for drugs almost killed you—you, my only son. All I ever wanted was one child, one son." He paused again, this time closing his eyes momentarily as if to recollect the memories of my entrance into the world. "When you were born, I used to brag to everyone that one day you were going to be somebody. And then, I almost lost you before your life had a chance to really begin."

As he wiped away the trickle of tears, I could feel his pain. That was the first time I had ever seen my dad cry, and my heart truly went out to him. My eyes watered, too. Both of my parents muddled through very tumultuous lives as adults, thanks to the merciless entanglement of drug addiction. As a newly married couple, they reached the height of their turmoil in 1969, a time when heroin was devastating the black communities, especially in the housing projects of Chicago.

Thinking back to the 1970s made Dad angry. He was angered by what was, in his opinion, government's active role in the late 1960s and early 1970s when heroin was being ushered into low-income communities. As a result, it seemed only a matter of time before this horrible drug began destroying the black family nucleus. While he understood that no person or government should take the blame for his own decision to shoot up, my dad still hated the government for what many believed was its role in conspiracies against the black community.

All the historical precedents of attacks and oppression in our neighborhoods nationwide supported these beliefs.

I share my dad's point of view on the atrocities blacks have suffered at the hand of other citizens and sometimes our own government. From the brutal bombing and desecration of Tulsa, Oklahoma's Black Wall Street in 1921[1] to the inhumane, secret syphilis experiments on black men in Tuskegee from 1932 to 1972, and the horrors of the Vietnam War from 1959 to 1975 and its destructive aftermath. He lost all trust and hope in "the establishment." His sentiments were certainly shared among our community as a whole; this was especially true when the empowerment movements of the 1960s, led by various activist groups (such as the Black Panthers) emerged, and the powers-that-be viewed them as just another criminal element to be harshly dealt with. Government officials were too busy being fearful of the Panthers to ever recognize them as the "agents of change" that they were. Originally, they mainly wanted to better things for their community and their people, so many of whom were tired of hundreds of years of subjugation and abuse.

As I sat and listened, Dad went on to tell me about the first time he stopped using drugs. "One day, when you were about a year old, I was coming out of the bedroom where your mom and I would usually shoot up. That room was separated from the rest of the apartment by a hanging beaded curtain. You would often crawl up to the doorway and look at us through the beads while we were getting high. There were times when we couldn't even stop to move you, so you sat there playing and watching while we shot up our heroin. Sure, I felt embarrassed and ashamed, but that's the way it was." He paused and said, "Addiction itself overrides even the firmest moral compass."

Dad looked like his mind could have drifted, but he quickly got back on track with the story. "So anyway, one day I walked out of the room; you were sitting there with a string loosely wrapped around your arm poking it with a pencil. I couldn't believe what I saw! I fell to my knees, tears running down my face. I grabbed the pencil and string, picked you up, and just held you tightly. That's when it really hit me that I had let my horrid life affect my boy. I swore at that point that I would never do drugs again, and I went cold turkey." He closed his eyes momentarily and shook his head. Apparently, that image of me with the pencil and string struck him as profoundly this day as it had those many years ago.

"Unfortunately," he continued, "your mother had a tougher time trying to quit."

He spoke regrettably. "She tried to go cold turkey, but it was rough: the sweating, the sickness and everything else that goes along with it. It was really, really tough for her. I still sold drugs at that time. On occasion, I would leave and when I came home, your mother would be gone. She would later return, shuffling in, eyes half-closed, mumbling and saying, 'Sorry, Sam, I just couldn't take it.' Your mother was so beautiful. She had the prettiest skin, such big, brown, alluring eyes, a gorgeous smile, and a wonderful, big afro. I was so in love with her; I think I'll always be. I didn't know how she got the drugs, and I never asked."

Dad shared more, "One day there was a sting going down, and the police raided the whole apartment building. I heard them coming up the front and as I ran to the back, I realized they were coming up that way, too. The only choice I had was to jump out of the window, so I did. I then ran across the field, but they caught me. I went to jail. My life of pimping, drug dealing, using, and all that street stuff had finally caught up with me. That's when your mother sent you to live with your grandmother. You were just a little more than a year old."

So, that's how it all began. Just into my second year of life, not only was I almost violently killed, but my father sat in jail, and my mother's young life went astray. I then got carted off to the first of many places I could never really call "home." This was just the beginning of lots of disturbing and destructive disconnects all because of drugs.

As it's been shared with me, both my parents were using heroin prior to my mother getting pregnant but I've always wondered if my mother was "using" while pregnant with me. Getting that sort of information directly would not have been easy, since this is certainly not a piece of one's history anyone is proud or anxious to share. No one else in my family had any definitive information either; thus, it will remain a perplexing and unanswered question for me. The fact that I've faced several health challenges throughout my life that have puzzled doctors leads me to believe I entered this world a heroin baby. So, I suppose you could say that the curse of drugs haunted me from the moment my life began.

Project-ed Beginnings

My grandmother, Dorothy Holloway, lived in the near west side Chicago projects called the ABLA Homes. ABLA is an acronym for four different housing developments located on one site: Jane Addams Homes, Robert H. Brooks Homes (and the Brooks Extension), Loomis Courts, and Grace Abbott Apartments. Built in 1938, this was Chicago's first public housing project.[2] Just to give you an idea of its immensity, each development within ABLA consisted of various numbers of buildings, up to as many as thirty-two. Together, this one complex housed 12,000 residents in approximately fifty buildings! Unfortunately, there were many more projects close to this size throughout Chicago. We lived on Racine Avenue in one of the three high-rise buildings that made up Robert Brooks Extension, the newest addition to the complex. I say "we" because that's where I was carted off to live with my grandmother before I reached two years of age.

I remember Grandma's apartment number was 507. Her place consisted of two bedrooms, a kitchen, a living room and a bathroom. Funny how that apartment seemed so big to me back then. Oh, the joy of the forever innocent childhood vantage point, having no real perspective on big or small, rich or poor, good or bad, high or sober, loving care or neglected love!

Grandma's place housed lots of people at all times, mainly due to the fact that my uncles lived there from time to time: Uncle Bill, Uncle Eddie, and Uncle Dobie. One of my aunts, Aunt Betty, lived there, too. Without a doubt, she was the meanest of all my aunts. Unfortunately for me, she was also the one who watched me when Grandma went to work. My mother's other sisters, Aunt Bob and Aunt Hannah, popped in all the time to visit. All of them were born in a small Alabama town east of Birmingham; it was called Wedowee. As it was told to me, most of the black folks there were sharecroppers. Even my mother picked cotton as a young girl. My great-grandparents, Lee and Mary Wilson, were sharecroppers and had settled there to raise their family. I remember one of my great-aunts talking about her father who became blind as he got older. I later learned that his blindness was due to untreated syphilis. Though my family history is scant, I can't help but feel a connection to those black sharecroppers who were recruited for experimentation with this same disease originally in the 1920s at the Tuskegee Institute, which is only 78 miles from Wedowee. Virtually, no African-Americans could afford healthcare at that time, so the invitations for free examinations, along with food and transportation, were often readily accepted by people who were so poor.3 The history I do know is that my grandmother and all but one of her siblings moved to Chicago with hopes to find better jobs and a better life.

My mother's family was a pretty close-knit bunch, and they spent a lot of time together. As a result, I played with my cousins, Skeet and Charmaine, all the time. They were the children of Aunt Bob and her husband, Uncle Larry. We were practically raised as siblings except for the fact that they didn't live in the projects. The funny thing is, if you ask Skeet and Charmaine where they grew up, to this day they would emphatically say, "The projects." That's just how much they hung out there.

Skeet and I somehow stumbled into trouble all the time. At least it seemed that way by the daily "whuppin's" administered by Aunt Betty. Once, he and I scurried around the apartment in the middle of the night while everyone else slept, at least we thought everyone else was asleep. We played "ghost" by covering ourselves with sheets and running from room to room. All of a sudden, Aunt Betty popped up in our path as we darted past.

"Get y'all black asses back here!" she declared loudly and sternly. We instantly complied. "Now, stand right here, God damn it, and don't move!"

Scared as could be, we just knew we had a big one coming. Instead, Aunt Betty proceeded to the bathroom and then back to bed. She left us standing there at attention, and we dared not ask when we could move. It seemed we stood there for hours as we watched what we dubbed our own personal "Creature Feature Show." The stars of our show were the rats running to and fro. They were everywhere! A rat would run from the kitchen, around the corner, and down the hall to the bathroom. Then a mouse would follow. One or the other would run back to the kitchen while two new ones appeared. They represented our own live "Hot Wheels" track since we couldn't afford a real one.

So as not to be left out of the "show," the roaches scattered in full force as well—on the floor, on the walls, everywhere. We observed whole families of black ones, brown ones, and even albino ones! I often wondered why rats and mice never ate roaches. That certainly would have helped us out. Their bellies would be full without messing with *our* food. Our cracker and cereal boxes on the cabinet shelves always had rat teeth marks gnawed through them.

I don't know about Skeet, but that night I wished we had suffered one of Aunt Betty's whuppin's and were sent to bed rather than having to stand there any longer. Entertaining or not, those rodents proved very frightening to a young kid from this floor level perspective. Usually we watched them from our bed, which I realized that night was a lot easier to do.

Our bed offered a certain solace from those rats and roaches who stepped up their ownership role at night—with a lot of attitude, I might add. It was so much attitude, in fact, that going to the bathroom in the middle of the night challenged my cousins and me to have to make a decision. On those nights when we just couldn't hold our pee any longer, we contemplated two options: get up and go to the bathroom, or pee in the bed or closet. Our consequences: a rat bite or an Aunt Betty whuppin'. We generally chose the whuppin's.

As though the "wish fairy" heard me, one of the mice kept sniffing his way closer and closer to us until Skeet finally jumped and screamed loudly. On that note, Aunt Betty sprang up, and out of nowhere a belt slashed down on both of us in a ferocious fury. She beat and cussed us so badly you'd have thought we set the house on fire or something. We hopped around that floor, as if engaged in a tribal dance, while she continued to strike us, threatening, "Stop crying, 'fore I give you something to cry about!" I never understood why grownups said that, as if their crazy-ass beating was nothing to cry about! Finally, we got sent to bed.

The next morning, my underwear felt wet on one side. Immediate panic overcame me. The last thing I needed was another whuppin'. I turned Skeet over, and his underwear was soaked in the front. "Skeet, wake up. You peed on me!"

"No, I didn't; you peed on me!" he countered.

It obviously didn't matter who peed on whom because Aunt Betty unleashed another beating on us both. I never counted, but to say I endured hundreds of whuppin's in the five or six years that I lived there would be no exaggeration. They happened for all sorts of reasons: wiggling while getting my hair combed or braided, not taking a long enough nap, peeing on myself (for which I felt some slack should have been given because of the rats-in-the-bathroom issue), not eating all my food, playing too loudly, or any number of other things typical little boys do.

Unfortunately, there are no pictures of me until I'm 5 or 6 years-old; however, I am constantly reminded by my family that I was an extremely skinny little boy with a slightly protruding stomach, a 'big' outy for a navel, and huge brown eyes. I've joked with my family that I could have been a poster boy for Ethiopia, yet when I think about the images I've seen of starving children whose distended stomachs are due to protein deficiency, it might not be such a wild stretch. With all the whuppins I got, I'm surprised my frail, little body managed to handle all the punishment.

I know it sounds crazy, but in hindsight I truly appreciate Aunt Betty— a teenager at the time—having taken that primary responsibility for raising me, given that my grandmother worked all the time and my mother only came to visit me. Like any child, I wanted so much to be with my mother all the time, not just during visits. My cousins had their mothers, and I wanted mine.

My mother had three brothers and three sisters; most of them had different dads. In fact, she never knew who her real father was, and my dad's father walked away from his family when my dad was born. Therefore, I never knew my paternal or maternal grandfathers. They said Grandma Holloway was a little "loose" in her day. I don't like revealing that description since she is, after all, my grandmother. But, how can you argue with facts? Having seven children by five or six different men does make some kind of statement.

During one of my mother's visits, almost all six of those siblings were there at Grandma's. For the most part, everyone was in a pretty good mood. That is, until my mother said she was going to take me with her. That opened a tsunami of yelling and cursing. After a series of verbal exchanges, my mother grabbed me and said, "Let's go, Jemal!"

I was so happy. Finally, I was going to live with my mother! She pulled me toward the front door. Just as she did, my Grandma grabbed my other arm and while screaming at my mother, pulled me in the opposite direction. I can't remember exactly what she said, but it was something like, "You're not taking him anywhere!"

My mother pulled harder, and we inched closer to the door. Suddenly, all my aunts started pulling alongside my grandmother. Did anyone stop for a moment to think about me stuck in the middle of their tug of war? I began feeling like that Stretch Armstrong® action figure toy that had considerable stretching ability. The fact remained, though, I wasn't a toy; I was a real boy with real feelings, and some pretty empty feelings at that time, as I recall. The more my aunts began winning the tug of war, the more I wanted to be with my mother. "C'mon, Mommy," I thought to myself, "you gotta win. I wanna go with you!" That thought was abruptly interrupted by a loud scream.

"Aghhh!" My mother grunted forcefully amidst shattered glass everywhere and blood trickling down her forehead and face. Someone—Grandma or one of my aunts—had hit my mother on the head with a glass pop bottle! I couldn't believe it!

Thoughts raced faster through my mind. "Why are they doing this to me and Mommy? Why are they fighting over me? I want to be with her. Why couldn't they see that? Why was that so wrong? Why did they make my mommy bleed?"

I wished with all my might that my aunts would give in. Instead, my mother gave in. After being hit with the bottle, she let go of me, grabbed her bleeding head and ran out of the apartment.

"Mommy!"

I truly can't remember if I just thought it or actually blurted it out loud. Either way, in that single moment, I felt so loved, so wanted, and yet, so scared and disregarded. Although my arms ached slightly, that pain was only temporary compared to the stronger, more permanent pain felt inside of me.

Looking back to that day, I know my grandmother and aunts cared about me enough to do whatever they could to protect me. It sounds strange, but yes, they protected me from my own mother. I later learned she was still on drugs at that time, so I suppose going with her would not have been best for me. But, try convincing my young heart of that.

JEMAL OMAR GIBSON

Distant Dad

My dad got out of jail after doing almost two years. Upon his release, he visited me every now and then at my grandmother's house. Whether enjoying a visit from my mother or from my dad, the experience brought with it the same horrible ending: "Good-bye, Jemal. Be good, baby. See you next time."

Each good-bye formed a gaping, emotional hole—a pit deep inside of me. That painful hole was deepened and widened a little more with each visit. I wanted so badly to be taken away by one or both of them. But that never happened, no matter how hopeful I remained.

As a result, my emotions stayed in constant transitional mode. In other words, all the natural inclinations of a child to want his parents, need his parents, and love his parents were put on hold for me, over and over again. That hole quickly filled up with feelings like dejection and unhappiness. Fortunately though, with so many cousins to play with and adult relatives to rely on, dejection and sadness didn't stand a chance to shape me—well, not outwardly, anyway.

My inner workings were a totally different story. As a society, we've come to accept the fact that there are no quick fixes to the emotional trauma a child goes through when separated from his or her parent(s). It can take months, years, or who knows how long to heal the scars of abandonment; however, with life as it was in the ghetto, there appeared to be no *long* fixes either. No one in the projects goes to a psychiatrist or therapist to work through those kinds of things. No one asks, "How are you feeling? How are you coming along?" You just deal with it the best way you know how—yes, even as a small child.

Whether or not my grandma or aunts and uncles cared about my transitional emotional state, I'll never really know, although I'd like to believe they did. What I do know for sure is that nothing was ever done to try and correct it. Just suck it up kid. Get over it. Look around you—most kids in the projects don't have their daddies—you're no special case. So what, that your daddy hasn't seen you in months. So what, that your mamma chooses a needle shoved in her arm instead of you cradled in her arm. So what? If your parents really cared for you, they'd be here to take you away for good, not just to visit. That was the kind of rationale the world tried to feed me. But, I knew otherwise—even as a little kid, especially as a little kid. Deep in my heart, I knew my parents loved me and wanted me to be with them. Somehow though, that knowledge wasn't enough to keep me from chasing the love that was needed to fill that gaping hole. Neglect builds a deep, dark cave that is always looking for light.

This same chase for love and light would continue well into my adulthood. Along the way, it surfaced in every one of my relationships, whether with a family member, friend, or love interest. To this day, most people don't understand a part of me that is still affected by all of this. How can I expect them to understand it when I barely understand it myself? Yes, I overextend myself to everyone in my family, as though I have an obligation to do so. I suppose what looks like obligation on the outside is really that same love-chase still going on inside. It's sill looking for validation in order to fill that hole.

I remember one cold day when validation definitely didn't come. I awoke that day with a song in my head: "My daddy is coming to get me! My daddy is coming to get me!" I could hardly wait to see that orange station wagon (1972 AMC Hornet) drive up in our parking lot. I anxiously peered out the door for hours, which seemed like days to a five-year-old! Eventually, Aunt Betty had to go somewhere. She knew the drill regarding my dad and wasn't about to have her day's plans spoiled by waiting there with me for something she knew probably wouldn't happen. Since she was the only one home with me, she told me to stand outside in the breezeway and watch for my dad.

I remember being so cold out there that I wanted to go inside my neighbor's apartment to warm up. At the same time, I didn't want to miss seeing my dad. I clung onto the fence that lined the breezeway as the wind tried to knock me off my stance a of couple times. Back in the day, most project buildings sported fences that kept the porches enclosed and protected. The irony, of course, was that the fenced-in look resembled prison. Sadly, for many young men and women growing up in those projects, the fenced-in conditions mentally prepared them for their transition into their later home: the jail cell.

After awhile, my neighbor (nicknamed Baby) saw me shivering outside even though I was wearing a winter coat. She opened her door and invited me inside. Beaten down by the cold wind, I quickly accepted. Baby was a few years older than me in years as well as in street-sense. When we all played outside, she would let Skeet and me take turns putting our hands down the front of her panties. Skeet and I would giggle as we did it, our little members becoming aroused in the process. Lord knows we were not aware of any wrongdoing. It was just common behavior. Most of the kids in the community engaged in that and more. Looking back, of course, I'm saddened by that form of street play. Not just by my own participation in it, but I'm also disheartened thinking of the stolen innocence of so many young children.

While perched on my knees on the couch in Baby's house, I kept a clear view of the parking lot. I inspected every car that pulled into the lot, thinking each time, "The next one will be him; he has to be coming!" Finally, after numerous false alarms, he made it! It was definitely his station wagon pulling into a spot. I hopped off that couch still clad in my coat, ran to the door, flung it open and stepped out onto the fifth floor breezeway with a big smile on my face. But no dad. The car was still there; he wasn't. Where could he have gone that fast? "Surely, he must be coming upstairs," I thought. So, I waited and waited, once again in the cold winter air.

Once it was obvious that he wasn't coming up the stairs, I sadly went back into Baby's apartment to wait at the window. After what again seemed like hours, I spotted him by his car. Here we go again. I hopped off that couch, ran to the door, stepped outside, and this time began yelling down at him as he got in the car. I figured he'd be gone by the time I made it down the flights of stairs so my strategy was to yell for him. "Daddy! Daddy!" The only problem was my squeaky little voice couldn't be heard that far down and across the front courtyard, especially with the noise from Racine Avenue's traffic.

He drove away without ever hearing me. He drove away without even looking up toward Grandma's apartment, let alone coming up there to visit me. I held tightly onto that fence. Through a few big tears, I watched his car drive out of the parking lot and turn down the street. Once it was out of my view, the floodgates of tears opened, and I cried and cried.

Kids are ever so forgiving—sometimes to a fault. I remember after crying, I became angry, but only for a short time that day. My anger was quickly replaced with gratitude as I delighted at the opportunity to just see my dad, even if it was only from a distance.

Project-ed Behavior

Skeet and I had a blast playing in the projects throughout my early childhood. Many times, our other same-aged cousins—Kim, Darnell, and Elonda—would visit and play, as well. Lots of children hung out in those courtyard areas day and night, especially in the summer months. There were no video games (and, in some households, no TV) to keep us inside.

Nestled in that sixteen-story building (with approximately twenty apartment units on each floor), were many other families just like mine. In other words, crowded! Some units easily housed three generations of people. At any given time, you'd find parents, kids, grandkids, aunts, uncles, grandparents, friends, plus whoever was dating any of the above, all coming and going. You never knew who really lived there from one day to the next. Thinking back, I don't know how we coexisted in such close quarters. Like most children, though, we had fun and remained oblivious to the crowded conditions, especially when no different conditions presented themselves for comparison.

Eating government cheese, bread, and peanut butter, and using water in our cereal was the norm. I hated the powdered milk Grandma tried to pass off as the real deal, so my cereal actually tasted better with plain water. Who invented that stuff, anyway? I haven't checked lately, but certainly they couldn't still be giving it away, could they?

When Skeet and I were about four or five-years-old, we had girlfriends— the twins from our building. Boy, were they cute! We played together all the time, mostly singing songs like "Three Bind Mice," while skipping down the porches on different floors. Having so many floors at our disposal made Hide and Seek our all-time favorite game. To pick who was "it," we counted feet while chanting, "Engine, engine number nine, rolling down Chicago line. If the train should jump the track, you won't get your money back..."

It really never mattered who won Hide and Seek, or any of the games, for that matter, because just *playing* the games always led to "catching" a girl. When we caught a girl, we kissed that girl. That action ultimately led to "getting" a girl. Getting a girl meant "juicing" a girl. I can tell you that, unfortunately, juicing in this case had nothing to do with healthy drinks!

Among the kids in the projects, "juicing" was slang for having sex. Usually though, among the much younger kids, it consisted of merely rubbing genitals. You may be wondering, "How did you even know what to do at just four or five-years-old?" That was easy. Remember, Grandma's crowded apartment only had two bedrooms. My bed was a little couch in Aunt Betty's bedroom. At night, Aunt Betty's boyfriend, Junior, would come over, and I'd see them doing it all the time when they thought I was asleep. One time, while curled up on the couch, I awoke in time to see Aunt Betty lying on her bed wearing only a towel around her waist. As she removed the towel, Junior got on top of her, and they rocked and moaned.

I suppose other juicing lessons presented themselves to me, as well, but I just happen to remember the ones by Aunt Betty the most. Being the good student that I was, repeating those lessons came quite easily. While playing "hide and go get it" with the twins, I would catch one of them in the project hallway. Once the coast was clear, we'd pull down our pants, place body to body and pump back and forth, making the moaning noises, of course.

No one ever told me *not* to do it. No one ever taught me about restraining and abstaining from sex. So, there we were—adults, teenagers and children—all enjoying sex, with no real regard for or understanding of its full context or prerequisites in our lives. We lived our lives as one big experimental, juicing, melting pot.

Lack of space for adults to do adult activities and children to do children's activities remains to this day one of the many negative consequences of this subculture created by such condensed living arrangements. The English Encarta Dictionary defines subculture as "an identifiably separate social group within a larger culture, especially one regarded as existing outside mainstream society."4 Could that have been part of the intention behind public housing? To purposely separate us from society's mainstream? To create conditions designed to perpetuate identifiably negative influences that would be carried down from generation to generation?

I have heard about an experiment conducted using rats in simulated project housing environments. Scientists created a caged model consisting of six rows and six columns and placed rats in them. Over a period of time, they observed high degrees of violence, sexual aggression, and ultimately insane behaviors. If that is really true, then it's puzzling why the powers-that-be thought the concept of public housing would be a good thing. Why was it allowed to continue in that form for so many years?

Now, I know public housing is not unique to the United States. Countries all around the world share this concept as well: Canada, France, Singapore, South Wales, China, New Zealand and the list goes on. However, not being knowledgeable of statistics from those places, I can only speak regarding the evidence shown here. A 2002 study by the Justice Department's Bureau of Justice Statistics (BJS) shows us that in the U.S. one out of every one hundred and forty-two adults is in prison.5 But when you break down that population further, you find that the black male is 8.5 times more likely to be there than the white male.6 That is an astoundingly ugly reality, but it doesn't stop there. In 1990, federal drug sentencing was 49% higher among that black population even though more whites than blacks were initially arrested on drug charges.7

Of course, there are many different factors to consider; however, the bottom line is our judicial system unapologetically works against the low income and black communities. So, when looking for a cause, I believe fingers can point directly back to this subculture where young people are trapped in dire situations created by the socioeconomics of public housing. Look at all the major U.S. cities like Chicago, Atlanta, New York, and Washington, D.C. and you'll see cookie-cutter results.

In other words, within those various cities, it doesn't matter whether it is cold climate or warm climate, southern state or northern state, or even the financial wellness of a particular state. The common thread among those cities' housing projects is an extreme amount of crime, violence, murders, teen and unwed adult pregnancies, drug and alcohol abuse, prostitution, single parenting, high unemployment, health issues and financial woes. All those things tie back to one thing: a poverty mentality in public housing. It's not just a lack of finances that causes the problem; no, it goes deeper than that. The culprit is the whole mental state of a person. The mental state, mind you, which is developed from birth in the confines of the projects.

The good news is that a few folks *do* manage to stay clean and stay out of trouble in the midst of those adverse conditions. As a result, they escape and enjoy all the benefits and privileges mainstream America takes for granted— and sometimes even more than the average person. We hear the rags-to-riches stories all the time. Are those people just plain lucky? Is it pure destiny? Is it hard work? Maybe it's a combination of all of these elements.

The reality from the standpoint of a child from the projects is that I experienced the same madness as the adults. Statistics show that typically adults can't overcome those negative conditions. If *they* can't handle them, how could they expect *me*, as a child, to handle them? Or did they?

Stolen Innocence

Skeet and I were often sent upstairs to "the candy store" on the seventh floor of our project building. The resident there, Ms. B, sold just about anything you could want or need in a pinch—bread, cereal, cornstarch, soda pop and all kinds of candies and snacks. No one ever questioned where she got all her goods. I'm pretty sure their origin was simply "understood." Bottom line is, in a neighborhood like that, any time you could get what you needed without having to leave the building, you had a good thing going, so you didn't rock the boat. Today, however, I'm sure that store wouldn't stand a chance against some neighborhood watch whistleblower.

One particular day, Grandma told Skeet and me to buy her some Orange Crush. As usual, we eyeballed all the candy Ms. B had. There were Squirrel Nut Zippers (Squirrels), Chick-O-Stick, Now and Later, Big Bol bubble gum, a variety of penny cookies, and much more. She had everything! After salivating over it all, we paid Ms. B for the Orange Crush. I grabbed the six-pack from her hand, and Skeet and I headed downstairs.

As we approached the sixth floor, two teenage boys jumped out of nowhere yelling, "Give us yo' money!" One boy was kind of chubby and the other one just plain ugly.

I froze right in my tracks. Didn't move; couldn't move. Didn't say a word; couldn't say a word. Same for Skeet. In our four to five years of hanging around those hallways, that had never happened to us before. Of course, the odds weren't in our favor, given the conditions, so it was bound to happen sooner or later. Still, it caught us off guard.

"Give us yo' money 'fo we kick yo' ass!" they repeated.

Suddenly, I snapped back into reality, just as tears welled up in my eyes. Through it all, I tried my best to look strong and act tough. Not only did I fear a beating from those teenagers standing in front of us, but I feared, even more so, the wrath of Grandma if we didn't bring back her change. Messing with her money warranted a sure beat-down in her book.

I finally spoke up in my strongest yet squeakiest voice possible, "We don't have any more."

The chubby boy, who was apparently the leader, spoke harshly to the ugly one, "Check their pockets! Check their socks!"

They quickly patted our pockets, checking the front and the back of both of our pants. They pulled down our socks. We felt trapped in that predicament forever, and of all times for there to be no one in the hallways.

Ole' Chubs grew angrier and continued his screaming, "I know ya'll got money!" He looked at my hands, one balled in a fist, the other gripping the six pack of pop.

"Let me see your hands," he snapped.

"I don't have anything," I sheepishly replied, with "lie" written all over my face.

He pried open my hand just enough to see the coins tightly clutched in my sweaty palm that was holding the pop. He then yanked open my fingers which made me almost drop the pop bottles. It definitely would have been tragic to walk into Grandma's house with no money *and* no goods. Soon, I began crying hard. I looked over at Skeet, and he cried harder. So much for us looking strong and acting tough.

Once they gotten what they wanted, the boys ran down the stairs and disappeared from our sight. Skeet and I held hands as we walked slowly down to Grandma's. By the time we got to her door, the crying ceased, and we didn't utter a word.

Grandma opened the screen door for us, and our long faces and a few leftover tears immediately revealed our misfortune. "What's wrong?" she quickly inquired.

We spoke in whiney unison, "Someone just took yo' money."

"What?!" Her loud voice caused us both to jump back.

I kept wondering what else I could've done to keep Grandma's hard-earned money. A dozen or so "would've, could've, should've" scenarios floated through my mind. Imagine my deluge of emotions; I was terrified by the violation of robbery, remorseful over what happened, fearful of the anticipated punishment, and saddened over being punished for something totally out of my control.

"What happened?" my older cousin, Reggie, chimed in, as he ran to where we stood.

"Someone took Grandma's money on the stairs." I stated just the facts, leaving out the crying and scared part.

"Who?" yelled our other cousin, Samuel, who had overheard from the kitchen and joined the crowd now formed at the front door.

Skeet and I shrugged our shoulders. Because of my fear, I honestly forgot what they looked like, except that one was chubby, and one was ugly. I offered that description to my cousins.

"Come on, let's find them!" Samuel said to Reggie, as they both took off running out the door.

I handed my grandmother her pop and inched by her. Fortunately, I did not get punished for mishandling Grandma's money. Sadly, though, I don't remember being consoled, held, or hugged, either, after such a traumatic experience. It's not that Grandma didn't love us, but perhaps she thought it was no big deal, having grown immune to those types of experiences. As I write about that robbery today, even *I* don't think it seemed all that bad; after all, they spared us a beating. Nonetheless, from a little child's perspective, it *was* a big deal! Money wasn't the only commodity taken that day. A piece of Skeet's and my innocence was stolen which, unlike money, can never be replaced.

As I look back at that event and the many others to follow, it saddens me to think about what must have been stolen from those robbers psychologically for them to act out in that fashion at such an early age. More than likely, after robbing fifty cents from little five-year-olds, they graduated to armed robbery or maybe even worse crimes.

I pray that Chubby and Ugly had an intervention that somehow turned their lives around. If so, they could be sitting on this very same airplane with me as I write this memoir. If not, they could be in a jail cell next to one of my cousins, Reggie or Samuel. Remember, Reggie and Samuel were the two who went looking for our offenders that day. Yes, they were my heroes—at least that day, anyway. A third scenario for those young robbers is, perhaps, they are dead.

From 1978 to 1987, homicide was the leading cause of death among African-American males aged fifteen to twenty-four and occurred at an alarming rate of seventy-three percent.[8] No doubt most of that was done at the hands of their fellow "brothers." Being in that age group during that time, my robbers could have easily become part of those statistics.

A New Union and a Reunion

One day, something very strange, but good, happened. My grandmother and I went to a lady's house on the other side of town. The lady greeted us at the door and introduced herself to me as Tee, my grandmother's sister. I could barely pay attention to her introduction because my eyes were too busy taking in the grand surroundings. In my brief, but full, six years of life, I had never seen anything more beautiful, except on TV, of course.

Several very cool looking cars were parked outside of Tee's townhouse in the serene, dignified neighborhood. Everything inside seemed remarkable as well. There was real wood-crafted furniture, lots of pictures and paintings on the walls, and it was very clean with a fresh scent about it. It looked so different from my grandma's house in the projects. They represented two totally separate worlds.

I observed toys galore—two drum sets, some bikes and toy cars—a kid's wildest dream come true. "But what kid did this all belong to?" I wondered.

Just then, my mother came out of the kitchen. "Mommy!" I ran and jumped into her arms. Everything I'd seen so far in that home paled in comparison to seeing my mother. What a surprise! Seeing her made me so happy. I don't recall how long it had been since our last visit, but it seemed like a very long time—long enough that I almost thought I'd never see her again.

As I hugged my mother, a boy came downstairs and said, "Hi," in a very friendly manner. Immediately, I envied him as I thought about how lucky he was to be the owner of so many cool toys. I'm not sure who did the introduction, but I do remember them saying, "This is your brother, Anthony, but everyone calls him 'Ant'."

"What?" I thought, "A brother? I don't have a brother, other than Skeet. He's the only one I call brother. I've never seen this guy in my life." Even as I thought all of that, I couldn't shake a strange sense of familiarity when I looked at Ant.

As it turned out, Ant really was my brother. I later learned we shared the same mother, but he had a different father, Donald Walker. Apparently, Ant lived with our mother and my dad until I was just a few months old. From there, he moved in with Tee.

The whole thing, frankly, had me confused and somewhat jealous. "If this *is* my brother, why does he have all of these toys and his own room, and I basically have nothing, not even my own bed? Why aren't we living together like brothers do?" After I quieted all those thoughts, I immediately liked Ant and was grateful that he came into my life when he did.

That new union with my new brother was one of the coolest things ever to happen to me. I looked forward to getting to know him, although I wasn't sure how that would happen since we might as well have lived on two totally different planets. But just when I thought meeting Ant was the coolest thing, something else happened to actually top that. My mother came to get me!

Yes, my mother and I were together again, for good. It was the day that I had waited for all my life, the moment that I dreamed of and cried out for. It finally arrived and, truthfully, I can't even remember any details of the event! Perhaps the elation of the whole thing caused my brain to go haywire for those moments or hours or days.

In any case, I do remember that shortly thereafter, we were living in Peoria, Illinois as I celebrated my seventh birthday. I enjoyed the little party in my honor; I enjoyed the recognition of my special day, but most importantly, I enjoyed living with my mother. She was the best birthday present I could ever receive.

My brother, Ant, soon came to live with us, which was icing on the cake. That almost qualified us as a whole family, like what Charmaine and Skeet had. Having my very own brother meant the world to me at that age. I remember following Ant everywhere, that is, until he got tired of me hanging around. Like older siblings tend to do, he ditched me for his buddies at every opportunity he could.

During that summer, Ant got his wish. I was out of his hair most of the time because I began going to work every day with my mother. As a single mom, she couldn't afford a babysitter for both of us. It was great that she had the type of job where she could take me along.

In Peoria, my mother worked at a drug rehabilitation center called Stonehedge where she was once a patient herself. The facility was filled with some very nice people. My mother always introduced them to me as "Aunt" or "Uncle" So-and-So. In a short period of time, I became nephew to a whole slew of recovering addicts. Those aunts and uncles took daily doses of Methadone to help them transition away from the illegal drugs. I remember it so vividly, watching them all line up in a single file line like kids at school; one after another stepped up to a door with only the top half opened, got their cup, drank the methadone while standing there, and then returned the cup. That was the routine every day and sometimes a couple times a day.

In daily group sessions, I watched people cry and lament over their lives, lives damaged and, in some cases, totally obliterated as a result of their involvement with illegal drugs. "I starting drinking; then I started smoking marijuana. When I needed something stronger, I started doing drugs. Then I lost everything in my life." It was both peculiar and sad how those words reappeared like a broken record out of the mouth of one recovering addict after another, sitting in that mournful circle.

Some shared details about their loss. Some remained reserved, refusing to open up until they had a chance to size up the group. Most had a long way to go to learn to trust people, to trust life. Sometimes as part of their session, they would take turns standing on chairs blind-folded, then falling backwards as those standing behind them would catch them. As part of their journey to trusting again, they had to believe that these comrades, who were also somewhat strangers to one another, would catch them before they hit the floor. I felt moved by it all but, of course, oblivious to the privilege of being vicariously exposed to that self-empowering treatment. I knew then, at that very young age, that I never wanted to use drugs.

I always enjoyed the sessions when they sang. Their favorite song was "You've Got a Friend," written by Carole King in 1971 and taken to the top of the music charts that same year by singer-songwriter-guitarist, James Taylor. I can still hear them singing that in the circle,

"You just call out my name,

And you know wherever I am,

I'll come running, to see you again.

Winter, spring, summer, or fall,

All you have to do is call,

And I'll be there, yeah, yeah, yeah.

You've got a friend."

That magical song united and encouraged them, and perhaps did so for recovering drug addicts all over the world, in quite an amazing way. No doubt, it had a lot to do with the fact that James Taylor himself battled heroin use in the years just prior to making that song famous. I believe all music is spiritual, meaning that it contains energy that exists in a different dimension. That song, infused with such passion by Taylor and the overcoming of his own difficulties, served to minister to so many people. Many were people who perhaps never even knew who James Taylor was, let alone that he had similarly suffered.

Whether my "aunts" and "uncles" were singing or speaking, tears were the norm at every meeting. Thank goodness that all of their tears were not sad ones. Some tears accompanied joyful testimonies shared by those who came to the session in a great mood. Perhaps, they were finally getting a grip on a new life. Or perhaps, the methadone was finally taking effect. In either case, the sad people and the happy people all made promises to never do it again, and they really seemed sincere when they said it. I assume my mother and father made those same promises.

Stealing Innocence

One day during the summer of my eighth year, Cousin Samuel visited us in Peoria from Chicago. He and Ant were both about thirteen-years-old, and were rather fond of each other. Talk about two boys who stayed in trouble, especially while hanging together! That particular day started out hot, and the temperature seemed to escalate by the hour. The neighborhood swimming pool served as the only logical respite on days like that, so that's where we headed. We arrived there only to discover that every other person in the area opted for that same relief. In spite of the crowded conditions, we enjoyed a fun afternoon, that is, until we returned to the locker room to dress for our mile-long trek back home.

Someone had stolen all our money right out of our lockers. The worst part was that it took so much effort to "earn" that money in the first place. We earned it by looking and acting pitiful around the house until my mother either felt sorry for us or grew tired of us in her face and forked over fifty cents each, enough to pay to get in the pool and buy candy afterwards. That strategy worked better than begging. On a real good day, we could sweet-talk seventy-five cents out of her. Either way, we really depended on that little bit of change to supply our post-swimming hunger, and suddenly we had none.

"I can't believe someone would steal our money!" My voice quivered, as I fought back tears. Ant and Samuel, on the other hand, were far from tears. They looked downright angry. We left the pool that day in morose silence with growling stomachs and a simmering anger.

I picked up a stick as we walked. Later, I dragged it across the railing of a bridge we had to cross. Halfway across the bridge, my stick's rhythmic output was interrupted by Samuel's arm stuck out in front of me like a railroad gate, causing me to jerk back. I hadn't noticed the little white boy approaching us in the distance, since I had fixed my eyes on the highway below us and was daydreaming while watching the lines down the middle.

As though my brother read Samuel's mind, he nodded in agreement almost before Samuel opened his mouth to declare, "Let's take his money."

I didn't really think they meant it until the little boy got right in front of us and, sure enough, Ant demanded, "Give me your money!"

"I don't have any," the little boy replied.

Next, Samuel made the request expecting to draw a different response. At the same time, Ant reached toward me, shoved me forward a bit and ordered, "Hit him, Jemal."

"Hit him? Why would I do that?" I thought to myself. I stood frozen. I had the stick in my hand, so hitting him would've been quite easy. I looked at Ant and Samuel.

They both glared at me and commanded, "Hit him, Jemal! Hit him!"

I stared at the boy, who we had cornered by this time, and he looked beyond scared. He cried as his only defense against us three offenders who were all bigger than him *and* black (which always added an extra element of fear considering the mindset we dealt with in that low-income part of Peoria back in the 1970s). I felt like crying, too, faced with such a huge dilemma for an eight-year-old.

Ant and Samuel had a soft heart that day for the little boy and for me. They stopped forcing me to hit him, and they did not hit him either, nor did they hit me, which I really expected to happen once I chickened out on them. Instead, they quickly rummaged through the boy's pockets, only finding a single dime. They released their prey with a shove to his back, and we continued our walk home.

I felt pity toward the little boy and anger toward Ant and Samuel. All that effort and emotional work-up over a dime? I knew Ant and Samuel sought retribution and retaliation on the heels of our own money being stolen; however, I refused to accept harming an innocent party as consolation. Three of us ganging up on that one boy made me think back to the first time Skeet and I were robbed in our hallway in the projects in Chicago. That is a terrible thing to experience at any age, under any circumstance.

We had traveled only a couple more blocks when a police car stopped beside us, and an officer stepped out of the car. He asked us some questions to which I let Ant and Samuel provide all the answers. I guess the answers they gave weren't good ones, since that officer put us in his car and took us the police station. It was my first time in a squad car. As I sat there scared out of my mind, I thought that I was simply too young to be there.

Apparently, our released victim had run and told someone about his dime being stolen. The police looked like they wanted to lock us up in a cell to teach us a lesson; instead, they directed us to a bench in the hallway, called my mother, and told us to sit there until she came for us.

As though it wasn't torture enough being in that predicament, we now had to suffer the anxiety of waiting for a whuppin'. When my mother finally marched through the door, I knew that look on her face. It was the "no words needed" look that a black Mama masters all too well. It clearly announced, "Wait 'til I get yo' little black asses home!"

For some reason, I don't recall getting a whuppin', but when reminiscing about that event years later, Ant and Samuel remembered the whuppin's. Did it teach them a lesson? Did they become repentant, the way punishment should make a child feel? I can't speak for them but, punishment or no punishment, that episode touched me to the core of my being." Having now been both the victim and a perpetrator of robbery, it felt horrible. Period. It didn't matter that only a dime was involved. It was the principle of it.

It's amazing to think how the lives of several people experiencing the same incident can be shaped by that event in totally different ways. Those ways, or directions, then place a person on a roadmap of life that often has no U-turns. "For as a man thinketh, so he is," the scripture goes. But, I can affirm that, "For as a *child* thinketh, so will he be."

What a Real Family Feels Like

Later that year, my mother remarried. My mother and father had been divorced for many years by that time. I believe their marriage began suffering a slow and painful death from the moment Dad went cold turkey from drugs and Mom didn't. He tried to assist her in overcoming her addiction, but proved unsuccessful. Although he kept trying, he knew all too well that she had to first have the desire to change. The drug addiction, along with Dad's two-year jail time, cooked up a great recipe for a failed marriage.

Mom was clean from drugs when she married Elvin Farmer. He was a decent guy who made a decent living working in the railroad industry. His company, The Burlington Northern Railroad Company, was newly formed at the time in an industry emerging from a decade of struggles using plenty of mergers as its revival plan. The government had even stepped in with subsidized funding for the rail lines, and later deregulation made operations profitable once again. I'm not sure how secure Elvin's work position remained through all that; I was too young to know or care. However, I wasn't too young to know that he made life fairly comfortable for us, for a change.

In spite of everything good about him, Elvin joined our family as "the enemy." First of all, in my little eight-year-old mind, his entrance on the scene meant I would never see my real dad again. Secondly, I had grown accustomed to taking orders from my mother only. That set-up worked just fine for me; no two-parent process to work through every time I wanted something (its flip side, however, was that with only one parent, my mother usually couldn't afford to buy the things I wanted). So Elvin, as the new man of the household, would naturally expect me to take orders from him. That would throw everything off. After all, would he first find out what *our* rules were? Or would he insist on enforcing *his* rules only?

Lastly and most importantly, I revolted because no one asked my opinion before they made their decision to get married. No one asked me whether I wanted a new daddy! We had finally started to feel like a real family—Ant, Mom and me—why couldn't it stay just like that?

I cried when my mother broke the news to me and Ant about her upcoming union. When she asked why I was crying, I whimpered and whined through all my concerns, articulating them as best as an eight-year-old could. My mother comforted me and, more importantly, assured me that her getting married did not cancel out my ability to be with my real dad again. It simply meant I would have two fathers.

After the dust of the new marriage settled, I gave Elvin the benefit of doubt as a father. He didn't let me down. He lovingly took care of us, financially and otherwise. Soon, all my previous notions regarding what constituted a real family, gave way to what actually *was* a real family for me: a father, a mother, and a sibling, all under the same roof! Now, that felt good—like a real family should. I even started calling Elvin, "Dad." My real father didn't appreciate that one bit.

Our new real family took family portraits, went on family trips, and for the first time that I could ever remember, purchased a Christmas tree for the holidays. That alone measured high in my book! Every Christmas thereafter, we celebrated as a family, complete with decorations, big meals, and gifts. The number and quality of gifts surpassed anything I'd ever received before.

To this day, though, there are two things Elvin gave me that I cherish more than any of all those many Christmas gifts. One was the nickname that he dubbed me with: Mal (pronounced mall). People still call me that name today. The second thing was the most beautiful baby sister, Eboni, whom I call Ebi. Words cannot express how much I loved her from the moment they brought her home. As the big brother, I immediately felt obligated to protect her and guide her. I taught her how to count, how to say her ABC's, and everything I thought she needed to know. In fact, her first spoken word was—you guessed it—Mal.

About three years after Ebi's birth, the unthinkable happened—my mother left Elvin. As a child, I didn't know any details about the breakup. Later, however, I learned that he had been an addict prior to marrying my mother. Somewhere along the line, they both relapsed. Elvin lost his job, and things started to spiral downward. My mother then caught him having an affair with a white woman, and he was history.

After Mom and Elvin's divorce, we moved from a nice complex called University Apartments to a new housing project called Village Green, on the south end of Peoria. The family life I had come to love and enjoy no longer existed. In its place stood the same daily struggles that plagued us before. Only this time, there was an additional child and no job for my mother. She no longer worked at Stonehedge; therefore, welfare became the inevitable substitution. We once again said hello to government food: cheese, bologna, cereal, staples, and other necessary handouts. It reminded me of life at Grandma's, and the powdered milk was back in our cupboards!

My mother forked over food stamps to Ant and me like other kids got allowances. Food stamps spent like real money, so I didn't care. It allowed my favorites to keep coming: Hostess apple pies, Snickers candy bars, and Jolly Ranchers—nothing nutritious, but pacifying all the same. My life with a dad in the house had been pacifying and comforting, as well, but those few good years of normalcy ended with the same old curse—drugs.

First Time Fishing

My brother, Ant, was a very likeable person, and he played football in school, a winning combination for easily making new friends. Some of his close buddies included Todd Wright, Lester King, James King, and James Mays. He also stayed connected with his old friends: Boobie, Lil Johnnie, Melvin, and Paul. As a very perceptive young kid back then, most of Ant's friends left lasting impressions on me—good and bad—which is why I remember so many of their names to this day. I observed what they did and said every time they came around. One such occasion was when I went fishing for the very first time.

That particularly beautiful summer day, I got to hang out with my brother and his friends. That alone was perfect, but then they told me they were going fishing. The fishing excursion bumped the day up from perfect to paradise. At ten years of age, I had never been fishing before, but always wanted to try it out.

The entourage included two brothers, Kevin and Kendall, and a boy named Anthony Farmer. I found it quite amusing that the boy shared my brother's first name and my mother's new married last name, though he wasn't related to my mother's husband, Elvin. Kevin and Ant were both fourteen-years-old; Kendall and Anthony were sixteen. We piled into Kendall's car and drove quite a distance to their favorite fishing spot. I'm sure they were annoyed by my repeated inquiry, "Are we there yet? Are we there yet?"

Finally, we pulled over to the side of a much smaller road. The boys had already begun talking trash about who would catch the biggest fish and who would catch the most fish. Forget being the first or having the most, I just wanted to catch something and make my brother proud of me.

Everyone grabbed their poles out of the trunk, along with a tackle box full of fishing accessories and headed toward an open field. That's when it dawned on me that I didn't even have a pole. What was I thinking? How could I participate with no fishing pole?

Just then, my brother noticed my puzzled look and said, "I got you covered, li'l bro," as he handed me an extra pole from the trunk. My brother, my hero! A mile-wide smile grew across my face, and it stayed there as we ran to catch up with the other guys.

We trudged through a huge cornfield and finally crossed over into a secluded, woodsy area, hidden from the world. I thought that certainly water had to appear somewhere soon. Just then, the ground suddenly dropped off, and lo and behold, a few yards below us there was a small, serene pond. It was a pretty steep drop to that water, and it was obvious that it would take some skill getting down without tumbling forward. The guys knew to continue a little farther along the edge where an area that was not so steep allowed easier access to the pond.

Once we all made it to the water, we prepared our poles. Kendall opened his container of worms, and everybody reached in to grab one—everyone, that is, except me. They were nasty, squirmy little creatures all covered in slime and dirt.

Ant took one worm out and pointed it at me. "This is how you put a worm on a hook. Ya' better learn fast, 'cuz I ain't gonna be doing this for you all day."

He then took my rod and showed me how to cast, first holding down the button, and then releasing it as I threw it over my shoulder. It looked pretty simple; operative word is "looked." There was nothing simple about it for me. That point of release challenged me, but I kept at it. After throwing it only a few feet out, getting it stuck on someone else's line, getting it stuck on my own shirt, and nearly making my brother's hat my first catch, I finally cast my line successfully in the water. Wow, I was fishing! Well, at least that's what *they* called it. *I*, on the other hand, called it waiting, and it seems like that's all I did.

After about twenty minutes or so, one of the guys yelled, "I got one!" He then reeled his fish in. As we envied his catch, we all cast our lines toward that same spot as if a school of fish was just hanging around in the same area where their buddy had been snatched. I started to get the hang of things, and fishing seemed kind of fun.

We laughed, joked, and talked about each other's mamas. We called it "signifying" back then. "Doin' the Dozens" was another name for this competitive jabbing. Most people in my family and neighborhood signified with "yo' mama" jokes. For example, "Yo' mama so fat that when she gets on the scale, it says 'to be continued'" or "Yo' mama so ugly that when she walks into Taco Bell, er'body in there runs for the border." The list of jokes covered categories from ugly to fat, dumb, and short; you name it, there's a joke for it. We would come up with some super funny ones that would have folks rolling on the floor laughing.

But just like most things that are so very funny, the jokes are usually done at the expense of people's shortcomings, which is exactly why it shouldn't be done. Unfortunately, "Doin' the Dozens" developed from a very ugly origin in African-American history. During slavery, the deformed slaves, or the too old, too short, or simply not-up-to-par ones, were sold in batches of "cheap dozens," hence the joke's name. What a terrible stab at one's self-esteem. But as kids, we didn't know any better, so we had some great one-liners spewing back and forth at that fishing hole that day.

Suddenly, out of nowhere, in the midst of our laughter, an old, wrinkly-skinned white man appeared at the highest part of the ledge waving a huge machete. He started yelling at us. "All right you kids, git yer poles outta dat water! Yer not 'posed to be fishing here; dis here's private property! Gimme fifty dollars each or I'll call the cops!"

All the guys frantically gathered their stuff and scrammed. Kendall beat everyone, jumping up over the ledge and across the field. I glanced around for Ant, but couldn't see him. Fear instantly swept over me. I slipped as far under the ledge as possible to escape the old man's view, until I could get to the part of the dirt wall that was easier to climb. Racing through my mind were visions of the old man slicing all of us up as he swung his over-sized machete.

I dug my fingers deep into the dirt to hoist myself up, but kept slipping back down. Sweat started rolling down my forehead as I tried to accomplish the climb while juggling the fishing pole. Horrible thoughts continued, "What if everyone left me? How would I get home? What would this old man do to me?"

Just then, Ant's right hand reached down and grasped mine, and with one good tug, he snatched me up over the ledge. Boy, I was happy to see him! He hadn't left me after all. I don't even know why I thought he would. Ant had always taken care of me, and he was my hero that day!

Once on my feet, I took off running, pole and all, passing both my brother and Anthony Farmer. That was easy to do since both of them were a little chunky in size. As I got closer to the car, I caught up with Kendall who was running back from the pond a second time. Apparently, in his haste, he had forgotten his tackle box and had to go back for it. He always was a fast runner.

The old man kept yelling and kept coming toward us, albeit in slow motion, or so it seemed. For sure, he wasn't about to catch us. Still, we quickly tossed our gear in the trunk and clumsily pushed each other into the car. Ant noticed that I never reeled in my line, so it stretched along the ground back to who knows where! He snapped the line, threw the pole in the trunk, and we joined the others already in the car.

We drove a little distance out of harm's way, and then pulled off the road onto someone's deserted private property to catch our breath. After a minute or two, we all burst into laughter, everyone sharing his version of what had just gone down. We all gave Anthony Farmer a hard time, mocking him because he had yelled back at the white man, "I'm going to call my mama! She's a lawyer!" You could tell he was on the brink of crying when he said it, scared like all the rest of us that the man would somehow make good on his promises. We teased him so badly, his laughter almost turned to tears.

As everyone piled out of the car, my brother told of his lifesaving heroics, yanking me up over the ledge. I was never more thankful to have a big brother than at that moment. I appreciated him and mentally placed a hero's crown on his head.

In that very next moment, something happened that totally caught me off guard. Kendall reached in his pants pocket and pulled out a tightly rolled joint. He lit it, inhaled long and hard, held his breath briefly, and while exhaling the smoke, passed the joint to Kevin. Kevin put the joint to his lips, mimicked Kendall, and passed it to Anthony Farmer. Anthony Farmer took a couple quick "hits" off the joint, and passed it to my brother.

Right then, everything went into slow motion as my eyes stayed glued to my brother. Surely, he's going to hand it right back to Kendall, I thought, but he didn't. Instead, he slowly lifted the joint up to his lips, sucked in a couple of times, squinted a bit, and puffed up his cheeks like Louis Armstrong on his trumpet. After a couple seconds, which seemed like forever to me, he blew the smoke out. Done like a pro.

Tears immediately rolled down my cheeks. I couldn't believe my brother was smoking dope! How could he, especially after all the years of knowing what our mother went through? While he wasn't at her job all the time, he was there enough to remember hearing all those people tell how they lost everything and destroyed their lives because of drugs. What was he thinking?

Anthony Farmer snickered and nudged Ant's arm.

"Ant, look at your brother."

My brother turned around and saw my tears and my confused stare. Those tears spelled pain—the pain of him and me missing out on a childhood together, the pain of years of not living with my mother or father, the pain of not knowing what a real family feels like. On top of all that pain, I certainly didn't need the extra inner turmoil of seeing my brother enjoying drugs.

Ant handed the joint to Kendall, put his arm around my shoulder, and led me away from the group. "What's wrong, bro?" he said.

I distinctly recall my response to his question. "Don't you remember what they said at mommy's job? First you start with drinking and next comes smoking weed; then, it's onto the harder stuff, with a little bit of drugs here, a little bit there. Before you know it, your life is ruined. I don't want you to ruin your life, Ant," I sobbed.

"I won't ruin my life," Ant assuredly stated. "This was my first time. I promise I won't do it again."

"You promise?" I asked, wiping the tears off my cheeks with my shirtsleeve.

"I promise," he replied.

I later found out that the weed smoking session by the car was *not* Ant's first time. More important to note, he didn't keep his promise to never do it again. That day, the hero's crown I had just placed on the head of my fourteen-year-old brother began to tarnish.

That's Just the Way Life Is

Throughout my childhood, I lived in numerous homes between Chicago and Peoria, Illinois. I attended at least seven Peoria grammar schools (Franklin, Tyng, Roosevelt, Thomas Jefferson, Whittier, Wilder Waite, and Charles Lindbergh) and then high school at Richwoods. Military brats had it easy compared to me. Sadly enough, all those moves made it extremely difficult to develop long-lasting friendships. You can only claim "friends for the moment," compliments of a transitory childhood. As a student, you see other teenagers pal around in the hallways or cafeteria with their best friends from first grade. In contrast, you meander like an outcast, waiting on one of the cliques to invite you in.

To help avoid that situation, I looked to sports as my catalyst for making new friends. When I moved to Village Green, I changed to my final grammar school, Charles Lindbergh. That was when Jimmy Roberts and I became best friends and stayed close for three years.

Both of Jimmy's parents worked at Caterpillar, the manufacturer of mining and various types of mining and construction equipment. His family lived up north in a very nice home in an upscale neighborhood.

Our meeting was rather ironic, given the fact that prior to meeting Jimmy, my brother and I had once received candy from his house at Halloween when we lived in Candletree. Our modest dwelling was in the community right on the other side of a wooded area that separated our neighborhoods We trekked through those woods to Jimmy's world because we knew trick or treating among those rich people would net us the "good" candy. You know the ones: Snickers, Kit Kats, M&M's, and other popular brands.

The first time I rang the doorbell at the Robert's residence, I was shocked to see a black kid (Jimmy) answer the door. I thought, "What?! A black kid in this rich white neighborhood?" That was all new to me. He had donned a Dracula costume and dished out "good" candy from a large bowl. He and I made eye contact with no exchange of words. He may have sensed my thoughts.

On the way home, I talked about that kid in the Dracula costume over and over. I told Ant, "One day, I'm going to buy me a house over there." That affirmation of mine spoken into the universe brought me into that neighborhood, not as a homeowner (since I was still a kid when it happened), but as a sleepover guest many a night at Jimmy's house.

Some other close friends I had growing up in Peoria were Cornelius "Corny" Taylor and Dante Labbe. Corny lived next door to me in the Village Green projects; Dante lived around the corner. I regret losing contact with them. I was informed that Corny served in the Army somewhere and Dante, the Navy. We simply let life sever our ties. Now we are different people, living different lives in different worlds. Even with Jimmy, it's no longer the same. He still lives in Peoria with his wife and kids. Years after moving from Peoria, I saw him a time or two during visits back there. It was obvious that time and distance had melted away the childhood bond we once cherished.

In spite of my new "world," at times I love to travel down memory lane to my old one. When I do, I catch myself laughing out loud remembering the adventures of riding our bikes, playing basketball, chasing girls, and being threatened by Juandale, the neighborhood bully! I swear he and his brother, Mousy, must have been on steroids at age nine. With muscles galore and attitudes the size of Texas, they ruled our neighborhood. They had an older brother nicknamed, "Shotgun," who was a teenager about the same age as my brother. I always wondered how a teenager got that type of nickname.

One such trip down memory lane reminded me of a not-so-nice time period when I experienced my first couple of negative racial encounters. I was in the eighth grade, where I played on the school's basketball team. After one of our practices, one of the guys on our team, Jeff Rail, called someone a nigger. It caught me off guard. Instantly, offense rose up in me along with the urge to fight.

"What did you just say?" I prodded.

He stammered slightly, "I didn't mean you; you're not that kind."

"Well, what is *that* kind?" I questioned angrily.

Before he could answer, the bell rang, and we dispersed to class. Perhaps that was best. After all, we were on the same team and didn't need to drum up dissension. Besides, I figured that's just the way life is, so I let it go.

I was also co-captain of our team that year. High school coaches came to our basketball games and often told me I was pretty good. I ended the season on a great note, and lots of people favored me to win Most Valuable Player (MVP). Much to my chagrin, at our awards dinner, Coach Frank presented the MVP trophy to Dan Shekelton and the Best Man trophy to Jeff, the nigger-caller. I couldn't believe it, and neither could some of my teammates who felt I had been incredibly cheated.

I didn't whine or complain too much about the coach's decision that night. That incident, coupled with a few other observances, led me to believe that his prejudiced ways wouldn't change. No matter how hard I played the game, he would not award me a trophy. No amount of anger on my part would cause him to admit to that characteristic shortcoming, either. I realize now that was rather presumptuous of me as a fourteen-year-old, and I could have been wrong. Nevertheless, I let it go at the time.

As the sayings go, "Turnabout is fair play," and "Fairness can be relative and time-sensitive." Therefore, as fate would have it, a few months later at freshman try-outs at Richwood High School, Jeff Rail didn't make the team. And, Dan Shekelton didn't play much during the freshman basketball season. On the other hand, I started and even played with the sophomores on occasion.

Those significant incidences taught me that racially biased thinking will always be among us. That's just the way life is. The big question is, "How do we as so-called victims deal with it?" Do we fall into its trap and become bitter, or do we use it to push ourselves to become better?

That Dog Ain't Mine

While in Chicago for a couple of weeks during the summer, I enjoyed great times with my cousins: Kyk, Edward, and Bryan. We were all between twelve and thirteen-years-old, and I would spend a few nights in a row at Aunt Shirley's house. Edward was her son, a really smart kid who used good grammar. As a result, folks who knew him considered him a nerd. In our neighborhoods back then, it was not fashionable or "cool" to speak proper English or enunciate one's words clearly. If you did, you got labeled a "white boy." I know, because that's what my brother and his friends used to call me. The teasing became so bad that I tried to use slang or speak poorly, just to fit in. Unfortunately, that craziness continues today among children in lower income communities and schools.

Not only did Edward speak well, but he also had a passion for animals and could talk about almost any animal in great detail. Whether it was birds, snakes, cats, or dogs, or any other creature, he knew lots of stuff about them. Not surprisingly, Edward wanted to be a veterinarian when he grew up.

We liked helping Edward with his dogs. I say "his," but in actuality, I don't recall where Edward got the dogs he always had with him. No one ever knew where he kept them, either. The funny thing is, he would leave the house without a dog and come back with one! We would each walk the dog and act like it belonged to us. In trying to keep up with Edward, we would act as if we could train the dog, as well. "Sit. Stay. Come." Over and over, we would repeat those commands. "Sit. Stay. Come."

One particular day, Edward, Kyk, Bryan and I walked his Pit Bull near

Independence Boulevard and Homan Avenue. As we strolled around with no real direction or purpose, we came upon a group of older guys standing on the corner talking. Since their ball caps were turned to the right, they must have been black Gangsta Disciples. The four of us were well-known in the area because of our cousins, who were gangbangers and sold drugs, but we didn't know these guys. They didn't know us either, so instinct told us right away that they weren't going to just let us freely walk by.

None of the four of us claimed to be fighters, so we certainly weren't about to pretend at a time like that with guys who were much older than us. As we approached those guys, we could feel each other tense up. As we walked past, I waited for the infamous question, "What you ride?" That meant, "What gang are you in?" The only correct answer would be the name of the gang *they* were in, and if you said you were in it, then you were challenged with secret questions that supposedly only those gang members knew. Most of us non-gang members knew those questions anyway but dared not ever repeat them. Besides, you never knew if the guys were "false flagging," which meant pretending to be in one gang but actually in another.

As we walked past those guys, the question never came. I couldn't believe it. I sensed them staring at us, though, and then I heard a little mumbling. As cool as we tried to be, meandering on by, I'll bet we were just as green as a lightning bug in the summer night, flashing: "Scared! Scared! Scared!!" A few more paces down the street—still nothing. Great! My rapidly pounding heart began slowing back to its normal pattern.

As I recall, that racing, pounding heartbeat occurred quite often living in the hood. You could face a situation like ours up to ten times a day, and each time your adrenaline would kick in as though preparing for a life or death situation. Many times, it was. And, we were just kids—twelve- and thirteen-years-old. Should anyone, especially a child, have to live like that?

I once briefly shared with a colleague at work about how I had a very difficult and poor upbringing. And he, like some of my other white friends, began sharing how tough *his* upbringing had been. I never wanted to downplay their struggle because every struggle is different and real to that person. I can't say mine was worse than someone else's because you never know how different situations may impact someone as an individual. I always listened intently, but at some point, they all started sounding the same:

"We were dirt poor. We lived in a small house and never had new clothes, only hand-me-downs from older siblings." Or:

"We lived on a small farm and raised some pigs, a few cows, and some chickens. We hunted deer, rabbit, and squirrel and went fishing all the time. There were times when I would lay out in a field and wonder what I would do with my life."

No doubt, each of those scenarios may have truly been a struggle; however, the challenges of my upbringing seemed entirely different. I couldn't lie in an open field or leisurely hunt possum for dinnertime stew. No, my neighborhood likened more to a jungle with scary predators all around trying to hunt *me*. I was their target for drugs, sex, money, or gang affiliation. A small apartment usually housed several family members at once, along with roaches and "supersized" rats, generally the size of squirrels. Almost every week, I dodged bullets from a neighborhood feud. Almost every day, I heard of someone I knew who'd been shot, stabbed, or sent to jail.

Call me biased, but being white and poor with the world at your fingertips to conquer, if you can figure it out while lying quietly in a field with a blade of grass hanging out of your mouth, seemed a whole lot easier than being black and poor in a cramped environment wondering if the next interaction you have with someone on the street will lead to a fight, flight, or life or death situation. Of course, I'm not implying that all black people who are poor have it that bad. Neither do I believe all white poor people have open fields to lie around in. It just seemed funny to imagine how my white colleagues, after knowing me only in the work environment, might react if they ever knew the truth about how I used to live and what I used to be exposed to.

As my cousins and I, along with the Pit Bull, passed those thugs on the corner, one of them yelled, "Give me that dog!" Before he could finish his sentence, we darted into a full sprint, running down the street with them chasing us. Edward's dog led the way. At first I thought, "Some Pit Bull; if he were so tough, he would have been protecting us, not running in front of us!" I later had to chuckle as I considered the possibility that the smart Pit Bull knew the trials of the ghetto as much as we did. He knew they wanted to "dognap" him to make him fight, get scarred up, and possibly die, too. That's why he outran us!

We turned a corner and yelled to each other to split up. Since I knew they were after the dog, I made sure to go in the opposite direction from Edward. The last thing I needed was to get beat up over a stupid dog that wasn't mine. Just as I figured, the guys kept chasing Edward and the dog, and none of them came my way.

I ran under a viaduct and hid. I didn't know which direction Edward had continued in or if he would circle back through an alley, which meant they could still possibly run my way. I remained crouched in a runner's position, prepared to go again. After a few minutes of eyeing both entrances into the viaduct, watching cars drive by, and wishing I could just hop in one, I figured the coast was clear. I remember being really scared. Kids were always getting beat up, hurt badly, or even killed over small stuff like this. And, I didn't want to die. My heart pumped harder and faster. I knew I had to get to a safer spot.

Although the coast was clear of thugs, apparently the ground wasn't clear of debris. I jumped up to start running and stepped on a piece of glass. I screamed loudly and instantly became more nervous about someone hearing me than about the glass in my foot, so I crouched back down and sat quietly. I felt my heart racing back into flight mode, ready to take off at any moment should one of them come around the corner. I am not sure how much time lapsed, but suddenly a stabbing pain in my foot shocked me back to reality. I had almost forgotten I had stepped on the glass. When I looked down at my foot, blood covered the ground around my shoe. When I turned my foot to the side, I saw the thick piece of glass from a wine bottle sticking through a hole in my Converse. I didn't even realize I had a hole in them until then. I pulled the glass out and sat back in sheer pain.

I figured the longer I stayed in that spot, the more I risked crossing paths with the gangbangers again, so I jumped up and starting running. Each step I took, searing pain sliced through my foot as though the glass remained lodged there. I ran all the way to Edward's house, just a couple of blocks away where the other guys had already gathered. They thought the gangbangers caught me, since I never made it back to the house. I told them what happened and showed them my foot where blood had now soaked through the white part of my converse. Aunt Shirley took one look and immediately ordered me to sit down. She briskly retrieved a towel from the bathroom and knelt down in front of my chair. She slid off my shoe and peeled off my bloody sock. She began gingerly wiping the blood off my foot.

"Baby, you know you got holes in your shoes?" Aunt Shirley inquired.

"Yes Ma'am," I replied, as she continued wiping and dabbing.

At that moment, I felt a real loving tenderness from her. She didn't chastise me for being careless. She didn't make me feel like I could've and should've avoided stepping on glass and having holes in my shoes. That one very gentle childhood moment created by Aunt Shirley still stands out in my mind today, juxtaposed with the numerous negative ones generated from other times when I had hurt myself and there was no one there to care.

For instance, one of my most vivid memories of injuring myself took place in the projects when I lived with my grandmother. Skeet and I played "Superman" with the garbage chute. In the projects, you just dropped your garbage down a chute in the wall at the end of the hallway. That practice of hundreds of people dropping (sometimes un-bagged) garbage and dirty diapers in one central location in the building, served as the culprit for the constant horrible stench in the project building. Aside from the smell of urine in the stairwell (and my uncle's stinky feet), that had to be one of the worst smells anywhere.

I would hang onto the handle of that chute with both hands, my body stretched out, and Skeet holding my feet up in the air, simulating flying like Superman. One time, he let go of my feet by accident, and I fell. I thought it was fun because I was actually flying like Superman. So I said, "Let's do it again!" And, we did. But, the next time, I let go of the handle before he let go of my feet and I fell face first and hit my chin on the concrete floor of the hallway. Blood went everywhere! As I walked home crying, I remember my Aunt Betty yelling, "What happened?"

Skeet and I nervously mumbled the sequence of events through our tears, fearing major punishment for playing with the garbage chute. I can't remember if we got a whuppin', but I do remember being yelled at harshly. No loving, no hugging, just yelling. My medical treatment consisted of toilet tissue and tape strapped on my chin. Of course at that time, I didn't think anything odd about that treatment. Today, however, with the tale-tale sign of a very noticeable, several inches-long scar under my chin, I know that stitches would've been more appropriate. Most parents or guardians would not have hesitated to take their child to the emergency room if that happened. Apparently, my guardians operated under a different premise: Ghetto Doctoring 101. You get taped up, yelled at, and sent to bed.

Aunt Shirley's attentiveness that day made me feel so loved in such a special way. I know Grandma and Aunt Betty loved me too, but Aunt Shirley showed me a different type of love, a tender love I had never experienced before. Needless to say, I developed a fondness for her that she probably never knew from that simple act of kindness.

While wiping my foot, she noticed a piece of glass still lodged in there which explained the continual pain. She managed to get the remaining piece out, and then bandaged up my foot and made me something to eat. I hobbled around on my foot for several more days until we went back home to Peoria. Once there, my mother took me to the doctor to make sure I didn't get lockjaw or something. Good thing she did because the doctor found yet another small piece of glass still inside my foot. He determined that the hidden glass had cut a nerve in my foot. Unfortunately, that severed nerve caused permanent damage, preventing me from bending several toes on my right foot. All of that happened because some gangbangers wanted Edward's dog. But, I guess it could have been worse had they caught us that day.

Where's Ant?

I entered my freshman year at Richwoods High School when my brother was a junior. He had failed a couple of grades, so the family joke was I would graduate before him, even though he was four years older than me. During that period, my brother and his friends stayed in trouble. That's too bad because they all played football and were good at it. Ant could have let an athletic scholarship become his ticket out of his life of nothingness. Instead, he regularly smoked weed, took speed, broke curfew, and came home drunk.

Ant inherited an additional partner in crime—our "play" cousin Tyrone, also known as Ty or T-Bone. Ty's mom, Aunt Dee, was one of my mother's good friends from Stonehedge. I loved Aunt Dee. In prior years, while my mother worked, Aunt Dee would pick me up from school, take me to get ice cream or candy, and we would just hang out. Later, Aunt Dee experienced some personal difficulties. My mother reciprocated, and without hesitation, our home became Ty's home.

Ant did a pretty good job at keeping me away from his drug activities, since I would be the first to let him know my negative feelings about the whole matter. However, every now and then, Ant, Todd Wright, Lester King, and some of his other friends would strap me down and blow smoke in my face until I got high off the fumes. Later on, after sobering up, I could tell my brother felt bad about doing that sort of thing to me. I know he really wanted me to be cool and participate like some of his friend's little brothers. For instance, James and his little brother,

Rodney, often got high with them. Sort of an inner city rite of passage, I suppose, that an older brother proudly sees his younger brother through. Well, I chose to abandon that particular tradition of the "hood."

My childhood exposure to the devastating effects of drugs really deterred me from ever being interested in them. At an early age, I developed a philosophy pertaining to drugs that has stayed with me forever and literally saved my life. In choices where others saw joy, I saw destruction. It was just that simple.

One afternoon, my mother, sister, and I were sitting at home watching TV when we received a frantic phone call from Deloris, one of Ant's classmates. "Where's Ant? Where's Ant?" she exclaimed hysterically in between sobs.

"I don't know," I replied, confused at her distraught questioning.

More frantic words came bellowing through the phone's receiver, "Lester, Boobie, and James were shot down in the Harrison homes! Two others were shot, but have not been identified!"

My heart dropped to my stomach and then raced all over the place. "No, no! This ain't happening!" But, everyone knew Ant and his crew were inseparable, so the likelihood of one of the two unidentified guys being Ant became great. I told Deloris to hold on as I shoved the phone in my mother's face, quickly repeating Deloris' story.

Mom listened on the phone and cried. She thanked Deloris, hung up quickly, and then dialed St. Francis Hospital. The hospital couldn't, didn't want to, or weren't allowed to divulge any information. I can't remember which it was; either way, we didn't know if Ant was even there. Our phone must have rung fifty times, all from Ant's friends, asking us questions we couldn't answer and giving us bits and pieces of what they had heard.

Finally, the evening news anchorman reported, "Several teens have been shot and one killed." He sounded so nonchalant. Naturally, it's their job to not get emotional. Besides, that sort of thing got reported all the time. But those were people *I* knew and loved. There was nothing nonchalant about it! My heart sank again as that report reverberated in my head.

I used to have different nightmares about something like this happening to my brother. One such prevalent dream had me waking up screaming night after night. In that dream, Ant and I would be walking out of an apartment building past a garbage can. Somehow, I knew there was a gun in that can, and I would yell at him to get the gun out of the garbage can. By the time he heard me, it was too late, and someone else would walk past him, reach in the can, get the gun, and fire at him. That's when I would wake up screaming, "Get the gun out the garbage can! Get the gun out the garbage can!"

With all the bad news swirling around at that moment, I couldn't help but think that my reoccurring nightmare had become reality. More news came to us from various sources. James Mays shot and killed; Lester King shot in the chest; Boobie shot in the leg; one unidentified person shot in the leg. I just knew the unidentified person was Ant but at least he was alive!

Wow! I couldn't believe James Mays was dead. He and I shared the same birthdate, May 25th, but a different year. He was only eighteen-years-old—a life barely begun. I remembered, years prior, when he first told me his date of birth on the city bus. I felt a kinship to him, partly because of that and partly due to the fact that he allowed me to feel cool without having to smoke like everyone else. He always let me be me, without judgment.

Lester remained in critical condition at St. Francis Hospital. My thoughts slipped back to when James, Lester, and Boobie started hanging out with my brother. Years of memories resided in and between them all. They spent many nights at our house and hung around us all the time. I took it for granted that I'd always see them.

As more information poured in, we learned the shooting involved gang activity. The guys doing the shooting were the Disciples, a gang from Chicago. Ant had always been affiliated with the Vice-Lords, who also originated in Chicago, so I assumed the rest of his friends were Vice Lords, too. Some words were exchanged when the two groups walked past each other, and the Disciples turned around and started shooting. My brother's entire crew had been shot.

My mother finally decided to go find Ant. She stayed out all night, so I figured she located him at the hospital. When she made it home the next morning, she reported, "Anthony is OK."

Total relief swept over me as I heard those words I'd been anxious to hear for over twelve hours. "Well, where is he?" I asked.

"He's in jail." My mother's tired response reminded me of how much stress all that must have caused her, first thinking her son dead, then finding out he's in jail!

"What? Why is he in jail, Ma?"

"Rape," she replied, slowly shaking her head in disgust. When my mother had arrived at the hospital, one of Ant's friends told her where he was rumored to be. I can only imagine relief and anger clamored for space in her mind at that precise moment.

Ant and Ty only stayed in jail for a day or two longer. A white girl my brother dated had told the police both my brother and Ty had raped her. In other words, they "ran a train" on her. Apparently, the girl's parents found out their daughter had had sex with two black guys and made her report it as a rape. Fortunately, my brother had letters stashed in his room from that girl talking about the other times they had been together sexually and how she liked it. One note pretty graphically explained what she was going to do to Anthony and Ty the next time they got together.

Based on those letters, both of the boys were freed. Based on our wonderful judicial system, if my brother had *not* kept those letters, he and Ty would've been in jail for a very long time. I must say that was one time I was glad he ended up in jail, as the alternative would have been death or serious injury like his friends. I'm sure his girlfriend's parents never knew that forcing their daughter to lie saved my brother's life that day.

With Money, Trouble Came a' Knockin'

I heard my mother in her bedroom one day, whining and moaning for hours. I felt bad because she sounded horribly ill, and I couldn't help. I knocked on her door from time to time, but she never answered. Finally, enough was enough; I had tolerated her painful groans as long as I could; now I had to do something. I cracked open her door slightly to see if I could help. As I peeked in, I noticed her tossing and turning in her bed while totally naked. I quickly shut the door, embarrassed at catching her vulnerable like that. I got scared, hoping she didn't see me, since I knew better than to open her bedroom door without permission. Whatever was wrong with my mother, it was bad.

"Something is wrong with Mommy. She is really sick. You can hear her moaning and stuff and she's been at it for a while." I dumped that frightening observation on Ant as soon as he came home from hanging out with his boys. Ant headed toward her room to see about her. I abruptly intercepted his path explaining that I'd already tried that.

Just as we discussed options, my mother's boyfriend, Larry, knocked on our door. We let him in; he halfway spoke to us and then made a beeline to our mother's bedroom. I hated Larry. I trusted him only as far as I could throw him and, perhaps, not even that much. Ant could see right through the guy, too. Probably, everyone could—everyone, except our mother.

My mother met him after her car accident. Months earlier, a truck had run a red light and broadsided her small Chevrolet Chevette as she and my sister drove across an intersection. My mother was badly injured, suffering broken ribs, a broken jaw on both sides, and lots of bruises and contusions. When we visited her in the hospital, she had tubes sticking out all over her body and her mouth wired shut. Ironically, my little sister escaped with only a few scratches.

My mother settled out of court for $70,000.00. To us at that time, it represented a whole lot of money! With the right kind of help, it could have represented freedom. Never had we imagined owning that much money at one time. My mother immediately spent some of that money on necessities such as furniture, a new car for herself, a car for Ant, and several other things. She told us she put some in savings accounts and money markets for all three of our college expenses. Our life actually began to seem normal. No doubt, money played a big role in that. Nevertheless, as the saying goes, it's not how much money you have that matters; it's how much you keep—which brings me back to Larry.

Soon after Larry showed up on the scene, my mother started staying out late, a lot. When she did come home, she had obviously been drinking—a lot. Oftentimes, in the wee hours of the morning, she would sit in the living room, nodding off and speaking gibberish. Other times, she would come near my bed, when I was supposedly asleep, singing lyrics by Anita Baker, "My angel, ooh angel. You're my angel, ooh angel…" Even in her drunkenness, I enjoyed her singing to me. "If I could, I'd give you the world. Wrap it all around you…" Although they were just lyrics, and she couldn't sing, somehow I believe she meant those words from her heart; she really would've given me the world if she could have. Perhaps that's why that song is among my favorites to this day.

Next, she indulged in spending sprees. My mother started buying "stuff"— like clothes for herself and gadgets for Larry. It didn't matter what; their arms cradled loads of bags each time they came home. I became a little jealous; no, a lot jealous is more accurate, and rightfully so. Ant shared my sentiments. He and I both knew Larry did not have my mother's best interest at heart. Money fueled that relationship.

That particular day, Ant and I watched as Larry slipped into our mother's room where the moaning and whining still lingered on. Within a few moments, like magic, it stopped. Shortly thereafter, the two of them came out of the bedroom and headed out the front door without a word. No "Good-bye," or "I'm OK," just a slammed door.

As soon as the door slammed shut, Ant got up from where he was sitting and told me to follow him. He opened our mother's bedroom door and went in. I hesitantly followed, as I knew we weren't allowed in our mother's room when she wasn't there. That would surely result in a whuppin' or some kind of punishment if we were caught. Ant opened her top dresser drawer, lifted up some clothes and from underneath them, unzipped a little pouch. He told me to come closer, but I wanted to be in a good position to run out, just in case my mother came home. I leaned over just enough to see inside the drawer and observe the pouch. I could not believe it.

My eyes immediately teared up just like when I saw Ant smoking weed. Again, my mind went back to seeing all those people at those meetings talking about how they'd lost their families, their houses, and all their possessions because of drugs. Inside that pouch were needles, a rubber hose, and a package that I assumed had drugs in it. My brother closed the pouch, shut the drawer, and we ran out of that room.

Once back in our bedroom, Ant stated the obvious, "Mommy's back on drugs."

I don't know why he made that unnecessary statement, unless verbalizing it helped him face the reality of what we feared all along. I knew that with drugs came trouble. We were headed for trouble alright, and trouble soon came.

As I reflect back on the events in my life, I can say with surety that sometimes trouble comes our way due to our most innocent ignorance. Too bad, though, that the innocence factor alone isn't enough to block the consequences.

One such innocent mistake on my part occurred when my family prepared for a trip to Chicago one weekend. As we packed, my Uncle Jerry stopped by to visit. He used to live at Stonehedge. Before my mother came in the room, I told him we were going to Chicago to visit family for the weekend. After he left, my mother scolded me for sharing that information. I didn't understand why, especially since it was just Uncle Berry. She said, "Never tell people we're going out of town."

We returned from Chicago a couple of days later to a total mess! Someone not only broke into our house and stole everything, but they ransacked and trashed it, as well. They wrote expletives all over the walls, such as, "F**k you b***h!" I later figured out the answers to the two main questions I had regarding that crime. Why would someone do that to us? One word answer: Jealousy. What did my mother do to make someone write those nasty things about her? Two word answer: Have money.

I sensed my mother's anger toward me for many days, and it caused me major feelings of guilt. She never said anything directly to me, but I could see it through the pain on her face. She never said anything about Uncle Jerry either, although we all knew he was involved. After that, I never saw him again. I guess he was no longer my uncle.

You hear people say they feel violated after a home robbery. Well, violation is really the only word that fits the feeling and even that falls short of the heart-wrenching toll it takes on your spirit and your trust in mankind. I knew it all too well, since I obviously didn't learn my lesson as a child and had to experience that betrayal again as an adult. Needless to say, nowadays no one ever knows when I'm away from home.

Returning our home back to normal after that trashing was no easy feat. That's when it became apparent that the $70,000 awarded to my mother was all used up, in just one year. Larry was gone, as well. He had appeared and then disappeared in the same timeframe as the money. Once again, we were broke.

Christmas was right around the corner, and being broke at Christmastime was no joyful matter. To make things worse, I dated a girl at that time, and I knew she expected a gift from me. Sherri Smith was one of the prettiest girls I had ever laid eyes on. What she ever saw in a poor, skinny kid like me with braces on his teeth, I'll never know. She had a very sweet disposition, which is why I tried to do everything possible to impress her.

For instance, as our first date, I treated her to the movies. The movie we wanted to see was R-rated. Being under the restricted age limit, we purchased tickets to a PG movie and sneaked into the R-rated one. Soon after the movie started, as we inched close together in our seats, a very observant usher, having spotted our exploit, came down the aisle with his flashlight. He asked for our tickets which, when produced from our pockets, clearly displayed PG across the top.

As though being escorted out of the movie theater wasn't bad enough, I then had no money for a back-up plan. Our rides wouldn't be there to pick us up for two hours, so I managed to spread the few dollars that I did have over the two-hour period. Pretty much, a few dollars can only buy you a couple of pops and a couple of games on a pinball machine. I felt like such a loser by the time her mother came to pick her up. A little voice in my head said, "See, this is why pretty girls don't date guys like you."

Several nights before Christmas, my mother came home and gave me a bottle of perfume to give to Sherri. What a lifesaver! I immediately wrapped it, anxious to present it on Christmas day. I then noticed my mother had lots bottles of perfume and cologne. So, we wrapped gifts for lots of people, which I thought was really cool. She even gave Ant and me our own bottles of Polo for Men. It was the first bottle of cologne I ever had.

Back at school after Christmas, Juandale, the neighborhood bully, created one of my most embarrassing moments. He told everyone that my mother was a thief and that she had stolen a bunch of cologne and tried to sell some to his dad. He even said she got busted and had gone to jail. He exposed that bit of trivia with everyone, even Sherri. Talk about humiliating! I wanted to beat him up, but my skinny frame against Mr. Muscle Head would've caused more disgrace.

I never validated Juandale's claims about my mother, but the likelihood of them being true was certainly great. I knew she had previously gone to jail a couple of times, but I never knew the charges. I don't believe she stayed in there long, but it would explain why some nights she didn't come home. At times, my brother, sister, and I got by on our own, no questions asked of her and no complaints made to her.

It's strange how some things take root on a subconscious level and don't materialize or blossom until later in life. Even though I can now afford to pay for any perfume on the shelf, a sense of embarrassment and shame still creeps in at the thought of such a purchase. Therefore, when buying gifts for women, perfume is very rarely a choice I make; most often, a nice watch or some clothing will have to suffice.

No Home Sweet Home For Me

Things got really bad for my mother because of her drug relapse. She decided to admit herself into a treatment program, but the facility's location took her to Chicago. Since I only had several months to go to finish out my freshman year, my mother, brother, and sister moved to Chicago, and I stayed behind with our next door neighbor, Ms. Olivia. She was a very nice lady, a mother of three kids, who assured my mother that one more kid added to the mix would be no problem. To help "seal the deal," my mother gave Ms. Olivia all of our furniture. Ms. Olivia put most of it in her bedroom and loaned that bedroom to me. It saddened me to be separated from my family, but at least my mother's furnishings dulled the pain.

I quickly found out why Ms. Olivia said one more kid would be no problem. She never really supervised me. Maybe she was giving me space; maybe that's how she parented. Therefore, at age fourteen, I pretty much supervised myself. I came and went as I pleased, hanging out all hours of the night with girlfriends and some of my homeboys.

One day, I went to get my hair cut at the barbershop where I had been a patron for many years. As I sat in my barber's chair, he and a couple other people near him began looking around for something. Soon, I joined in the search, and we all started scanning everything in the room. I didn't even know what we were looking for, but continued right along with the others. Out of the corner of my eye, I noticed someone pointing at me. All of sudden, everyone stopped talking, ceased looking, and started laughing.

One of the guys even got next to me, tilted his head back slightly, sniffed in a couple whiffs, then frowned at me. Talk about being embarrassed! Even though I didn't know which of my body parts smelled, I put two and two together and realized that I was definitely the culprit. I sat there for what seemed like the longest haircut of my life.

When I finally got finished, I nonchalantly walked out of that shop. After turning the corner, I took off running to Ms. Olivia's house. I darted upstairs, slammed the door closed to the bedroom and began examining my body. I smelled myself everywhere, not detecting what they obviously did at the barbershop, that is, not until I pulled off my shoes. Then it hit me like a Mack truck. Wham! An extremely foul odor burst forth from those shoes and blasted my nostrils. Why hadn't I smelled that before? Fortunately or unfortunately, I couldn't smell my own body odor as well as others could.

There I sat, a humiliated, hygiene-challenged young teenager, trying to make sense of his growing body, trying to make sense of his whole world. Sure, my mother told me not to wear my shoes without socks, but I didn't know the sweaty, smelly, embarrassing consequences of not obeying her. Besides, if she wasn't there to enforce that and other rules, what good were they?

I stuck my hand in my shoe and felt something. I thought, "Why do I have mounds of crap in my shoe?" I scraped and scraped the insides of both shoes with my fingernails. Loads of caked-up dirt crumbled into the trashcan creating a noteworthy pile in there. During that process, I no longer felt independent or able to totally take care of myself. That was the first time I remember desperately wanting to reunite with my family.

At that point, I had lived with Ms. Olivia for a number of months, hanging out all night doing whatever I darn-well pleased and saw some of my friends go to jail for criminal activity. Thank God, I didn't find any major trouble to get into, and trouble didn't find me. However, I realized I needed to make a change before that was no longer the case. Since it didn't seem my mother would be able to get me anytime soon, I reached out to my dad.

Initially, my dad sounded very angry at the prospect of me being left in Peoria for months without a real guardian. He told me several times he would come and get me, but apparently something always sidetracked him. It reminded me of when I was a little kid waiting to no avail for him to come and pick me up at my grandmother's in the projects.

Finally, the day came when he actually did show up at Ms. Olivia's house. Words cannot explain how happy it felt to be leaving with him. Through no fault of Peoria's, my abandonment left me with a bad taste about that place so I vowed never to return, though I have a few times as an adult.

Back in Chicago, my dad struggled to make ends meet. I moved in with him in his studio apartment at the Flamingo building on 55th and Lake Shore Drive in Hyde Park. To a teenager, the sixteen-story building with an awesome view of Lake Michigan in trendy, cool and upscale Hyde Park felt heavenly. Compared to Peoria and the Chicago projects, I couldn't call it anything less. To Dad, however, his studio was small enough as it was and definitely too small for the two of us. I didn't care about being cramped, as long I lived with him. After a while, though, it proved simply too much for him, and I got shipped off again.

As a result, I went to live with Aunt Enner and Uncle Wright. Everyone referred to Aunt Enner as Enner. Even her kids called her Enner. The same was true of Wright. His first name was Louis, but everyone, even his kids, called him Wright. As in most cases, they weren't my real aunt and uncle. Enner and Wright were two more friends from Stonehedge in Peoria; however, they were not addicts like my other aunts and uncles from there. They lived on the West Side of Chicago, near Christiana and Homan Streets, with their six children: Kenny, Kennethe, Kykhoura (Kyk), Kita, KyKujichagulia (Kuji), and Kykiamisha (MiMi). One of their sons, Kyk, was my age and size, so we shared everything from a bedroom to underwear.

I loved that they always had a houseful of people and treated everyone as family. That made for a fun atmosphere, unless, of course, you got in trouble with Enner. Enner reminded me of Madea (the hilarious, pistol-packing grandmother character in Tyler Perry's stage plays and movies). She loved everyone in the neighborhood and would help anyone, but you had to watch out; she could chop you down in a heartbeat. She would curse you out so badly that you wished you had gotten a whuppin' instead. But then again, her whuppin's weren't anything nice, either. Not only were they intense, but you got the cursing along with it; a curse word accompanied each swing of the belt, her hand, her shoe, or whatever was closest at the time.

Kyk and I became really close, like brothers. The Hip Hop craze and break dancing dominated the music scene back then, so Kyk and I formed a little crew that would battle kids in the small grassy area that divided the wide boulevard where we lived. Kyk lead the group because of his creativity, his dancing skills, and his love for music. He constantly gathered new music and developed new dance routines for us.

Once summer rolled around, we didn't have a whole lot of free time to develop our dance crew since Enner hooked me up with a city-sponsored job. She lied and told them I was sixteen-years-old when actually I had just turned fifteen. I worked at a youth center at Homan Avenue and Thirteenth Street called ABC. Its sister center was BBR, located nearby off Independence Boulevard. Both of those centers were a part of the Chicago Youth Centers organization that acts as an oasis for many at-risk children living in neighborhoods where poverty, drugs, violence, and under-performing schools are the norm. It was the coolest job ever because we either did activities all day in the center, went on field trips, or went swimming. The important thing was it kept a lot of kids occupied constructively and, in the process, increased the self-esteem of the attendees and the workers.

Everyone who lived with Enner that summer worked at ABC. Who knows how she managed that, but she knew a lot of people and knew how to make things happen. Wright exposed us to some extremely valuable life skills, as well. He would sometimes make us stay in the house for hours on a beautiful summer weekend to teach us meditation and memorization skills. We had to practice until we got them right. All the other kids seemed to hate it, but I loved it. I never complained and simply found myself fully engaged.

I firmly believe my appreciation of Wright's time and the attention he paid to us is what kept me loving what he taught, as well. Some of the kids never had to experience the pain of living without their parents, torn apart by drugs, crying their eyes out at night from missing them, or wondering if they would ever see them again. And yet, there I was again, only this time as a young man experiencing that same inner pain. Even though I dealt with it differently, it was the same old pain.

While we meditated, Kyk snored, and the other folks fidgeted around on the floor. I took in all the directions given by Wright and went to that place in my mind as he instructed. It was an escape from my painful reality that I desperately needed and wholly welcomed.

To this day, meditation remains one of my lifelong practices. Many times, when I mediate with the intention of falling asleep, I dream about solutions to my problems. I am forever grateful to Wright for blessing me with this invaluable skill, and I am forever grateful for them inviting me into their home.

Academically Inclined

In the summer of 1984, as the start of my high school sophomore year approached, the Chicago Public Schools went on strike. That's when my mother arranged for me to live on Chicago's Far South Side with Aunt Bob and Uncle Larry, parents of Skeet and Charmaine. That way I could attend their school, Thornton Township High School, located in the suburb of Harvey. Their family lived in a nice house on the corner of 105th Street and Indiana Avenue in an area nicknamed, "The Wild 100's."

Life in The Wild 100's truly lived up to its name, offering the potential for extreme violence at every corner. No doubt, that was the handiwork of gangs and drugs. West Side or South Side, it didn't seem to matter where I lived because that same evil spirit plagued yet another black community. Nevertheless, the prospect of once again hanging out with Skeet and Charmaine far outweighed all the dangers of living there.

I was fifteen-years-old and, up to that point, had lived in over a half dozen homes—first with both of my parents, then with my grandmother, back with my mother, left with Ms. Olivia, a short time with my dad, on to Enner and Wright, and now Aunt Bob and Uncle Larry. What a journey of constant disruption! As an adult, I have come to realize that this disruptive mechanism has allowed me to easily adjust to circumstances in everyday life. I can be laid back and go with the flow, be the life of a party, or start a revolution. I call it my survival instinct, and it kicks in whenever I need it.

I enjoyed that school year the most, and it showed. Perfect attendance, high honor roll, basketball team starter, and track team member; I engaged in so much and excelled! In almost every subject, I competed against my really smart friends: Toni, Cordia, and Sarita. Doing such became my self-administered method of discipline. What's funny is that they probably had no idea I competed with them. I just admired how smart they were and felt I could be just as smart.

Constantly going up against them transported my sense of competition to a whole new level. For the first time in my life, I recognized that my ability to compete intellectually was as strong as my ability to compete athletically.

Thornton Township brought me some meaningful and life-long relationships, as well. One was with Illandus Hampton, a basketball teammate of mine. We are still great friends to this day. Another such connection was to Twila, a cousin whom I had never spent time with before. She was the daughter of my mother's brother, Eddie. I became as close to Twila as I was to Skeet and Charmaine. She is an exceptionally loving and kind person.

One time, the family celebrated Uncle Eddie's birthday as well as his sobriety at Uncle Larry and Aunt Bob's house. Uncle Eddie asked me to walk to the store with him, and he bought a half pint of liquor. On the way back, we ducked into the alley and he drank the whole thing down—straight—non-stop! He gave me $5, and told me not to tell anyone. Well, I told Skeet, who hustled me out of $2.50 to keep the promise. Unfortunately, my Uncle Eddie died of liver failure due to alcoholism when he was just forty-nine years-old.

Uncle Larry and Aunt Bob were extremely involved in our educational welfare, as well as our extra-curricular activities, something I was certainly not accustomed to enjoying. Uncle Larry took us to school almost every day and made it to most of our sporting events. Even as an officer for the Chicago Police Department (the second largest law enforcement agency in the nation and consequently one of the busiest), he was never too busy for any of us kids.

I firmly believe Uncle Larry and Aunt Bob's physical presence and moral support proved catalytic to my academic excellence. Yet, that same supportive environment found Skeet struggling with his grades, and Charmaine producing B's and C's at best. Unfortunately, there is no guarantee of the same performance results from different children within the same household even when receiving the same care and attention. It just doesn't work that way.

However, in spite of our varying school grades, as adults, the three of us have succeeded in our very different paths. Today, Skeet is a terrific father of five children and has been a diligent bus driver for the Chicago Transit Authority over the past fifteen years. Charmaine followed in her father's footsteps and became a police officer. She also achieved a master's degree while raising a beautiful daughter. Both my cousins have traveled to many places around the world and have provided wonderful, supportive environments for their children, much like their parents did for them.

To this day, I am extremely indebted to Uncle Larry, Aunt Bob and my cousins for their role in my life, not just during the nine months I lived with them, but before and beyond that as well. My thank yous to them may never be enough, compared to all the great lessons in life they have provided for me. One such lesson, that I incorporate into my own parenting, is to not look at the actual grade on a child's report card as much as the effort put forth behind achieving that grade.

In essence, the academic grade is not the most accurate yardstick with which to measure the potential of a child. The true measure of accomplishment is shown by how he or she understands and uses the power resting within to develop a productive, meaningful, and sustainable life.

Home Again. . .

My mother finally got out of treatment and once again secured a place for us all to live on Chicago's West Side. It had been quite awhile—almost two years— since my mother, brother, sister, and I all lived under the same roof. During her stay at the facility, my brother lived with Aunt Tee and my sister with Enner. I, on the other hand, ran the gamut of changing homes.

We moved into a basement apartment in the 5700 block of Washington Boulevard, between Waller and Menard Avenues, one block north of Madison Street. The one-bedroom floor plan actually resembled that of a studio apartment because the bedroom walls were more like glass doors on both sides allowing you to scan the whole apartment from the bedroom. Only four windows in the entire apartment, two in the front and two in the back, gave us a reprieve from the drab feel of a basement. However, those were hardly what most people would call windows since each one equaled the size of a car door window. That must be the reason why to this day I love houses with lots of windows and why I prefer those windows to be free of blinds or drapery.

Rats and roaches came along with the signed lease, just like in the projects. That being the norm, I didn't focus on them or anything else negative. Instead, after moving furniture in, I rummaged through a couple of large, plastic bags of clothes and things and reacquainted myself with my personal belongings. I'm not sure where they had been stored over those two years, but reuniting with my own possessions, slight as they were, felt great. My favorite boom box radio, my 13-inch black and white TV, my Atari, and a few other things. Man, was I happy to see those things!

Unless you have experienced it firsthand, you can never imagine what a strain it is to live under another person's roof for years on end. Bottom line: "their stuff" will always be "their stuff," and you are at the mercy of them and "their stuff." I know my aunts, uncles, cousins and friends meant well, but I learned to never underestimate their possessiveness. The TV channel changes in the middle of whatever you're watching because it's their TV. The dial on the radio changes in the middle of your favorite song because it's their radio. One day, you're told to help yourself to the fridge; the next day, you get a tongue-lashing for eating what they intended to eat because, after all, it was theirs. I would imagine that happens in any home, but maybe I became extra sensitive to it because at the end of the day, it was never my home. Needless to say, it felt good touching and seeing things that truly belonged to me.

It also felt great having my mother back home. Just the thought of going to bed and waking up knowing we were all in the same place was extremely comforting. If I weren't so consumed with having my family back, I would have been more aware of our new neighborhood. But the truth was, I didn't pay much attention to it, so our surroundings didn't seem so bad, not at first, anyway.

That neighborhood showed its true colors as the days went on. Drug dealers on almost every corner talking smack, "Got that fire bow to make your nails grow," or "Got that fire bow to make your hair grow." "Fire bow" meant good weed or marijuana. Those statements got folk's attention because long hair was fashionable back then for black guys. They would go to the hairdresser to get their "butter" whipped, fried, dyed, and laid to the side. Finger waves were really popular, as well, for the processed hair. But if you gangbanged, a five-point or six-point star in blue, red, or gold glitter was what you had outlined on a portion of your head showcasing who you represented. Ant typically got his hair done to represent the Vice Lords.

Nothing I saw on those streets surprised me anymore, but what really caught my eye soon after we moved in was a nice surprise on the inside of my building.

Her name was Sylvia, and she lived upstairs from us. Sylvia was about two years younger than me, very interesting, and really cool to talk to.

Sylvia and I would sit out on the front steps and just ponder life, school, and street stuff. We often watched in bewilderment as a crack head stood on the corner of the alley and the street with her two naked children begging for money to clothe them. As soon as she got enough money, she would run into the crack building next door to get high. It was despicable. Sylvia, who already had a child, never understood how a mother could do that to her herself or her children. Neither could I. I could tell Sylvia didn't like school and assumed that she probably was not doing well, but that didn't matter to me. We connected in other ways.

After only living there for about a week, my mother, sister, and I arrived home rather late one night to an opened back door. Someone had literally kicked in our door! Being in the basement would allow anyone to kick on it all day long without ever being heard. We slowly walked in and found our things strewn all over the apartment, that is, what little was left. In the sitting area where I slept, my radio, TV, and Atari were gone. I could not believe it. We didn't have much, and now what little we had was taken away. How quickly the joy of being back together diminished under the cloud of vulnerability—compliments of the ghetto!

Even though things improved when we moved to a second floor apartment in the same building, our living arrangements still saddened and angered me. Fortunately, in the midst of those feelings came inspiration; I felt inspired to succeed, no matter the cost, and motivated to be of help to my family when I got older.

"Someday," I told myself, "we will no longer need to be grateful that we at least have a basement studio apartment with a few car door windows. Someday, we will not have to deal with the rats and roaches on the inside and the thieves and thugs on the outside. Someday, we will no longer be victimized by stolen goods or stolen dreams—dreams lost by getting hooked on drugs, selling drugs, or gangbanging." Those were the circumstances in which I found myself, yet was determined to rise above. One day, I was going to rescue my loved ones from that hellhole we called life.

Inner Search

I began to spend more time with my dad, especially on Sundays—thanks to his introduction to church, to which he then introduced me. The church was Unity Church of Chicago, located then on Chicago's North Side in the Old Town neighborhood. It has since moved farther north and has a thriving congregation on Thome Avenue where the sign reads, "The church of love and laughter." There, I gleaned spiritual truth and divine principles through the positive and enlightened teachings of the pastor, the late Mike Matoin. An extremely intelligent and incredibly funny man, he used to say he had 88 unrelated jobs until God dragged him, kicking and screaming, to the ministry. He put love and laughter and practical applications of Biblical truths in all his messages instead of the traditional fear and guilt. That made it so easy for me to learn about my inner self and my oneness with God.

Having the discipline to search for and then connect with a divine inner spirit was made possible through my ability to meditate for long periods of time. I again thank Wright for training me how to do that several years prior, when I was just fourteen-years-old. That discipline, coupled with the newfound knowledge of who God was to me personally, changed my life forever. I actually looked forward to Sundays. That time not only allowed me to see my dad, but the hours we spent together at a restaurant after church discussing mind improvement principles, really created a tighter bond between us.

Dad was introduced to Unity Church by his ex-girlfriend, Debbie (now

Maeve), who remained a close friend to him. I remember meeting Maeve when I was about eight-years-old. She lived with my dad, and we shared time together on a number of occasions when I visited him. In college, she had majored in communications, so she helped Dad in his early singing career with publicity, photography, and bookings. She worked for a Chicago radio station and was given tickets every time there was a big concert or theatre production in town. So, while Dad struggled getting his own singing career underway, he got to see Sammy Davis, Jr., Count Basie, Johnny Hartman, Joe Williams, Nancy Wilson, Frank Sinatra, and many others, plus plays and musicals at all the top Chicago theatres in the late '70s.

In fact, Maeve was part of an interesting group of women: Maeve, Dana, and Pint. These three women all happened to be white, attended church together, and hung out together. Each had dated my dad at some point in their lives. My dad loved each of them, in different ways and for different reasons, and they have all stayed connected in varying degrees for over thirty years.

Dana dated my dad around the time he got out of jail. She was Jewish, and her mother was one of the only Holocaust survivors in her entire family. While she hardly ever brought up that subject to me (maybe because I was too young to understand), it always fascinated me to know that a piece of such important first-hand history was within my reach. Dana once spoke to my dad about adopting me so that the three of us could live together as a family. But, my mother would never have gone along with that plan. It was Dana, with her big heart, who got my dad to move to the suburbs, out of the city and his old drug haunts. She connected him with his first real job, and got him to enroll in college to earn his degree. On a vacation to the Virgin Islands in the early '70s, she got him onstage to sing at an open-mike club, and the audience screamed for an encore. It was the beginning of his vision of himself as a performer.

Then there was Pint, a supportive, motherly figure to me as well, and a soul mate to my dad. She stayed with him for many years throughout most of his ups and downs, and as he put it, was "the wind beneath his wings." Unfortunately,

Pint's father was very racist, so she hid that long-term relationship from her family. I can't even imagine the pressure that must have put on her, and my dad. But according to Pint, her father would have denounced her if he had ever found out she dated a black man.

I appreciated each of these women and their interest in my dad's spirituality and self-improvement because they influenced his interest in my exposure and development in those areas of my life. He used to suggest books for me to read to help me strengthen my mind and see myself in a lifestyle beyond poverty and beyond mediocrity. The first two books he ever gave me were a Unity book titled, *Lessons in Truth* by H. Emilie Cady and *The Road Less Traveled* by Scott Peck. After reading Peck's book, I started writing my success lists, otherwise known as affirmations. I wrote those lists every year, sometimes twice a year, and still do today.

My affirmations consisted of things I aspired to be, desired to own, or set out to achieve. That list looked something like this:

I am an honor roll student.

I am loving.

I am wealthy.

I am inspirational.

I am a District Sales Manager.

Through the years, I have written hundreds of affirmative lists. It is important to both write them down and say them out loud, which I would do throughout each day. All of my friends and family have seen my lists because I have them everywhere—on my bathroom mirror, in the kitchen, on my car steering wheel, in my wallet—everywhere. I believe that autosuggestions (messages from your conscious self to your subconscious self) are amazingly powerful; therefore, I learned to focus and train my conscious mind because the subconscious mind follows the orders of the conscious mind without knowing whether the information fed to it is real or not. To date, every affirmation that my subconscious mind received has come true—every single one! I'm constantly feeding it new ones, as well.

When I first began the process of this belief system, it took special effort on my part to watch everything I said. I had to be careful about what I suggested and affirmed to myself in order to accept the positive and block the negative. After things started coming true on my list, I had personal proof—my own personal testimonies—that thinking that way truly worked. That made it easier to adopt that practice, as well as continue it to this day. I also developed an insatiable appetite for reading authors who focused on spiritual belief and self-help strategies. Authors such as Napoleon Hill, Emmet Fox, Eric Butterworth, Charles Filmore, Venice Bloodworth, James Allen, Tony Robbins, Les Brown, Marianne Williamson, and others are all favorites of mine.

Years of practicing my spiritual walk—starting at Unity Church and continuing through today, attending Christ Universal Temple or Hillside International Truth Center—has helped me to interact with people from a much more loving and forgiving perspective. For the most part, I was always a pretty good kid; I was never a troublemaker and was always respectful to my elders. But, I knew there had to be more to life than being a good person. Establishing spiritual principles and a new way of thinking has allowed me to operate on a deeper level, so that my actions toward people come from a higher realm. Learning those principles really came in handy for what I was about to go through.

The #20 Madison

My dad had fallen in love again—this time with a black woman, named Lynn. It shocked me, since I had only seen him with one other black woman, besides my mother. Lynn was fine with a really nice figure, beautiful, light brown eyes, and a heart of gold. I really took to her kind spirit.

Basketball season was quickly approaching, and there I was wearing last year's gym shoes. All the other guys wore their brand new Air Force Ones. I had constantly wondered, since the start of the school year, how I could get a pair of them before the season started. Even though I worked steadily throughout the summer, I couldn't work night shift during the school year, primarily due to playing sports. The money I saved, I quickly spent on a few school clothes and supplies. Those $100 gym shoes did not make the list—that would have been three days worth of pay.

My thoughts kept going to Lynn. I never really asked her for much. She often helped out of her own free will, or perhaps it came with some urging from Dad. Nevertheless, one day I got up enough nerve to call her and ask her for the money to purchase a new pair of Air Force Ones. To my amazement, she quickly consented with, "Come on down and get a check from me at work."

I hopped on the #20 Madison Street bus to the McDonald's which was also on Madison Street, right off of Pulaski Avenue. On bitterly cold days like that one, I loved the convenience of that #20 bus line; it was within a block of my home and within a block of the McDonald's. Its route is straight on Madison

Street, going from Michigan Avenue downtown all the way west to the suburb of Oak Park. Therefore, at almost any time of the day, the bus remained crowded.

I also rode the Madison street bus every day to get to school at Whitney Young. My stop was Madison and Laflin, and I remember it so vividly. On most days when I got off the bus, a transvestite or two would be prostituting themselves on the corner. Sometimes I actually saw them hooking up with johns, mostly guys in trucks. These "gender illusionists" (a euphemism I heard recently), were really scary to me because they looked to be 6'2"–6'3" and extremely manly. After seeing me on such a regular basis, they got friendly, and as I would walk by them feeling a little intimidated and ready to run, they would say things like, "Get that education, baby; you don't want to be out here like us when you get older." Well, they never had to worry about that, but after awhile I realized I never had to worry about them. Actually, I began to feel sorry for them seeing how their lives had turned out. While they were rooting for me, I was always secretly rooting for them, hoping that some day they wouldn't have to live the life they must have felt stuck in.

Lynn was very busy when I arrived at her store, but she still took a moment from her work to keep her promise. She handed me the check written out to my school, and I stuck it in my pants pocket without even looking at it. With a motherly kiss planted on my cheek, I headed right back out to the bus stop.

I was settled in my seat, and the bus had traveled down a few blocks when a guy got on selling gloves. He stopped where I sat and asked if I wanted a pair. Thinking about the cold weather outside I said, "Yeah, let me see the gray pair." He handed me the gray gloves. They were nice, and they actually matched the coat I was wearing which was a hand-me-down from Ant. I figured I could look pretty good with color-coordinated gloves. But when I attempted to put them on, all the fingers were stuck together like mittens instead of individual fingers like gloves.

"Hey partner, all the fingers are stuck together." I said, as I waved the gloves back at the street hustler.

He glanced at the gloves and then back at me, and just by the way he glared, I could sense something wasn't right. He snatched the gloves from me and ripped each finger apart. At that point, the fingers were now torn, and I didn't want the gloves at all. And, I'm not even sure why I showed interest in them initially, since I didn't have any money anyway, just a check in my pocket. Stupid me. But, that crazed man looked furious, as if *I* had torn the gloves.

Still glaring at me, he demanded, "Scoot your little ass over."

I slowly slid over, thinking, "Oh no, here we go."

He stuck his hand in his pocket and then that pocket against my side.

"I gotta gun, and I will shoot yo' ass if you say sumpin'." He rambled on, "I just got outa prison, and I don't give a damn 'bout you, you li'l punk motha-f**ker. I kill li'l motha-f**kers like you!"

He continued to ramble on about getting out of jail and killing me. He spoke in a gruff, semi-hushed tone, so as not to allow everyone on the bus to hear. Others heard enough that I thought any minute someone would report what was happening to the bus driver or yell at the guy to leave me alone.

Instead, no one did anything. Of course, that was back when cell phones were not commonplace. So, unlike today, you couldn't call for help from your own safety zone. No, to be a Good Samaritan back in the day, you had to put your own body in harm's way—hence my dealing with that situation alone.

Tears rolled down my face as he continued, "B*tch ass nigga. You want to f*ck with me, I oughta shoot yo' ass right now!"

I thought about the reality of that whole situation. I recalled several young guys killed in the past few months for their gym shoes, coats, and other personal belongings. I could not believe I was about to become one of those victims. I definitely knew I didn't want to become another dead youth statistic from the ghetto. My heart began to race as fast as my tears flowed.

He asked, "You got any money?"

"No, I don't have any," I quickly responded. I had the check Lynn had given me, but I didn't consider that as money. In hindsight, I suppose by not disclosing it, I was resisting and potentially putting myself in the same predicament as the other young boys killed earlier that year, but I really wanted those Air Force Ones. Stupid me.

Next, the guy said, "That's a nice coat. Give it to me."

I couldn't believe what I had just heard. "But, it's cold outside."

He requested it again, "Give me the motha-f**king coat!" I knew he wasn't playing as I felt the gun in his pocket being shoved deeper into my side. In single-digit weather with the wind chill below zero, I gave him my coat.

"You still f**king with me. Ooh I swear I oughta blow yo' li'l ass away, say one word, say one motha-f**king word."

Then, he said, "That's a nice sweater homeboy. Give me that sh*t too."

I looked at him, thinking, "You can't be serious; it's freezing outside!" But, I dared not say a word. I obviously moved too slowly for him, so he said it again, with more force, "Give me that f*ckin sweater!". I took my sweater off, leaving me wearing only my tank top, pants, and shoes.

The robber got off the bus at the very next stop which was somewhere around Lockwood Avenue. I sat stunned, staring out the window as the bus continued to roll down Madison Street.

One man stopped by my seat while he prepared to exit and asked if I was OK. He seemed a little too hurried and disingenuous to really care, but I answered anyway, barely in a whisper, "I'm fine."

It was broad daylight and below zero outside. I sat half-naked on the #20 Madison bus that was full of people who didn't care that I just got robbed. I guess I should've been grateful that the gym shoes I wore, and the ones I would soon buy with Lynn's check weren't stolen from me also. More importantly, I should have been grateful that he did not shoot me, but gratefulness was certainly not one of my sentiments in that moment.

Then, that inquiring man put his hands on my neck, fondling my necklace, as if to inspect it. I really couldn't believe it! Did I look like a gazelle that had just been wounded by a lion? Was I now a helpless heap of carcass to this approaching hyena? Once he realized my necklace was about as thick as a piece of floss and had little or no value, he removed his hand and continued off the bus.

We finally got to Menard Street, and I rushed off the bus. The wind whipped brutally across my bare arms as I walked slowly, still in shock. The reality of the cold didn't totally register. About halfway down the block, I noticed my mother's boyfriend, Berry, walking toward me. Once he realized it was me, he sped up his pace until he reached me and said, "Jemal, where's your coat? Where are your clothes? What the hell happened?"

I came out of my daze and cried out, "I was robbed on the bus by a man with a gun!" He put his arm around me and briskly walked me home. Fortunately, it was only a block away. My brother was at the house, and when I told him what happened, he ran out the door to the hood. That was his gang's turf, so he wanted to see what he could find out.

Nothing ever came of Ant's search. There was never any sign of that guy again, only the scarring left in my mind. After that experience, I never really spoke to strangers, especially on various modes of public transportation. That taught me that big cities are not places where you make eye contact with people on the street or carelessly bump into them.

To this day, I rarely speak to people on an airplane or in an elevator. I tend to keep to myself. This has been an ongoing issue that I'm still working to change. However, when you have felt the hard consequences of being open and trusting at the wrong times in a dangerous society, it disfigures the soul. Healing those wounds takes time; in my case, it is taking a long time.

The violence on Chicago buses continues to this day. In December, 2009, a thirteen-year-old cousin of mine and two of his friends were shot on a city bus on the South Side. As my family shared with me about his two gunshot wounds in the arm and one in the leg, it brought back some haunting memories of my own experience. Twenty-four years later, and I still cannot make sense of any of it. Thank goodness, my cousin and his friends recovered from their ordeal that day—physically anyway.

Work Ethics

My relationship with my mother at home resembled a rollercoaster ride, due to the turbulent relationship between me and her boyfriend, Berry. He was a recovering addict who I found to be arrogant, selfish, condescending, and downright mean. I despised the way he treated my mother—like a servant or peasant, not someone he loved. As long as he hung around, my days there were numbered. Dad and Lynn discussed living together and having me live with them. The thought of cohabiting in a peaceful family setting with dad captivated me so much that I dreamed of it day and night.

One day, Lynn took me to the place she wanted to rent for us. The brand new building on Roosevelt Road—The 1212 Building—was technically a part of Chicago's downtown with a dynamic view of the city skyline and the lake. It seemed like the perfect plan to me—the three of us in a luxury high rise. Truly, it felt like a dream come true.

I liked Lynn and began viewing her as my stepmom because she treated me like a son. She managed a McDonald's on the West Side, which was fairly close to where I lived with my mother. That made it convenient for me to see her often. In fact, she arranged for me to work there that summer of 1986 which proved a truly interesting experience.

My job consisted of basic cleaning duties; however, I aspired to be on the grill. A guy named Cal worked the grill, and I found myself fascinated with his burger cooking skills. Cal could place six burgers in each hand and slap them down on the grill in a rhythmic pattern: clack, clack, clack, clack—clack, clack! You could hear those burgers dropping throughout the restaurant. He provided a tempo that we all worked and moved to during our shift.

One day, I asked Cal if I could try flipping burgers. He stepped aside without hesitation, and I grabbed a stack of burgers in each hand. I thought about how cool it would be to have that job. I would make more money, and plopping food couldn't be as taxing on me as mopping floors. "Besides," I remember thinking, "what type of skill could it possibly take to drop burgers?" So there I went—clack, clack, clack! Each time I dropped a burger on the grill, my fingertips hit the hot metal. After a few burger drops, I just threw them on that grill. My fingertips burned as if someone held a match to them. I jumped and hollered, shaking my hands while Cal and a few others were cracking up at me. No wonder Cal had quickly given me a shot at his job.

My thoughts of working my way up to grilling burgers vanished pretty quickly. I grabbed my mop and went back to the floors like a puppy dog with his tail between his legs. As it turned out, I caught strep throat that same week and never went back to work. That ended my brief—but appreciated—career at McDonald's.

A couple of weeks later, having fully recovered from my illness, I desperately needed a job to replace my McDonald's income. My mother struggled to make ends meet. She passed out flyers when she could, while working as a maid at a small hotel. Then for some reason, she stopped working altogether. Welfare alone wasn't cutting it, so I knew she counted on me to pay for my own things. I couldn't look to my dad for support, since his singing career only peaked sporadically, leaving him to struggle financially, and he was dealing with his own difficult process of relapse and recovery. I couldn't ask Berry for anything because he and I were not close like that. So, there was no one for me to lean on financially to meet my needs.

One morning, Berry invited me to go with him where he worked and suggested that I could possibly get a job there. That caught me totally off-guard because of our volatile relationship up to that point. It surprised me that he would even try to help me. "It's good work, and you get paid every day," is how he explained it. "The work is hard but it beats doing nothing."

His last comment offended me. It seemed he insinuated that I enjoyed doing nothing. Quite the contrary, as an enterprising young person, I had always worked somewhere since age fifteen. I just happened to be in-between jobs at that moment. But, what use was it to argue with him? I simply said, "Sure. What time do I have to be there?"

He responded, "Five o'clock A.M., so be ready at four-thirty."

"I thought to myself, "Damn! Five o'clock in the morning? That's a real grown-up job." Still, I knew I couldn't turn it down. The next morning, I got up around four, got dressed, and stood ready to go by four-thirty. I noticed during the car ride to the job that Berry's disposition seemed to have changed overnight. He smiled, joked around a little, and was actually chummy toward me. I began to think he could really be an okay guy. Maybe I never really gave him a chance. Maybe we could develop a great relationship. No doubt, that would certainly make things more peaceful at home.

I never knew where Berry worked. I only knew he left home before I woke up in the mornings. When he came home, he showered, ate, got out his bucket and sticks, and drummed to songs by Tito Puente and other Latin artists. I had never known a black person to listen to so much Latin music. He always seemed to be in another world while beating on that bucket, acting as though he really played drums or bongos. What really perplexed me was that he couldn't speak a lick of Spanish. Go figure.

Within a short while, we pulled up to a place located on Halsted Street slightly north of Washington Boulevard. It surprised me to see the streets lined with cars and a long line of men standing outside the door of that small building. At such a crazy early hour of the morning with darkness blanketing the area, we stepped in line barely able to see past two or three people in front of us. A dingy little sign hung over the front entrance: "Windy City Labor Union."

Today, just a couple of blocks away stands Oprah Winfrey's Harpo Studio.

In the wee hours of the morning, a swarm of women typically form a line outside that front entrance, much like the line I stood in around the corner. The irony being that although the buildings were so close in proximity, the character, educational level, financial status, and social standings of each building's occupants were worlds apart.

Most of the men seemed pretty rough around the edges. I could smell the stench of alcohol and stale cigarettes on some, while others were obviously strung out on drugs. However, there also appeared to be a few guys like me—clean-cut and eager to work hard.

Once inside the building, the crowd doubled. Men were everywhere—sitting in chairs, leaning against the walls, perched on windowsills, and standing in small groups. There was a small bank teller type window at the front of the room, and quite a few men gathered there, as well. Behind the window, some white men in flannel shirts rustled about in a small office.

Berry nodded toward the fully occupied chairs, instructing me to find a seat or stand in the back. As he walked toward the window, he acknowledged guys, created small talk, and shook hands extended out to him, like some sort of rock star. He spent a few moments at the window, and then stepped away. A few minutes later, one of the guys in the office yelled Berry's name. Berry walked back up to the window, took a slip of paper from the man and then yelled out the names written on that paper, resulting in some high-five celebrations. Berry came over to where I sat and said, "Stay here. I told them who you were and they'll try to get you out on a job today." He then left with the men whose names he had called, and that was that. I had absolutely no idea what to expect from there on.

I sat in the back of that dingy, smelly room and saw the same thing happen over and over again. Some guy would be called to the window; he would then either read some names from their list or pick people he knew from the crowd. I finally asked the man sitting next to me what was happening. He told me that the guys who were being called to the window had been going there for a long time and had proven themselves to be hard and trustworthy workers.

They would be given a job. That job could be anything from setting up a trade show at the McCormick Place convention center to assembling things in a factory or hauling furniture for a moving company. In turn, those "lead" men would either choose some of their friends as their helpers or some guys who were friends of the men behind the window.

The way the guy next to me explained it, if you didn't know anyone already, you had to just sit there and hope one of those crew leaders would pick you to go on a job. At some point, they would run out of friends in the room and look for people who appeared to be willing to work hard and capable of handling the workload. Sometimes guys would go up to crew leaders and just ask to be on their team, to facilitate matters. The bottom line was the harder the crew worked, the better it made that crew leader look. If the crew leader looked good, he would get more job opportunities in the future. So, I figured out quickly that nepotism was the name of the "day labor" game. Knowing those rules, why then, didn't Berry pick me to go out with his team? He knew I didn't stand a chance against all the "regulars" there.

There I sat the whole morning, not being selected. It made me think of being back on the playground as a kid and waiting to be chosen for someone's team. Nine o'clock rolled around—still sitting. Only a few guys remained waiting for that call from the window. Those calls had died down to almost nothing. Guys started leaving, saying there was probably no more work left for the day. I finally made that same assumption and left at ten o'clock that morning, bitterly disappointed for a number of reasons.

First and foremost, I was disappointed no one picked me. I never experienced being that last kid picked for a team on the playground. Everyone wanted me on their team, and I felt those crew leaders should have wanted me also. Secondly, it angered me that I wasted an entire morning just sitting when I could have been out job hunting. Lastly, Berry totally misled me. He made me believe he was getting me a job when, in reality, he simply left me there without even explaining what to expect. I thought the whole thing was some real B.S. Something in me, though, made me determined to go back that next day and give it another shot. Aside from my pride being hurt from not being selected, I knew I could work harder than most of those guys at that place. For sure, I was more sober than most of them.

I hung around the house the rest of the day. I couldn't wait until Berry came back so that I could demand an answer as to why he hadn't take me out with him. When he got home, before I could say anything, he asked, "What happened? Did you go out?"

"No," I responded with much disdain.

"Well, better luck tomorrow," he said, with little sincerity. He retreated to his bedroom before I had a chance to say anything else. At that point, I decided I didn't need him. He apparently didn't care to do anything for me anyway. Maybe he was acting supportive to appease my mother.

The next day was the same as the first. It felt like the movie, *"Groundhog Day."* I figured I'd give it one more shot, and if it didn't work out, I would go find a real job. I went back that third day which offered more of the same until mid-morning, around ten o'clock. There were very few of us in the building when, finally, one of the guys behind the window called me up and asked me if I wanted to work. I thought, "What a dumb question! Why else would I be wasting my days sitting here in this dingy, smelly room?" But, I knew that was not the time to act like a smart aleck or be disrespectful.

"Yes sir," I replied.

"I am going to send you out on a job with a couple other guys. You'll be doing a move job."

"Yes sir," I said and thought to myself, "Finally!!"

I knew I had to work hard to prove myself for future gigs. The guys he sent me out with appeared to be regulars. They were all pretty straight-laced and didn't appear to be drug addicts or alcoholics. Once we got to the job, I realized the customer was a relative of one of the guys behind the window, a seemingly nice old lady. She lived quite a few flights up in a North Side apartment building. I spoke extra kindly to the lady saying, "Yes, ma'am" and "No, ma'am" every chance I could. When the other guys went on break, I kept working. When we were finally finished, the guys talked about how hard I worked, which made me feel good. Most importantly, I knew the report back to the main office would be positive. When we got back to Windy City Day Labor, the crew leader turned in a slip. They told us to have a seat. I knew we got paid every day, but I never thought to ask how much. That's just how bad I wanted work. It baffles me today about young black men set unreasonable standards and think they are too good for minimum wage, McDonald's, or other hard labor. It's a job—take it! Excuse my digression, but I've never understood disdain for work.

A few minutes later, the man at the window yelled, "Gibson!"

I walked up to the window, and he handed me a check for $35 and some change. "Heard you did a nice job out there today," he said.

"Thank you, sir," I replied, "I'll be back tomorrow."

I exited with check in hand, not realizing until I got to the corner that I now had to figure out where to cash it. I didn't have a bank account and neither did my mother. I used currency exchanges (as did most people in the hood) but decided to walk back to the building and inquire at the window how to cash my paycheck. I got the address of a corner store that cashed checks for Windy City Labor. The cashier there took my check, kept his service fee and gave me back $32 and some change. Of course, that money was already burning a hole in my pocket. Even that small amount made me happy.

I continued to arrive at Windy City every morning, getting up at four-thirty to help ensure that I would be called out on jobs. I worked a lot, at locations like McCormick Place, setting up trade shows, at distribution centers, and even delivering liquor to restaurants and bars. At that point, Berry had started working nights, so I was on my own getting to and from work.

As you can imagine, my work schedule put a damper on my ability to hang out with my friends and do things that teenagers enjoy doing during the summer. I didn't care because I was making good money. That money later helped me buy school clothes and school supplies for my senior year. Toward the end of the summer, I had a very interesting conversation with John, one of the guys behind the window.

John inquired, "Why do you come here? You seem like a good kid, and this doesn't seem like the right environment for you to be working in. What do you want to do with your life?"

I answered, "I want to go to college."

"Are you a good student?" he asked.

"I'm on the honor roll; I'm really good at sports; I'm also..." I was very proud of myself that I could say those things. A lot of kids my age never looked at grades as their ticket out of the projects and off the streets. Instead, they sensed that the grading system would always be against them, so why try any harder than just enough to get by?

John interrupted me, "I'm going to do you a favor. I'm going to put you on a steady job, but it's at night. You need to be there by nine-thirty in the evening. The place is called Romano Brothers; it's a liquor distributor. Then, in the morning when you finish, bring your ticket here. You will get paid every morning. Hey, don't tell them your age; you're supposed to be over twenty-one. Make me proud and work hard."

"Yes sir!" I exclaimed with extreme excitement. "Thank you sir; I won't disappoint you!"

I set out to build the reputation of being a good worker, and this was exactly what I accomplished. I no longer had to play games creating small talk with some of the guys or position myself where I could be seen, and in most cases, work three times harder than most of the people I went on jobs with. I was granted a steady job, and all I had to do was work hard in order to keep it.

When I got home, I excitedly shared the news with my mother. She then informed me that Romano Brothers was where Berry worked.

"Since it will be late in the evening, you can probably ride to work with him," she said.

"What time does Berry normally leave for work?" I asked.

"Around nine o'clock"

It was already late, so I could only get a few hours of sleep before starting my new job. A short time later, I woke up and got ready. Berry seemed to be pretty excited about me working where he was. I found that quite interesting, considering he definitely hadn't helped me get the job. However, I remembered that I was really practicing love and forgiveness, so there was no point holding on to any animosity that would destroy my peace and serenity. Things were looking up.

Enough is Enough

Berry and I drove to work together on my first day at the Romano Brothers, a liquor warehouse located off of Blue Island Avenue in a Latino neighborhood. Our job would be to load the liquor trucks. Berry shared with me how he had already worked himself up to "switchman" in a short period of time by working hard. His job was to switch the lever that would send different boxes down different lines at the warehouse.

You could tell he was really proud about that position as that title gave him a greater sense of worth at the job. I was pretty anxious to show him that I could work just as hard as he, so I gave it all I had. I also made sure I remembered what John at the Windy City Day Labor window had instructed me to do. He told me to keep my mouth shut about my age because, technically, we had to be at least twenty-one-years-old to work in the liquor warehouse; I was just seventeen.

Once we got in the warehouse, Berry showed me around and introduced me to everyone as his stepson. I got my assignment to work on the blue line. The blue line was one of the easiest lines. It had smaller trucks with fewer boxes of liquor to load. On most of the lines, workers paired with someone else. Seven lines were each named after a color.

I quickly noticed that all of the guys loading the liquor trucks were black, and all those driving forklifts, working in different areas of the conveyor belt, or any other operation within the site were white. They were union and we were day labor. It resembled the day labor office with the whites in the office behind the window arbitrarily handing out the jobs to the blacks on the outside. Oh well, I couldn't dwell on all the inequality issues in the world at that moment; I was just thankful to have a job. Plus, I needed to focus on proving myself at that place from the very start.

They paired me with a guy who taught me how to load the truck and stack the boxes properly to get the maximum number of boxes on a load. He also gave me all the "ins and outs" about the breaks, the break room, breakage area, and most of the other things I needed to be aware of. He seemed to be a nice, fairly straight-laced guy. I appreciated his thoroughness which helped me fit right in and feel comfortable.

As we prepared to start, he pulled a conveyor belt into the truck and before I knew it, boxes of liquor started rolling down: Carlo Rossi, Bartels & James, Peach Schnapps, Grape Schnapps, Peppermint Schnapps. So many brands I'd never even heard of. Most of my friends were already drinking on the weekends, but I hadn't started any of that yet, so it was interesting learning some of these names.

The night flew by pretty quickly, box after box and truck after truck. The work never stopped coming. Before I knew it, the clock displayed six-thirty, and the sun began peeking through. My first day was completed. I worked really hard that evening, once again trying to make a good name for myself. On our way out, something unexpected happened. As Berry and I exited the door, all of our bags and belongings were searched. Once outside, I asked him, "Why did they do that?"

He told me it was common practice because people stole liquor. Anyone caught with anything would be fired on the spot. I thought it kind of odd that Berry would not have warned me about something with such a harsh penalty like that ahead of time. He knew I didn't drink and was not a thief, but what if I fell under the temptation to take just one bottle for one of my friends? Deep down, I felt he really hoped I wouldn't make a successful run at that job.

Berry continued talking as we got into the car, "You'd be surprised at the number of alcoholics who work in liquor warehouses." He described how most of those alcoholics didn't need to steal anything because they drank all they wanted through the course of their shift. I got a chuckle out of that, as I already could see how it happened. If you broke a case of liquor, we took it to the breakage area to be repackaged, if possible. I could see guys breaking them on purpose and drinking out of the broken cases. There was no real accountability for that.

Once we got back to Windy City Day Labor, we turned in our slips and sat around while they processed our checks. It really felt good coming in that morning, knowing I held a steady job. I began to feel somewhat privileged among many of the other guys I saw arriving in the morning, waiting for work. Just the day before, I sat among them, waiting around, hoping to go out on a job.

John called my name, and I went up to the window. As he handed me my check, he said, "I heard you worked really hard, kid. Nice job." Mission accomplished.

My girlfriend that summer was Lisa Pride, a very popular and extremely beautiful girl at Whitney Young. Lisa lived on the West Side, had light skin and hazel eyes, and did not come from the usual middle to upper-middle-class family, unlike most of the other students at our school. Because of that, we felt a special bond; we understood each other's plight. She also had plans to escape her humble beginnings one day.

As my feelings for Lisa developed beyond what I considered a typical high school fling, I began to have thoughts of spending my future with her. After all, I worked what I thought to be a grown man's job—handling a night shift, getting paid everyday—I could provide for a family. Every now and then, I would think, "What if I don't go to college and just stayed at Romano Brothers? Then Lisa and I could get married." Fortunately, those thoughts only lasted a few moments. Reasoning soon kicked in, and I knew the money I made didn't justify putting aside other dreams and aspirations to take care of a family that early in my life.

As things sweetened between Lisa and me, my relationship with Berry soured. I sensed a shift in his demeanor overall but particularly in his attitude toward me. In fact, it wasn't just toward me; the negative behavior extended to my mother and my sister, as well. The more I tried to walk in love, as I learned in church, the more I could feel my patience with Berry growing thin.

One weekend, Berry yelled at Eboni over something minor she did. I can't even remember what it was she did, but I do remember him shouting, "You're so stupid!"

That did it! Enough was enough, and I was fed up! One of the lessons I learned from the empowerment books I read was to be careful of what you said to people, especially children. Young minds are not developed or astute enough to properly filter out the negative messages. Therefore, things you say to them or about them and the labels that you give them, if done consistently enough, will result in them becoming whatever you have verbalized.

I snapped back at Berry, "Don't call my sister stupid! She is not stupid; she is smart."

Berry countered, "I'll say whatever the hell I want to say to her! And who are you talking to?"

I grew bolder by the minute, "I'm talking to you, and you *won't* say just anything to her. You are not her father, and you have no right talking to her like that."

I could tell I really pushed Berry to the limit, standing up to him like that. At that instant, it became all about the ego. He got right up in my face, spitting his words, "I'm sick of your sh**! You want to be a man? Step outside and we'll handle this like men!"

"A'ight!" As I turned to open the back screen door, Berry hit me from behind. I stumbled out the door. I could not believe he struck me. A grown man hitting a kid with his back turned? What a coward!

I flung around and punched him in the face. Then I stooped down, straddled him around his legs and thrust him up against the wall. He kept hitting my back as I jammed my shoulder into his rib cage, trying to break a rib. Fortunately for Berry, my mother ran up behind him and tried to pry him loose. As I pressed into him harder and harder, my mother yelled, "Jemal stop it! Put him down; you're smashing me! Please stop!"

So I let go, and Berry plopped to the floor of the back porch. He jumped up, ran inside toward the front of the apartment. Whenever things got testy between us, he would go pull out his shotgun and start cleaning it, as if to send me a message. My street instincts told me to run in the opposite direction. There was no way for me to win by standing up to a man with a bruised ego and a loaded shotgun.

So, I ran down the back stairs. While doing so, I heard my mother screaming at her crazed boyfriend, "No, Berry! No, stop! Leave him alone!"

Hearing that, I ran faster, putting all my athletic talent to the test. I jumped past the last few stairs, darted through the narrow corridor between the apartment buildings and into the back alley. At that point, I couldn't distinguish between imagined and real footsteps behind me. I didn't want to stop and check, either. My heart seemed to beat a thousand times a minute. I was having my own personal track meet, tackling a 400-yard dash with ease.

Down the alley and across the street I sprinted, not stopping until I reached the end of the block. From that vantage point, I figured I would see him either walking or driving his car. After standing there for a few minutes, I went to a payphone and called my dad at Pint's. I rambled through the entire sequence of events, expecting (and hoping) him to say, "Stay right there; I'm on my way." But, he didn't. He just told me to go over to Tee's and not to go back to my mother's place. That's when I realized my dad was also exercising some of the lessons that he learned from Unity Church. The "old him" would've gone and beat the crap out of Berry. Dad adopted a new set of rules to live by. He knew that to take revenge or get involved in that type of foolishness and negative energy would have only resulted in negative consequences.

So, I went to Tee's house. Ant was there. After telling him what happened, he ran out of the house. While I knew nothing good was going to come from whatever Ant and his gang drummed up, I would be dishonest if I didn't admit that it felt good knowing that my brother jumped to my rescue without hesitation. After re-connecting with Ant, as a child, I realized I could always count on him to protect me.

One of my most memorable moments of Ant's protection occurred at a basketball game the previous year at Whitney Young. We played Crane Tech, the high school my brother attended. At one point during the game, a fight erupted. The entire gym was fighting; fans, players, and even our coaches were shoving people, trying to regain order. My brother and some of the Vice Lords came and encircled me on the court. In a way, I felt bad that I wasn't fighting with my team, but my brother wouldn't let me out of that circle. As the crowd pushed and shoved, he yelled, "Anybody touch my little brother, they gettin' they head swelled!"

That was my brother—Hollywood Holloway, as his boys called him. It felt cool when his friends referred to me as, "Li'l Hollywood." It made me feel like I had some street credibility, especially since I wasn't gangbangin' like they all were.

Berry would get what was coming to him if my brother caught him. I figured Ant would stop, pick up a few guys, and then head over to my mother's. I did not hear from my brother for a couple of hours, but my mother called and said that Berry's windows were busted out in his car. Fortunately for Berry, he was not at home because Ant knew he deserved more than broken car windows. Ant knew how Berry would make my mother walk to the store in the winter to buy groceries while his car sat parked out front. Ant knew Berry used abusive language with our mother and Ebi. Ant knew, just as well as I did, that Berry wasn't good enough for our mother. Unfortunately, our mother hadn't had that revelation yet.

The following Monday, I went to get my things from my mother's house, and my brother came along. Again, fortunately for Berry, he was not at home. My mother cried and asked me not to leave. I knew I could not stay where it was just a matter of time before something really bad happened to me. I also knew my mother must have felt she needed Berry; maybe it was to help with the bills or for her own emotional reasons. Bottom line, she never told me she would make Berry leave, so that made it clear to me that I had to go.

Aunt Freddie, my dad's sister, invited me to stay with her. She had four girls:

Yvette, Demetria, Latrice, and Doretha. My aunt also raised two other girls, who became like daughters to her: Stanlia and Cynthia Miller. Cynthia was extremely beautiful with a caramel-colored complexion and long hair. She was also quite sassy. She and I would later create an unbreakable bond of love and support. She worked for President Barack Obama when he was an Illinois State Senator. Back then, she would often tell me I reminded her of him. Back then, I had no idea who Barack Obama was. Once I found out, I certainly felt unworthy of her compliment. But that was Cynthia, always inspirational and supportive.

Upon moving into Aunt Freddie's home, she sat me down and laid out all the rules. That was the sixth or seventh household I had lived in, and all the "rules" speeches sounded alike: I must go to school; I had to get good grades; I must work; I had to help clean the house, and on and on. I later realized that the people who gave me rules really cared about me. In my lifetime, I've come across too many young people in homes without rules, without guidance, without love. Being grateful to have a roof over my head, I had no problem following any rules that Aunt Freddie set forth.

My first night going back to Romano Brothers since the fight with Berry naturally made me a little nervous. In Chicago, it wouldn't surprise anyone to see a newspaper headline that read, "Boy killed by mother's boyfriend." My dad often reminded me to not become a statistic, a newspaper headline. Good reminder, Dad, but how could a person be certain to avoid such a fate? If someone really wanted to kill you, there are a number of ways it could be accomplished without you standing a chance.

I figured I couldn't avoid him forever, and I certainly didn't want to mess up a good job over something that may have simmered down to nothing more than a leftover, slightly bruised ego. Still, a tremendous amount of anxiety welled up in me as I approached the warehouse. Once inside, I stayed very alert with my guard up, not knowing where Berry might pop up.

As I walked to my line, out of the corner of my eye, I noticed Berry walking toward me carrying a stick. I quickly turned to square up and tossed my duffle bag to the ground. He started yelling and cursing which drew the attention of several guys nearby. I immediately cased the room, looking for any object to pick up but couldn't find anything. Just as he charged me, a couple of co-workers dashed in between us. I had nothing to defend myself against him and his stick, so I was most grateful for their assistance.

Berry continued to shout, "So, you think you're tough? You want to f**k with me? I will hurt you!" He continued to bellow and, of course, I just couldn't let it be. So, I taunted him back, matching his sentiments.

"F**k you, old man! That's why I beat your old a**! You want another a**-kickin'? Uh? Let 'em go so he can come get another a**-kickin'!" This fired him up even more. What did I expect?

By that time, one of the supervisors rushed over and angrily told us if we didn't calm down, everyone would be fired. I picked up my bag and slowly backed up. The guys ushered Berry off. I felt uncomfortable the entire night. Working inside of a truck at the end of that conveyor belt put me in a vulnerable and defenseless position. I just hoped the fear of being fired would prevent Berry from seeking any further retaliation. My protective angels were with me that night on the job. I hoped they remained with me a lot longer.

Negative Influence

I had a friend named Eric, aka Cat Daddy. He attended Whitney Young with me and grew up on the West Side like me. That's pretty much the extent of our similarities. Cat Daddy harbored a real mean streak. He fought a lot and got in trouble even more. I don't recall if he ever started the fights, but he managed to be in them, nonetheless. I really liked him and had a sincere desire to help him do better in life.

One day, I decided to help Cat Daddy and get him a job at Romano Brothers. My reason was two-fold. First and foremost, he did need a job. The second reason, I admit, benefited me. You see, I figured at 6'4" and three hundred-plus pounds, Cat Daddy would make an excellent bodyguard for me, in case Berry decided to act crazy at work again. Berry would have to try something only one time before it would be his last with Cat Daddy around.

From one of the many books I read, I remember learning about the law of association. It makes you take serious note of who you hang around. Just by association, if you're not changing the folks around you, then they are changing you. In spite of what the experts said, I felt Cat Daddy and I defied that principle, in that we could hang out together and still maintain our two very distinctive personalities and characteristics, still accepting each other for who we were. There was one time, however, when I did allow his character to negatively influence me at Romano Brothers.

Cat Daddy came up with a scheme to steal some of the flavored Schnapps and sell it at school. Our friends didn't drink whiskey, vodka, or other strong alcohol, but most of them did drink the more sweet types of alcohol like Schnapps, Mad Dog 20/20, Boone's Farm, Brass Monkey, beer, and things along that line. I told Cat Daddy how my duffle bag actually had a secret zip-up compartment on the very bottom, making it ideal for hiding several bottles.

The security guards who checked our bags each morning seemed fairly nice. We sometimes engaged in small talk as they routinely did their job. I would open the top of my bag; they would quickly look in, briefly feel around, and let me pass through. I believe because of my age and good work ethic, they may have assumed I would not drink or steal at all. Therefore, their search of my bag was never as rigorous as their searches with others.

I decided to go along with Cat Daddy's plan, and I stole several bottles of the Schnapps. I quickly stashed them in the bottom of my bag, wrapping a T-shirt around each bottle to keep them from clinking together. Cat Daddy hid some in his bag, too. As we shuffled along in the line getting closer and closer to the security guard, I could feel my heart racing. I realized what I did was wrong, and I knew full well the potential consequences of being fired. When I finally got to the security guard, my heightened anxiety caused my heart to stop altogether. I tried not to look suspicious as I acknowledged him with a nod and scooted my bag toward him on the table. The guard opened my bag and put his hand in, while asking me how my night was.

"Just fine," I managed to answer in a nonchalant, matter-of-fact tone.

He slid my bag back to me, and I walked out the door. My heart, which seemed to have remained still during that whole process, started beating faster than ever. I let out a huge sigh of relief and rejoiced that I actually got away with stealing. Rejoice was short-lived.

The guilt of stealing immediately wreaked havoc on my conscience. How could I have done something so blatantly wrong just because someone suggested I do it? I couldn't believe Cat Daddy had that strong of an influence over me. For the first time, I began to truly understand the law of association and knew I had to make better conscious decisions to separate myself from people who could negatively influence me. I tried to separate myself from Cat Daddy after that. Fortunately, he made it easier on me by getting fired for continuously missing work.

Windy City Day Labor treated me well, so I never did anything again to jeopardize my relationship with them. I continued to work at Romano Brothers off and on during the school year if I needed the cash and if my schoolwork allowed for it. I would work through the night and then go straight to school in the morning. Sometimes, though, I opted to go home for a quick nap and miss Art, my first class before homeroom. I didn't do well in that art class mainly because of my absences, but at the time, I felt I needed money more than creative explorations.

Romano Brothers also let me work during the holidays. I usually worked a "double," meaning I would load the liquor trucks at night and then ride in the truck to the stores and restaurants the next morning to deliver the liquor. Working there really allowed me to establish a strong work ethic and a good reputation. I was able to take care of myself for the most part and stash a little away to buy things for college. To this day, I remain extremely grateful for the experience and security Romano Brothers gave me and for the income that kept me afloat during that time in my life.

Educated Thugs

While all of that tough life stuff raged on in my life—moving from home to home, conflicts with my mother's boyfriend, working long hours, being robbed at gunpoint—I felt grateful to have one constant. It was Whitney M. Young Magnet High School (Whitney Young). It had become the final destination along my primary and secondary educational journey. What a place to wrap up and put an exclamation point on my entire childhood learning experience as it proved to be a life-changing opportunity as well!

Enner facilitated my entrance into the school. All applicants are supposed to pass an entrance exam because it was a magnet school, but she knew Mr. Penny, the girls' swim and basketball coach. He pulled some strings, got me in playing basketball, and I didn't even have to take the exam. I love her for the way she really knew how to make things happen and will forever be grateful that she was my "educational angel."

Maintaining its prestigious reputation, even to this day, Whitney Young became Chicago's first public magnet school in 1975, with a few critics predicting its short-term demise. I suppose they based their forecast on the fact that the school's location was an inner city, burned out, vacant lot—compliments of the 1968 civil rights rioting. Perhaps they just didn't have faith in a plan to keep a school well diversified, yet academically competitive; after all, the prejudiced mindset of people because of the civil rights struggle proved very hard to change. Today, with its still well-diversified population, Whitney Young quiets all naysayers with its impressive academic standing as one of the best schools in the nation, according to a U.S. News and World Report.9

As I frequented those hallways in 1986 and 1987, I never once thought about the possibility that a future First Lady of the United States of America had graced those very same tile-floored hallways, using one of the very same lockers, just five years prior to my attending. But yes, Michelle Obama is among many intelligent and gifted alumnae who soaked up the excellence in education that Whitney Young has to offer and went on to create great and notable careers for themselves.

However, there was another side to the highly sought-after school that never got publicized; it was an ongoing activity that remained under the radar of those scholastic reports. Let's just say that I fought more in my two years at that school than I had in my entire childhood!

I started out at Whitney Young, as I did at all my previous schools, having to prove myself athletically. By that time, I definitely excelled at basketball. My ex-teammates and coaches knew it, too, since Jeff Smith and I stood out in every game during my freshman year at Richwoods High School. Yet, that didn't matter anymore. My contribution to our winning season my sophomore year at Thornton didn't matter either when I played with guys there like Trent White, Illandus Hampton, and Marcus Chapman. Fortunately, I was able to establish a starting position at Whitney Young. As usual, that made my transition into that new school quite easy.

Within those two years, I cultivated some of the most sacred and life-enduring friendships. James "Dave" Shanks, Jeff "JB" Beasley, Marc Christmas, Anthony "Tony" Hall, Andre "Scabini" Cunningham, Teddy Gilmore, Eddie "EB" Buck, and Marcette Magnum have all become like brothers to me. I often credit them with my success, as I emulated each and every one of them.

Our closeness even led us all to the same college: Florida A&M University (FAMU). We were absolutely inseparable. In fact, while we were in high school, we formed our own private fraternity called KDU. That acronym stands for Kappa Dammit Uh. Other members were Andre Thomas, Kameno Bell, Sammy

Smith, Koy Billings, Wesley Penn, Miguel Braun, Dan Fitzgerald, Anthony "Big Tone" and Henry Gray, just to name a few.

Those eight inherited brothers and I generated adventures galore! Mama Beasley (Jeff's mom) referred to us as "Educated Thugs." The police considered us "a gang." All of those guys were very smart and most came from middle class and upper middle class families, though if you heard them talk about their upbringing, they would tell about the struggles they experienced growing up. And yes, while some of them may have struggled, and I don't discount their personal stories, I would have traded in my family's financial situation for any one of theirs, in a heartbeat.

Most of them never really knew the degree of poverty I lived in, mainly because I never told them. They hailed from the prominent black neighborhoods like Hyde Park, Pill Hill, Beverly, and a few other areas on the South Side. Most of them never came to my neighborhood. None of us judged each other based on where we lived or what we wore, and these were reasons why our friendships grew so solidly.

It was a good thing they didn't judge me based on what I wore; otherwise, I would've never made it into their inner circle with my no-style attire. My mother's budget didn't allow for the designer labels that my friends and classmates sported—everything from Girbaud jeans to Gucci and Coach belts, Polo and Izod Shirts, and Louis Vuitton and Coach purses. You name it; if it cost a lot of money, the kids at Whitney Young owned it.

On the other hand, there I stood with my two pairs of jeans and one pair of slacks that my mother made me hand wash in the tub most of the time. My hand-me-down shirts from Ant were four sizes too big; yet, they dutifully served the single purpose of covering my frail looking body. For my high school senior picture (a mug shot that lives on to eternity in every alum's yearbook), I wore an old maroon and grey shirt, accented with my brother's skinny maroon tie, topped with his four-sizes-too-big, cream-colored sports jacket. Nevertheless, the guys and I were very tight, and they overlooked my fashion shortcomings.

Our "gang" had a girl crew as well: Yvonne Orr, Yvonne Lee, Latrina Jackson, Tina Taylor, Jana Johnson, Shelley Thymes, Tonya Smalls and Diana Shepard. Most of them went to FAMU, as well. We formed a close-knit circle. Actually, most of the guys dated the girls in the crew. Most did, but not me. At that time, I didn't dare attempt. My lack of cool clothing served up one dose of insecurity, while my braces dished out a healthier dose of hesitancy.

Though I was most grateful for the opportunity to even wear braces, I would have welcomed any sort of initiative by my parents to have them removed in due time. The real culprit, however, remained lack of money, of course. Approximately three months after receiving my braces was the last time money was available for regular orthodontic visits. So, by the time I attended Whitney Young, that five year-old metal apparatus in my mouth served no purpose whatsoever. My teeth could not have gotten any straighter than they did after eighteen months or so; yet, those braces stayed attached for a total of eight years. No enamel damage, fortunately, but definitely some self-esteem erosion.

As I mentioned, there was a side of Whitney Young most adults either didn't know about or simply didn't want to admit to. The fighting side. How the KDU crew found ourselves involved in so many fights, I don't know. There we were, among the top schools in the nation with students from affluent households, fighting kids from our rival school, Kenwood Academy, another highly regarded high school also with a financially well-off student body. It seemed to be a tradition of sorts passed down from generation to generation, sort of like the Hatfields and McCoys. It wasn't just boys, either; the girls also had their fair share of fights.

Unfortunately, we proved that fighting was not unique to lower-income schools since violence of varying degrees had become the norm in schools of all kinds across our entire nation. If it's not a rival school issue, then it's usually a gang-related situation or some neighborhood altercation between individuals or some-times even on-going family brawls. Whatever the setting, whoever the individuals, as with most fights, it's always a series of little things that lead up to the big "finale."

When we were seniors, one such situation with our rival school, Kenwood, appeared to be a hand-me-down issue that grew as time moved forward. I recall some people saying that Teddy threw an egg at a car that belonged to a Kenwood student as retaliation for a previous incident. Several days later, one of my classmates, Pat Barely, threw a party at his house and invited Whitney Young students as well as a few of his neighborhood friends. Word about that party got around to our Kenwood opponents who couldn't pass on an opportunity for more retaliation.

Like any high school's blue-light basement party, eventually boys and girls got cuddled up in various corners. Right when the cuddling was getting good, some Kenwood guys arrived and boldly walked through the party just staring at each of us without uttering a word. One guy stopped in front of me, opened his jacket, brandished a machete, closed his jacket and walked away. I didn't have anything on me that could serve as a weapon, so I certainly wasn't going to do anything foolish, like react. Those intruders slowly walked back to the stairs and once at the top, ran out of the house. All of sudden, like a herd of wild buffalo, my buddies and I ran out after them grabbing bats, golf clubs, and anything else we could find in Pat's basement and garage.

As we emerged outside, their whole crew stood at the corner waiting for us. We charged toward that corner like a bunch of rag-tag soldiers from the movie *Braveheart*, yelling and screaming like maniacs. Our scare tactic worked, and their crew hopped in their cars and sped off in different directions before we could even get to the corner.

One car, driven by Derek, headed recklessly toward Andre Thomas and me. Derek was a classmate of ours who we called "Sympathizer," because he hung around with those Kenwood guys. We jumped out of the path of that car just in the nick of time. As a spontaneous reaction, we both swung golf clubs at his back window, shattering it. Even though glass flew into the heads of the backseat passengers, Derek kept driving. Andre and I stood in the middle of the street feeling victorious, chanting, high-fiving, and carrying on like real street warriors.

Then came what we pegged "The Valentine's Day Massacre," which occurred during our school's annual Valentine's Day Dance. At that event, those same Kenwood guys busted out George Jackson's car windows in the parking lot. Later that night, a bunch of us drove to Hyde Park and found those guys sitting in a car. We rolled up on them about five cars deep, and they jumped out and ran. I'm embarrassed to say that we totally demolished that car. We busted every window, punched holes throughout, flattened the tires, ripped up the inside—thoroughly destroyed it.

The next night, their crew drove past Andre's house real slow, several cars deep, yelling out threats. So, of course, as feuds go, the KDUs had to react. I happened to be at a girlfriend's house that night and knew nothing about what was going down, but a few of our guys got together and planned an ambush—a *real* ambush.

Two of our guys went to the Hyde Park Square, a regular hangout spot for Kenwood kids, and stood at the corner of a major intersection. Taking the bait, the Kenwood boys chased our boys around the corner to an open parking lot where a lot more of our crew waited. Once they saw our group, they turned around and started running away, all except for one guy, named Mike. Mike wasn't aware that his buddies retreated, since he had run far ahead of them. By the time he did realize it and turned to run, it was too late. My boys were on him. They kicked, punched, and beat Mike so badly that they almost killed him. I'm not exactly sure, but I believe they broke his vertebrae, some ribs, an arm, and his jaw.

When the guys told me the next day what happened, I was so angry that I missed it. I really wanted a piece of that action. In spite of the fact that this feud between a bunch of revengeful sixteen and seventeen-year-olds had escalated to hatred, we were thankful that it didn't result in Mike's or anyone else's death. Our fights never resulted in any fatalities.

We were lucky, unlike what seems to be the case currently where students are getting killed over the same menial issues we had. For example, Darian Albert, a Chicago high school honor student, was killed during a fight outside of his school in 2009. He was hit in the head with a 2x4 and brutally stomped and kicked during a huge brawl involving many students. I'm sure no one meant to kill anyone, but those are the harsh, unforeseen consequences when engaging in that type of activity. Young people do not always think clearly about the effects of their actions.

That following Monday, all our crew wore ties, something we had planned to do before the Mike incident. We intended no symbolism behind it; we were just being "fly," as we called it. Later that morning, while in biology class, two police officers knocked on my classroom door. They asked for me. My teacher came to my desk and escorted me to the door.

One officer inquired, "Are you Jemal Gibson?"

"Yes sir," I cooperatively replied.

"You need to come with us," he commanded.

The two officers flanked me as we headed down the hallway. I could see several of my friends coming from different areas being led by either a school official or the police. We all had ties on, making it an unmistakable assumption that we were the "gang"—the educated thugs—sought after in the Mike incident. While we didn't know exactly what was about to happen, we knew it couldn't be good. As we entered a conference room, there finally sat the entire KDU crew.

The Police started off with the typical good cop, bad cop routine.

"If you don't tell us what happened this weekend, you are all going to jail! I mean it! A young man is in the hospital, hurt very badly. So, if you don't tell me what happened to him, I'll gladly throw you all in jail because I know you were all involved."

Now, the supposed "good cop" chimed in:

"Look, I know you guys are good kids; you go to a good school. We just want to hear what happened this weekend. Let me get the names straight. Who's Marc "Xmas" Christmas? Andre "Dre T" Thomas? Jemal "Big Mal" Gibson?

That police officer went through all of our names and included every nickname. After each name was called, we diligently raised our hands. He was so accurate with every name! I thought to myself, "How did he know that information?" Suddenly it came to me: Derek, the Sympathizer was now the Squealer.

They kept us in that room for what seemed like hours. No one gave up any information. When they got to me and asked about my involvement, I told them I wasn't there. Finally, they dismissed the rest of us but kept Dre and Dave.

Before we left, the principal lectured us about how ashamed and disappointed he was. I didn't listen to anything he said, as my mind was so "not there." Still angry that I missed the whole thing, I kept thinking about how I had let my guys down by hanging out with my girl instead. Had I been there, though, would I have gone along with the group's crazed beating, or would I have stopped them from thrashing that guy within an inch of his life?

I'm sure *none* of our crew intended to ever seriously hurt anyone. The most you usually expected to get out of those fights was a bloody nose or lip, not broken vertebrae. We always heard about teens being shot, stabbed, or even killed, but we never stopped to think about what led up to that final act—probably something small, just like in our case. What a rude awakening!

They took Dre and Dave to jail, but their folks posted bail and they were out later that day. From his hospital bed, Mike had identified the two of them and gave their names to the police. He stayed in the hospital for quite a few days, but did fully recover. I remember hoping and praying that he would get better because none of us were prepared for how our lives would have changed instantly if Mike had died or was paralyzed due to our silly school rivalry.

Dre and I were told we couldn't graduate unless we paid for Derek's car window. The new window cost eighty dollars, so my part was forty. It might as well have been four hundred dollars because I certainly couldn't come up with *any* of the money. Fortunately for me, Dre's mother graciously paid the entire bill.

Right after the Mike incident, I thought long and hard about senseless fights. Those brawls between our schools had gone on way too long and had gotten way too serious. That one episode could have dealt a totally different outcome for those Kenwood boys and for each of us. Unfortunately, there are too many times that the outcome is not good and not reversible.

Today, Dre is a successful orthopedic doctor. Dave, who served as an Airborne Ranger in the Army, is now an actor/producer in Hollywood. In one of his movie roles, he played the guy who stole the haircut in *Barbershop*. My KDU guys and I—yes, the educated thugs that we were—are the lucky few who managed to escape Chicago's city streets. It wasn't just the physical place that we had to leave; we had to break away mentally as well, leaving behind loved ones waddling in fear, resentfulness, and hopelessness.

Preparation is Everything

Attending so many different high schools didn't allow for much bonding with career counselors. Since no one reached out to me with necessary information on life after high school, it didn't occur to me to embrace it on my own. College? Yes, I'd thought of it many times, and knew I needed to go. But had I put together all the necessary steps to get there? No way. I had no real knowledge about higher education, other than I should go. No one in my family had gone to college in the traditional sense. For example, my dad earned his Master's degree in Psychology, but he did so at age thirty-something. Therefore, my family didn't know how to assist me in the transition from high school to college.

Even though I lacked official guidance, I learned some things about college from the KDU crew. Many of the guys had already filled out several applications to different schools, while I had no clue where to even get the applications. I inquired of fellow KDU brother, Dave, who responded rather matter-of-factly, "You get them from recruiting fairs and the career counselor."

What? I had no idea there *were* recruiting fairs. Those fairs had ended, so Dave gave me all the extra applications he had, mostly for schools I had never heard of. I filled them out quickly, hoping that I could get a few offers for basketball scholarships. While I served as captain of our team, I hadn't played much my senior year due to a thumb broken in a Christmas tournament. I started receiving many introductory letters telling me all about their schools. Some letters came from big schools like the University of Nevada, Las Vegas and Marquette

University, while others came from smaller, obscure community colleges.

Some of the letters I received were for possible cross-country track scholarships. Our cross-country team became the City Champion in 1987. It was my first year running, and I was the pick-off man usually securing our fourth or fifth spot. Points were awarded by the placement of the first five players from each team. Coach Wallace was a great coach and extremely motivating. His favorite saying: "Just get the next one." That meant just catch up to the next guy ahead. And that's exactly what I would do. With intense focus, I would hunt down the next one. I would watch his feet, measure his steps, match his stride, and then pick mine up. I always got the next one. I never lost to that next one—never. I believe that philosophy has helped me to this day to always focus on the next thing— the next assignment, the next project, the next development, the next promotion—with great intensity, until accomplished.

The only problem was I really did not like running—not cross-country anyway. All those miles, almost every single day! Running must be a God-given talent because I never practiced like my peers, yet I still excelled at it. I initially only did it for basketball conditioning, but the coach called me a natural.

I first ran three miles with my dad when I was just ten-years-old. I had never run any distance before; I didn't even know how far a mile stretched. That first long run created a memorable moment for my dad because he didn't expect me to keep up with him. He always jogged from his apartment in Park Forest South (now University Park) to Governor's State University where he attended school. It was a hilly route, considering how flat Chicago is. He said I never complained, not even once; I never asked him to slow down, stop, or rest. I just kept on running, like Forrest Gump.

Sometimes when I look back on that time, I believe I kept running in order to bond with my dad. He always had friends dropping by his apartment at different times. My infrequent visits with him were usually a few days or a week at the most—never long enough for me. While running with him, I had him all to myself.

I received those college letters, which appeared to be serious opportunities to run cross-country at various colleges, but I never followed up on any of them. I didn't know I had to respond. I only knew what I had seen in the movies. In the movies, the recruiters visited the athlete's home, and they shook hands to seal the deal. No one knocked on my door to talk to my mother and me about me attending their school. As a result, I figured such good fortune would elude me.

I respected my fellow KDU brothers' college knowledge, and they became my college counselors. Most of the fellas, as well as a large number of the girls in "our crew," selected Florida A&M University (FAMU) as their school of choice. "Wow, that would be cool," I thought. "Florida—warm weather, beaches, all my friends—I'm going, too!" That was it. All of my thoughts and preparations went into going to FAMU.

My most influential friend of the whole group was Dave Shanks. In fact, we all looked up to him because he seemed to be the complete package— intelligent, great communicator, loyal, handsome, a great athlete, and a chick magnet. I wanted to be like Dave. He and I ran cross-country together and, after winning City Championship, became inseparable. He really gave my college search a boost by giving me his extra applications. I am forever indebted to him for that favor, which he perhaps thought was a minor thing.

Dave pursued an Army ROTC scholarship to pay for school. He was the only one of our crew to do so. I guess the rest of us had no interest in the Army. Initially, I certainly questioned Dave's decision, primarily because of all of the stories my dad told me about his time in Vietnam from 1965 to 1966.

My dad's feelings about his military career were ambiguous. On one hand, he was so proud of his connection to the 173rd Airborne Division—The Herd. As a paratrooper, he often bragged that they were one of the "baddest" divisions in "The Nam." He talked about how they did two combat jumps but only received credit for one. He also talked about all the guys he grew to love as brothers.

Perhaps, Dad's loving feelings toward those guys created the paradox that was his experience in Vietnam; his pride could quickly turn to the visible pain and anguish the memories created. When the topic of his war buddies came up, he got quiet. There were horror stories of his friends stepping on landmines and being blown to pieces and of snipers killing many of his good friends. When his unit finally took the snipers out, sometimes they found children chained to trees, forced to be soldiers and die young, long before they could possibly understand why.

He also shared about how, as soldiers, they would be dropped via helicopters into fire zones where bullets and mortar fire were constant. Their only escape came as a wounded victim who would then be "choppered out." He said there were times he contemplated shooting himself just to exit the hell they were in on a continual basis. However, staying to protect his buddies always won over his mind's quagmire of fear, survival, and duty.

Dad had many war stories that almost always left him in sorrowful tears. Each time he finished sharing his military experiences, he would say, "I will never let that happen to you, Jemal. I will take you to Canada should there ever be another draft." My dad had never been drafted. In fact, he lied about his age in order to sign up. He was only seventeen-years-old when he shipped off to Vietnam from Okinawa in the first combat unit to enter Vietnam. He was one of very few returning veterans from his division. Most lost their lives in that jungle. Like so many others who survived the horrors of that war, he came home addicted to drugs and suffering from post-traumatic stress disorder (PTSD) off and on for the rest of his life.

I decided to go after the ROTC scholarship, in spite of all those stories. After all, my dad was my hero, and I wanted to be just like him. At least I desired to mimic all the good I saw in him, and his service to his country was good. I knew he would be unhappy about my decision, but in my mind, I kept asking, "How else will I be able to afford college?"

Once again, Dave came through in getting me the necessary paperwork. I filled out the ROTC scholarship packet that required three references. I requested the information from three teachers, but forgot to follow up and failed to receive one of the recommendations back in time to meet the deadline. At our graduation, all of the scholarship recipients were announced, and Dave got the four-year Army ROTC scholarship. I remember the crowd giving him a big round of applause. It always sounded impressive for anyone to get a four-year scholarship, regardless of the type. I was proud of Dave, yet disappointed that I did not get that award. Fortunately, a three-year one was still available, so I made a commitment to myself that I would apply for it once at FAMU.

On our FAMU applications, Dave and I had requested to be roommates. We created a packing list and split the items in half. For example, I bought the iron and he bought the ironing board. I couldn't send in my application during the school year because I couldn't afford the application fee. I was back at Romano Brothers working to meet all the financial requirements of preparing for college. Still, I seemed to lack all that was needed at the time it was needed.

The summer quickly drew to a close. It seemed so short, which I suppose could only be due to the fact deadlines and fees were hitting me left and right. I grew very nervous when I received a rejection letter from the School of Business and Industry (SBI) at FAMU. Initially, I thought that meant the university itself didn't accept me. I remember becoming very stressed out over what I would do next. I only applied at that one school, and classes were scheduled to start within a couple weeks.

Something had to give. I could not stay in Chicago. I firmly believed that if I stayed in that jungle with all the drugs and gangbangers, fighting with my mother's boyfriend while constantly stressed and victimized by the negativity surrounding me, I would not make it out alive. I knew I had to gain a new perspective on the entire matter.

I looked at the college entrance situation as just another challenge. I had already faced and overcome so many. I learned from my dad and from the Scott Peck book, *"The Road Less Traveled,"* that life is full of challenges—not problems. Because we will always have challenges, we should approach them with fresh optimism and bulldog determination to overcome whatever we're facing. I was so determined to go to FAMU that I figured I would just have to work through any challenges *after* I got there.

Find a Way

The first positive sign that my resolve and determination paid off was the general admissions acceptance letter I received from FAMU, just prior to leaving for school. I felt so relieved! That letter represented my ticket out of the ghetto. I embarked on a journey that no one in my family had taken before; however, my mother felt sad and, believe it or not, she and Berry tried to coerce me into staying in Chicago! They said they would buy me a car if I went to Malcolm X College or some other Chicago city college.

I don't know what got into my mother—and especially Berry—to want me to stay. However, I had learned over the years that those who love us the most are often the ones who hold us back from our dreams. Whether they do it consciously or subconsciously, it generally happens because our changing leads us to a higher level where we no longer desire to be with them as much because we have found so much more for ourselves. Also, when we improve ourselves, it shines an unwanted light on the problems and shortcomings of those around us who refuse to change. By nature, it's so much easier for our loved ones to want us all to stay in the pit where everything remains horrible, but familiar.

Nevertheless, as tempting as the car offer was, considering I had never had one before, I thought they were crazy for even thinking I would stay. Besides, based on my past experiences with them, I already knew the car would soon become an unfulfilled promise.

Finally, the day came for my departure to college. I planned to travel with one of my KDU fellas, Marcette Magnum (Cette), and his family. His family had a van, and so I gratefully accepted their offer for me to ride with them. We loaded up at Cette's house. I had my trunk filled with school clothes, school supplies, report cards and my FAMU acceptance letter, plus $40 in my wallet. Yep, that $40 constituted all that I had to my name. All my Romano Brothers earnings were prudently spent on the clothes and supplies I needed for school. To make matters even more challenging, I gave Cette's dad $20 for gas. I felt it was the right thing to do to avoid the impression that I was a freeloader. Of course, his dad didn't know he was accepting one half of all that I owned or I doubt he would've taken it.

The drive to Tallahassee seemed forever—over twenty hours. As we got closer, I began peering out the window for the beaches, but saw dry, slightly hilly land instead. I expected water—as in beaches or even the gulf—since we were in Florida. Obviously, I surprisingly learned that Tallahassee was not located in any coastal area of Florida. One would think that I would have studied something about the location I was moving to for the next four or five years of my life, so that I would know something more about it besides it being Florida's capital city, which was another surprise. It was just another example of my lack of awareness and worldliness. Despite graduating from the best magnet school in Chicago, I had not yet recognized how very isolating, hence crippling, our childhood environments can be.

We arrived on campus on a Sunday, so the Administration building was closed. We went to our dormitory to check in, and all check-ins were done at Gibbs Hall. I wondered if Dave made it onto campus, since we would be roommates. As we all stood in line, a guy in front of Cette dealt with some housing issues. Apparently, they did not have him assigned to a room. Since he had all of his paperwork, they gave him a temporary room assignment until things could be worked out on Monday. Cette was next and went through his processing with no problems.

My turn to approach the man at the check-in desk came, and my heart started beating a little faster. Hopefully, in spite of my late acceptance, everything was squared away for me, especially since I didn't have a parent with me. As fate would have it, they did not have my room assignment. I told the man that I was rooming with Dave Shanks, and he told me Dave already had a roommate assigned. My heart sank. We had purchased so many items to share. How would we manage if we were in different rooms? I showed the man a copy of my application with my request for Dave as my roommate, and he didn't look a bit sympathetic to my situation. I did not have a room. I suppose after hearing hundreds and hundreds of stories throughout that whole registration process, the workers grew numb to even the most unfortunate situations.

Next, the man asked for a check for my room and board payment. I told him I didn't have one and that it would be covered with financial aid. I also told him there must be a mistake with my housing, just like the guy in front of us. I then asked if they could give me a temporary room, as well, until I get everything worked out on Monday. He agreed, but told me if it was not done in a couple of days, I would be asked to leave the dormitory. I was relieved that I had a place to stay, at least for a couple of days.

I got to my room on the top floor with all my belongings, and found it empty except for its basic furniture. It was a new dorm, so all the furniture looked really nice and smelled really new. I claimed the top bunk. Built underneath the bed was my desk. I thought that was so cool; I had never seen a bunk bed like that. After unpacking, I went down to the main lobby to track down my fellas from Whitney Young. Almost everyone had arrived already. Dave and I were bummed that we weren't roommates, but quickly got over it with the excitement of being at school. I don't remember much about our first night, probably because I was focused on getting all of the challenges worked out the next day.

First thing Monday morning, I trekked over to the Administration building to get my financial aid worked out, to keep from being kicked out of the dorm. All the key offices of the university were located in that one building at the bottom of the hill. The long line that snaked outside the building and around the side consisted of students there for the same reason as me. I quickly got in line and waited, and waited, and waited. I actually enjoyed being detained for those two or so hours, as it afforded me the chance to do some serious people watching.

I had never before in my life been in one place with so many black people doing something so positive and transformative. I felt such a strong sense of belonging which just furthered my determination to get into that school. I don't recall seeing a single white person anywhere that day. That shocked me to encounter that in America where more commonly many places still exist where there are *only* white people and not a trace of color to be found.

That began my wonderful experience attending a Historically Black College or University (HBCU)—a solid oasis of black people, gathered for a common, uplifting goal: to educate or to be educated. As I stood in that line taking in my surroundings, I didn't speak to anyone. I was extremely shy, and I hated my smile. I still had braces on my teeth—now for the sixth year, and still serving no purpose. So, I just continued to absorb it all in silence.

That is, I didn't speak to anyone until the girl next to me introduced herself. Her name was Shannon Smith from Mobile, Alabama. Shannon was beautiful, light-skinned, with big pretty eyes and a thick southern accent. Her voice instantly convinced me that "country" could be sexy. My great-grandmother was as "country" as they came, having lived in Wedowee, Alabama all her life. She would say things like, "Dem boys chunkin' rocks at y'all." It always took me awhile to decipher what she said when first being around her. Just then, it dawned on me that *I* was now in the south, so I'd better use the politically correct term of "southern" rather than "country." As a Yankee, I reckon I had a lot to learn about the South.

I can't remember if she was in line for herself or with someone else, but Shannon truly mesmerized me with the way she looked and talked and how very smart she appeared. I sized her up as the kind of girl who dated athletes or light-skinned guys like Dave and Marc, not someone like me. Therefore, I enjoyed talking with her uninhibitedly, knowing I didn't need to try to impress her or anything. Shannon and I became very good friends over the years.

Unfortunately, twenty years later, Shannon, a wife and mother, was gunned down at her job just before the Thanksgiving holiday. She worked as a pharmacist at Shands Jacksonville Hospital in Jacksonville, Florida. As eyewitnesses recounted, the Friday before she was shot, Shannon had told an upset customer who had walked up to the counter that she needed to get in the back of the line to wait for her prescription. That enraged the customer even more. The following Monday, the woman returned, engaged Shannon in an argument, and when Shannon tried to diffuse the situation, shot her several times in the crowded pharmacy. Shannon later died in surgery.

They discovered that Shannon was pregnant at the time of her death. That whole incident really shook me to the core because she was my good friend; she was the first girl I met in college. After seeing so much violence growing up due to illegal drugs, it especially disturbed me that a senseless crime like that had to happen over legal drugs.

Finally, it was my turn to go into the financial aid office. I had no idea what to expect. I had all of my papers ready to go. Because we were so poor, I knew I was eligible for financial aid; it became a matter of filling out the paper work. As I sat down, the man behind the desk did not waste any time. He jumped right in asking, "How can I help you?" I noticed his nameplate on his desk. Mark Smith was his name.

I introduced myself by saying, "Hello, Mr. Smith. My name is Jemal Gibson, and I want to get financial aid to pay for school."

He then asked for my paperwork, and I handed him everything I had. He tossed a second question at me, "This is your admissions paperwork. Where is your financial aid paperwork?"

"I guess I don't have any," I sheepishly answered.

He then asked, "How much money do you have?"

"Twenty dollars," I responded, without having to think about it or count anything.

I remember him laughing. My heart sank into my stomach. At that point,

I knew there was going to be a challenge thrown in my path.

He asked again, "No, really how much?"

I repeated, "Twenty dollars."

"Where are you from?" he asked.

"Chicago."

"And that's all you came down here with?"

"Yes sir."

"Can you call your parents or someone else? Because I'm afraid you are going to need more money than that."

I told him, "I don't have anyone to call, and this is all I have."

He asked "What does your mom do?"

"She doesn't work. Neither does my father."

He finally spoke those dreaded words, "I'm sorry; I can't help you." He went on to tell me to get some more money from an aunt, an uncle or someone, but the words, "I can't help you" kept echoing in my head.

"Okay," was all I could muster.

I walked out feeling totally rejected and dejected. That explained the look that I noticed on the faces of a lot of students who came out from that same office. And to think I waited over two hours for that? Something came over me in that instant, and I decided to get back in line and see someone else. I thought perhaps if I did a better job explaining my circumstances that someone would understand and give me a break. That first man caught me off guard and all I could say was, "Okay." But it was *not* okay. Besides, I reminded myself, getting into FAMU was just another challenge, and I was there to overcome it.

I waited in another line for a few more hours. Quite honestly, it didn't seem that long because the people watching was great. Also, the wait gave me time to think about what I would say.

My turn came. I stepped in to the office and read his name plate: Bob Gibson. I thought, "Super! We could be related or something!" My strategy was to introduce myself and then ask him where he was from. Maybe in the conversation, we would find out that we were related or at least develop a relationship of sorts. It was kind of funny that I used the fake name, "Bob Gibson," when I worked as a telemarketer in high school because I found people often hung up before I could give my pitch when I used "Jemal" as my first name.

Before I could sit down and introduce myself, Mr. Gibson jumped right in like the other financial aid counselor and asked, "How can I help you?"

Using some of the information I gleaned from Mark Smith, I went about explaining that my mother hadn't filled out the financial aid paperwork because we thought I could do it on campus. I anxiously told him I was sure we would qualify because we were on welfare.

Before I could finish, he asked, "How much money do you have?"

Here we go again. I said, "I have twenty dollars."

Ironically, he too, laughed and repeated, "How much?"

I knew where that was headed. Couldn't those people learn some manners, so as not to laugh at someone else's plight? I repeated to him that I only had twenty dollars.

He basically regurgitated the same answer as the other counselor and then added, "You will need to go home and try again in January."

I walked away from that office with a heap of emotions welling up in me, ready to burst. I felt anger, sadness, defeat, jealousy. You name an emotion, I felt it. I tried not to look at anyone, as I walked down the long, winding corridor because the tears had started to run down my face.

All I could think about was living with my mother in the ghettos of Chicago like several of my cousins whose lives never reached the promise or potential their mothers had imagined for them. I thought about my Whitney Young friends who were there at FAMU and how embarrassed I would be telling them I had to go home because I had no money.

I had never told my friends my personal financial situation. I'm sure, based on my clothes and other situations, they intelligently deduced a long time ago that I was poor. However, I never confirmed any assumptions with anyone, nor had

I ever discussed my challenging childhood with drug addict parents. My friends would not understand what I went through growing up, nor would they believe I came with just $20. They all grew up with both their parents around or at least with employed single mothers. Many of them went to the same grade school and had been together at Whitney Young for their entire high school career. I, on the other hand, lived with almost every close and extended member of my family, had experienced a variety of neighborhoods, and pieced together my learning from seven different grade schools and three different high schools.

As the tears burst forth, I held my head down, too embarrassed to let anyone see me in my defeated state. I spotted a pay phone right outside of the building and decided to call my dad. Perhaps by some miracle, he had some money or could drum some up from somewhere. Funny thing was I really had no idea how much tuition even cost. My conversations with financial aid had never gotten to that point since I only had $20 and no paper work. I called Dad collect at Pint's place. That's where he was staying since he had gotten out of treatment for another relapse on drugs.

By the time he accepted the call, I was crying profusely and could barely get my first sentence out. He said, "Mal, what's up?"

I finally said, "Dad, they are sending me home because I don't have any money. Is there any way you can help me?"

My father was a prideful man, and I was his only child. He often talked about how I was all he ever wanted, one son. Hence, his favorite saying: "My Number One Son."

I know my request hit Dad like a ton of bricks. I now know that in that moment, my request for money that he didn't have, forced him to face his own failure as a father. He could not support his only son—his number one son—in one of the greatest opportunities of his son's life.

He was silent for awhile, and I waited for his response. I was hoping he would say, "I can get it; just give me some time." But, that's not what he said. Instead, he said something to me that was worth more than any money he might have been able to send.

My dad said, "Find a way, Mal; you have to find a way. You have been blessed with an ability to communicate with others. You're smart, you're handsome, and you're a great person. Believe in yourself. I believe in you. You are the most wonderful person I know. You've come through so much, Son, and this is just another situation to overcome. I believe in you, and you must believe yourself." He went on for a few more minutes, repeating all the outstanding qualities he saw in me.

As he spoke, the tears began to dry up, my eyes opened wide, and I raised my head. A small voice inside whispered, "You can't go back home; there is no home to go back to. Find a way."

In a stronger voice, I said, "Thank you Dad, I love you."

"I love you, too, Son."

Hanging up from that phone conversation, I felt like a new man. I felt like I had just come out of the locker room at halftime in a championship basketball game. He was right—I had personality, gifts, and big dreams. I had to find a way. I had to find a way. I kept telling myself that over and over. Suddenly, "a way" came to me.

I hurried back into that same building for a third time. That third time, I didn't wait in a two-hour line. I went straight to the information desk and asked if there was anyone else besides the financial aid counselors that I could speak to regarding trying to get into school. "Dr. Richard Flamer, Vice President of Student Affairs, is who you need to see," the clerk behind the desk told me.

"Yes!" I thought to myself, "someone else who could potentially help. It's not over yet!"

I went to Dr. Flamer's office, only to find another long line of students. It was getting late in the afternoon, and he probably had heard every story there was by now. I thought about leaving and coming back the next day, but I could not waste a single day because I would be faced with being kicked out of the dorm. Where would I go with only $20? It wasn't enough for a hotel or for a bus ticket back home. I had nowhere to go but in the line to wait and try again.

That time, I decided on a different communication strategy. As I stood there, I once again saw many students leaving, looking just as sad as those who had come out from the financial aid office earlier. I figured it was going to be tough. Finally, after an hour or so, it was my turn to meet Dr. Flamer. As I stood at the door, I realized that the man on the other side held the key to my immediate destiny. I thought more seriously than ever, "If I fail here, back to Chicago I go."

When I opened the door and went in, the atmosphere offered a different air. The office was much bigger, plusher, with a large desk and leather seats. Dr. Flamer had a rather jolly attitude and wore suspenders and a tie. Before I could say "Hi," he pointed to a chair, told me to take a seat and, sure enough, asked that same canned question, "How can I help you?"

At least when Dr. Flamer asked that question, his voice and demeanor seemed more pleasant and sincere than the first two men. I shared my story. That time, though, I felt the "go ahead" in my spirit to tell my complete story— more than I had ever shared with anyone in my entire life.

I began, "Sir, I am an honor roll student. I was captain of my basketball team and city champion in cross-country. My parents have both been on drugs for most of my life. My grandmother raised me in the projects of Chicago for six years until my mother got herself together for awhile. I went to live with my mother, but she unfortunately had many relapses. I've gone to eight different grade schools, three different high schools, lived with lots of different families but still managed to do well in school. I am a great person. I've never been in trouble with the law. My father just finished drug rehab and my mother is back on drugs again. She lives in the ghetto with her boyfriend who chased me out of the house with a shotgun after we had a fight. If I go back home, I will not make it. I will not live. Please don't send me home. Please don't send me home."

As I was catching my breath, I realized that I was crying. I must have been in a "zone" with my story because I had not noticed until I stopped that Dr. Flamer was crying, too. That gentle, wonderful man got up, walked around his desk, and reached out his arms. He gave me a hug, and I cried in his arms like a baby. "Please don't send me home, I have nowhere to go, please…"

It felt like an embrace that would happen between a grandfather and a grandson. Unfortunately, I never met either of my grandfathers, but I thought this must have been what it would feel like. After we stopped crying, he walked me out of his office with his arm around my shoulder and took me to the basement level where the Registrar's office was. He told the clerk behind the counter to make sure I was fully registered. He further instructed her to ensure I had a financial aid deferment, secured housing, the meal plan, and everything else that would help me to be a successful college student.

Before going back to his office, he turned to me and said, as a loving grandfather would, "Don't let me down, Son."

As we shook hands, more tears flowed as I thought about the opportunity I had been given, and I said, "I won't let you down, Sir. Thank you; thank you so much!"

I didn't let him down. I made the honor roll my first and second semesters. In addition to that, I received a three-year AROTC scholarship. I had found a way.

Alias, Jemal Gibson

Under the leadership of Dr. Frederick S. Humphries, FAMU had been labeled as the "Black Harvard," attracting more National Merit Scholars than Harvard for some time. To further solidify that distinction, TIME Magazine-Princeton Review voted FAMU as "College of the Year" in 1997.[10] Articles in various reputable publications have hailed it as the number-one college for African-Americans in the United States and as the school that awards the most baccalaureate degrees to African-Americans among all other educational institutions in the nation. I am proud to be a product of it all. I completed my sophomore year at FAMU, and things were looking very promising for me. I must admit that though my selection process for colleges consisted mainly of wanting to go to the same school as my high school KDU fellas, I valued my choice.

I had also just finished pledging into the Alpha Phi Alpha Fraternity and felt really good about myself. It's so funny because at Whitney Young, when we started our group called Kappa Dammit Uh (KDU), we all thought we would join the Kappa Alpha Psi Fraternity. However, once we got to FAMU, most of us became Alpha's. I can't really speak for my friends, but I changed my mind after a couple of opportunities to see the Kappa's up close and personal.

One such situation occurred in the fall of my freshman year when the fellas and I took a road trip to Atlanta to attend Morehouse College's Homecoming. While there, we got caught in the middle of a fight between the Kappa's and another fraternity, Omega Psi Phi—the Que's for short. The Que's beat the

Kappa's so badly, they were running and crying like real cowards. We had all experienced many fights in Chicago, but we'd never gotten beaten down like that.... well, maybe one time, but that's another story.

So right then and there, about half of us decided we didn't want to be part of any fraternity that got beat down like that, so we pledged Alpha. The others stayed with their original plan and became Kappa's.

In addition to the embarrassing beat down of the Kappa's, I found it hard to associate with a group whose mantra on campus was, "We smoke the dope, we drink the wine; Nupe, Nupe, motherf**ker, it's party time." Of course, I knew the chant did not reflect their organization's true motto or purpose for existence, just as I realized not all Kappa's did drugs. However, it was another clear example of how others viewed drugs as fun while I saw them as destructive. With my family's history of drugs, I felt uncomfortable about associating with them.

The Que's were always barking, slam dancing, and stepping. Now, I don't mind letting loose every now and then, but I have Que friends who are forty-years-old, still barking, howling, and "stepping" around my kitchen island as though they just pledged yesterday! Once again, I don't mind—to each his own—but after witnessing all of that, I felt most connected to the Alpha Phi Alpha fraternity's purpose of "manly deeds, scholarships, and love for all mankind."

During the time I attended, my FAMU chapter, Beta Nu, produced some successful contributors to society: Daryl Parks, a high-powered attorney in Florida; Kwame Kilpatrick, former mayor of Detroit; Vince Adams, international DJ; Will Packer and Rob Hardy of Rainforest Productions, makers of *Takers*, *Stomp the Yard, and Obsession*, just to name a few. On our organization's national level, who can argue with the amazingly great impact that change agents and fellow Alpha men including W. E. B. Du Bois, Martin Luther King Jr., Thurgood Marshall, and many others, have made across the globe![11] Again, I am proud to be associated with such high caliber men.

Between acclimating myself to campus life and pledging, I stayed too busy to go home for a visit until my sophomore year. I didn't go home that first summer because, in reality, I had no place to stay in Chicago. Finally, that second summer, I had an opportunity, so I took it. I still didn't have a place to stay for any long periods of time, so I just popped around staying with different family members. I would have stayed mostly with my dad, but his situation was rather shaky and definitely not conducive for visitors. However, the few weeks that I stayed with him were life changing.

One day we were chillin' in the office he had created at his girlfriend's house and he said, "Mal, how would you like to get those braces off?"

"Do you really have to ask, Dad? I've had them for almost eight years now; of course, I would like to get them off! "

"Well, you've got an appointment tomorrow with the dentist that I've been going to."

"Seriously? Thank you, Dad!!" I could hardly sleep that night. I kept getting up, looking in the mirror, and wondering what my teeth would look like.

The next day, we went to dad's dentist and not only did he take the braces off, but he did a complete work-up to give me a better smile. I had a permanent tooth that never grew in after I lost the baby tooth and another that never grew in fully. After a few weeks, and six or so appointments, I had gotten my gaps closed with crowns and additional work that gave me a beautiful smile.

Wow! I can't tell you what that did for my confidence. For a long time, I covered my mouth when I smiled, rarely spoke out in groups, and never looked people in their eyes because I was afraid they were looking at my mouth. But after the braces were removed, I became a completely different person. I couldn't stop smiling; I couldn't stop talking! The money for the dental work was the absolute best tangible gift my father gave me, which has had an everlasting *int*angible effect of enhancing my personality and elevating my confidence.

After that, I decided to go down to Peoria and spend some time with my brother, Ant, and cousin, Tyrone. I had not seen them in a very long time.

In Peoria, Illinois, Ant was known as "Hollywood Holloway" and Tyrone as "Ty" or "T-Bone." Unfortunately, they were also known by the police as notorious drug dealers. I guess my brother had made it. He always glorified that life, and now he was living it. When I got there, my brother gave me his Saab to drive. I'd never had a car before, so to have use of a nice one like that for a week? I was in heaven. Actually, that week started my love affair with the Saab brand; I've owned three since then.

During that week, I went all over Peoria visiting friends whom I had not seen in several years. I saw Jimmy Roberts, Kevin Heard, and the Linwoods, one of the largest families in Peoria. We were so close to the Linwood family that, like most black families, we called each other cousins. Then there was the large Burnside family. Boy, they were fighters. I got jumped by three of the Burnsides when I was about twelve-years-old. It was really embarrassing because two of the boys held me down, while their sister hit me multiple times. They dared me to hit her back or else they would beat me down. So, I didn't touch her; I just took the beating. I was told several of the Burnsides suffered violent deaths when they got older. It was sad to hear that, but it didn't surprise me, either. That's what happens with the large, hard-nosed, very tough families who come up in the inner city.

I surprised myself at how easily I got around town, considering I hadn't been there for years. I almost felt like I'd never left. Ant and Ty, who lived together, stayed gone—hanging out in the streets, naturally—so I basically fended for myself. Our paths crossed briefly at their house; it was usually when I was heading to bed, and they were heading back out after being home only a short while. They owned a couple of houses. I stayed at the one where they had two women living. Those women cooked for me and kept the house clean and always kept the fridge stocked. I assumed they were Ant and Ty's "do girls," but I honestly think one of them (if not both) were their prostitutes. Another street element my brother glorified.

One night, we were all at the house, and Ty said, "Let's go for a ride."

"Cool!" I instantly replied.

We hopped in the Saab. I drove, while he directed me where to go. We passed by the Harrison Homes, and Ty pointed out spots where they would hang out. I really didn't like the Harrison Homes. That's where my brother's best friends were shot in high school. We passed another block where a police squad car was parked on the corner. Ty told me to turn at the next corner. He started to look a little uptight as he told me to turn again, so I did. Finally he said, "Stop right here!" As I stopped, he jumped out and ordered, "Keep driving."

I was clueless as to what was going on, but I kept driving, thinking, "Knowing Ty, he's up to something." No sooner had I completed that thought when a police car zoomed up behind me with his lights flashing. I immediately pulled over and those lights, caught in my side view mirror, hindered me from seeing what the officer was doing.

As he and his partner got out of their car, another squad car suddenly pulled up in front of me. Both cops approached my driver's side window and asked for my license. By that time, there were at least three other officers surrounding my car with their hands on their guns. I obediently presented my license. One officer took my license back to the car while his partner stayed to talk to me.

"Whose car is this?" the one officer inquired.

At that point, my instincts told me to distance myself from Ant and Ty. "It belongs to my friend."

"What's the name of your friend?"

"Anthony Holloway."

He raised his eyebrows.

"Hmm, really? You know he's a notorious drug dealer, and you are driving his car. What are you doing down here, and why are you driving this car?"

"Well, I'm lost," I said. "I was trying to get to University Street to go out toward Richwoods and I've gotten a little lost."

A horrible lie—Richwoods and the Harrison Homes were on opposite sides of the city and not even on intersecting streets. But, I was committed to it as my story, so I had to keep it going. By this time, yet another car showed up.

A total of four cars had now appeared, all with white lights blinding me and blue lights spinning on their car tops.

The barrage of questions continued, "And what are you doing down here?"

I took a deep breath and responded, "I am here to visit my brother, Anthony Holloway, while I'm on summer break from college."

The officer squinted one eye and looked at me hard, "I thought you said he was your friend." Dammit! Busted in that lie. Whatever they'd done, whatever had happened, I was about to be connected to it somehow.

The officer then stepped back from the car and ordered, "Step out of the car."

I thought to myself, "Here we go. Hope I get out of this one!"

They ushered me to the back of the Saab, and told me to put my hands on the trunk and 'spread 'em.' As they began to frisk me, I looked straight down the block, and I'll be damned if I didn't see Ty sitting on someone's porch in the dark watching the whole thing. At that point, it occurred to me he knew we were about to get stopped and that's why he wanted out. He didn't warn me, tell me to be cool, run—nothing. A range of emotions surged through me—from fear to anger to betrayal—all while I tried to take in what was really happening.

The officer got rather demanding. "First, you said he was your friend; now, you say he's your brother, so you're lying. You better start telling me the truth or you're going to jail!"

"He is my friend, but we just call each other brothers because we were close when growing up. We don't even have the same last name." I stammered through a somewhat-good made-up answer, thinking a different last name would easily justify we were not siblings (of course at that age, I didn't know how common different last names were within families and that it really wouldn't justify anything to that police officer). While the one officer was asking me questions, two others were shining their flashlights in the car looking for something.

They asked, "Can we look inside?"

I said, "Sure." At that time, I wasn't knowledgeable of the law, or I would've known it was my right to deny them access to the car.

They opened the front and back doors and lightly rummaged through the car. I can't remember if they asked me or told me some of the things in the car were stolen, like the radio, the car phone, and a few other things.

"Look, I don't know anything about what he does. I'm just here visiting. I am in college in Florida and that's it." I felt I'd better start defending myself after being abandoned so unfairly.

The officer who frisked me started interrogating me as well. "Where are you trying to go?"

I learned quickly to keep my lies straight, so I said, "Out by Richwoods to see a friend of mine, Jimmy Roberts."

The first officer handed me my license back, gave me directions, and said, "If I catch you back down here in the Harrison Homes in this car, I'm taking you to jail."

I said. "Yes, sir."

I had to assume whatever background check they performed turned out good for me. But, of course it should have, since I did not have a record, I really did live in Florida, and I really was enrolled in college. Once I got back in the Saab, all the cars backed away, and I drove straight ahead. As I got ready to turn the corner, there was Ty sitting there watching. I kept driving. I drove back to the house in tears—tears of pure relief that I was let go, but also tears of anger because Ty had left me hanging like that. I'm really not sure what he could have done, but he certainly should have handled it differently.

When I got to the house, Ty had already called and told the girls he was on his way back and for me to wait for his arrival. When he pulled up in a car, I came out and charged after him, "What the f**k was up with that? Why did you leave me like that?"

"My bad, Li'l Cuz." He went to the back of the Saab, opened the trunk, and my heart sank. In the trunk were scales, plastic bags, aluminum foil, and lots of other drug paraphernalia. The scales had cocaine residue on them that even I could see in the dark.

I was so mad! If I were capable of beating Ty, I would've started kicking his ass right then. However, I knew there was no point getting big and bad because he would have squashed me. The only thing I could muster up was, "That's f**ked up!" And, I walked back into the house.

My whole life could have changed drastically that night. All I dreamed about, all I strived for flushed down the drain in an instant. Ty would have let me take the fall for him. I can only imagine how many young smart black men are in jail for stuff like this, taking the fall for family, not snitching and being promised to be taken care of while in prison and when they get out. That could have been me.

All of sudden, a thought rushed over me, "Why didn't the police search the trunk?" Even though they had me spread out across it, they could have easily told me to step aside. I would've done so, and it would've been a whole different night. "Thank you, Angels, once again."

The next day, Ty tried to make up for things by sending me shopping with his girlfriend, Bernice. She must have spent about $600 on clothes for me at Bachrach and didn't blink an eye! She just pulled out her checkbook paid for what I'd picked out, and we walked out smiling. I desperately needed the clothes for school. I generally went shopping after I got my "net check." This was the money left over after school fees were subtracted from grant and scholarship money. It seemed like every store in Tallahassee knew when net checks were mailed to the students because there were always huge sales during that time. Of course, being college students who were always broke, we'd shop and eat steak until we burned right through that net check, which never took long. I was so grateful I wouldn't have to be on that spending cycle, now that I had gotten those new clothes.

When we returned from shopping, I carried all my bags into the house. I never had anyone spend that kind of money on me all at one time, so I was pretty excited. It helped a little to take the sting out of what Ty did, but I still had a bone to pick with him. As I sat my bags on the table, I noticed a lot of mail there. Some of it looked like court papers, so I started snooping through them.

One of papers I picked up said, "Anthony Holloway, alias Jemal Gibson." Another read, "Tyrone Brown, alias Jemal Gibson." Court paper after court paper had various combinations of their names, but the alias was consistent: Jemal Gibson! Tyrone Gibson, Jemal Holloway, Jemal Brown, and other variations; I could not believe they were trashing my name! They knew I was trying to do something to better my life, to rise above the horrible conditions we were subjected to all our lives, and yet they were taking me down with them.

At that point, I'd had it. I packed up all of my stuff and told them to take me to the bus station. If I stayed any longer, I was either going to be caught up with them or they'd do something that would truly make me hate them. I told them how I felt, and all they could say was, "Sorry."

To try and make it up to me, they promised to send me some money for school. I didn't let them off the hook, either. When I got back to FAMU, I called and asked them for the money they were going to send to help me get through college for the semester. After about two or three phone calls to them, to my surprise, Bernice sent the money through Western Union. It was enough to pay my rent for my one bedroom apartment and all my bills for the semester.

It was a major financial relief. It helped me to focus on school instead of working a job for the semester. As an extra bonus, I was voted "best dressed Alpha" by the Alpha Sweethearts, as I sported all my new gear purchased by Bernice. I learned that shortly after that shopping spree, Bernice went to jail for writing bad checks. I felt bad, but I'm sure my clothes weren't the only thing she wrote bad checks for. That was my last visit to Peoria, Illinois for over a decade.

Where's Dad?

By the time I reached my junior year in college in 1990, my colleagues had labeled me an overachiever. I had pledged the National Society of Pershing Rifles (Pershing Rifles), Alpha Phi Alpha fraternity (Alpha), and had joined Chaires Masonic Lodge #259. In spite of all that those organizations required of me, I maintained Honor Roll status, served on the ARTOC Drill Team and Color Guard and worked a part-time job. At that point, I could not put another thing on my plate, except for Samantha Rolle (Sam). Sam was the prettiest, all-natural woman I had ever seen. With beautiful, flawless skin that didn't require make-up, and long, black, wavy hair that flowed down to the middle of her back, she seemed untouched and unscathed by life and all its weighty baggage. Her smile, which livened up everything around her, complimented her kind and gentle spirit.

Samantha and I dated off and on for a couple of years. She pledged Pershing Angels, the sister sorority to the Pershing Rifles. I believed she loved me unconditionally. In other words, she didn't care if I ended up as a total flop in life, which comforted me since deep down I'd always feared being one step away from the projects. But *she* never thought I would ever end up back there. No, Sam totally believed in me, praised me, and encouraged me—just as my dad did.

For awhile, Sam and I were inseparable, and I depended greatly on her love, inspiration, and support. She helped me to not be so uptight and concerned with what other people thought about me and about what I said, did, or wore. During many of our inseparable days, we would hop in Sam's old, blue Toyota Corolla and head to the beach.

There, we would fish, walk for miles, talk for hours, and sometimes even sleep right on the beach. We'd been known to even find a vacant rental house and sleep on their outdoor furniture, waking up only to start fishing again. The first time I ever went fishing was with my brother when I was ten-years-old; the first time I ever caught a fish was with Sam ten years later.

Autumn was well underway. An early snowfall caught Chicagoans off guard, making me even more grateful for Florida's contrasted temperatures and weather patterns. In fact, whenever I spoke with family from back home, weather often dominated the conversation; what I experienced day-to-day in Florida was much better than what I had known growing up in the Windy City.

One particular day, I received a phone call from Pint in Chicago, and weather never entered the conversation. Pint shared her concern about not seeing my dad in quite a few days. She heard he was spending time with Kathy, his ex-wife, although she couldn't confirm it. I believe my dad still loved Kathy well after their divorce, even though their physical connection dominated anything else (Dad confessed to me one day about how great sex was with her). Kathy was white, like most of the women he dated after my mom divorced him. I'm not sure how the two of them got into using drugs, but soon after their marriage ended, Dad went back into rehab.

Once Pint told me who Dad was with, she didn't have to say anymore. We both knew that meant drug use again. For the first time, I confided in Sam regarding my family background. Actually, it was the first time I shared detailed information about my family with *any* girlfriend. I told her that I needed to go find my dad and she responded with, "Let's go." I loved that about her.

The next day, Sam got her car serviced, and we were on the road. As we neared Illinois, the snowfall became brutal and never let up the entire distance into Chicago. I remained very nervous most of the trip. Making a nine hundred-plus mile road trip in *any* car in adverse weather is a challenge, let alone in a small, old compact Corolla with very bald tires. At various times along the way, I didn't know if the car would make it with all the slipping and sliding on the road. To top it off, the defroster didn't work well, so we couldn't see out of the side and back windows and just barely out of the front. We persevered and made it there with no incident.

As soon as Pint met Sam, she fell in love with her, just as I had. I think Sam reminded Pint of a younger version of herself. They both had sweet and kind dispositions, and both found themselves unconditionally involved with Gibson men.

Pint confirmed that Dad was using again. Even though I already sensed it, hearing it made it very real, and I broke down. I suppose those emotions were a combination of the news and pure exhaustion from the long road trip. But, Dad had been doing so well. How could he have fallen off? I asked where he was. Pint gave me the address and the directions, and I drove there right away—alone.

The late hour made it very difficult for me to read the addresses, but finally, I found the house and rang the doorbell. I could actually see Dad through the glass-paned front door, sitting in the living room, watching TV. He had a forty-ounce bottle of malt liquor sitting on the table next to him as he sat there smoking a cigarette. Although I had hoped Pint was wrong, seeing him sitting there drinking and smoking indicated he had relapsed. After his last time in treatment, Dad had ceased both of those vices because they were triggers for him.

I rang the doorbell again because he didn't move the first time. Hesitantly, he got up and walked toward the door. When he opened it, you would have thought he saw a ghost. "Mal?"

"Yes, Dad. What's going on?"

He looked back at the forty-ounce on the end table and the cigarette in his hand and knew there was nothing he could say. He diverted, "What are you doing here?"

"Pint was worried about you, and she told me how to get here," I began, "so I drove up from school to find you and figure out what's going on."

He stood solemnly in that doorway, never inviting me in. Finally, he broke his silence, "I will come see you at Pint's tomorrow."

"OK. I love you, Dad," I replied.

He closed the door slowly with a look of shame and disgust. I could see the tears forming in his eyes. I'm sure he never thought I would show up late at night in the middle of my semester to find him.

Dad knocked on Pint's door early that next dreary, gray, and cold morning. When I answered, he wouldn't come in; instead, he asked me to walk with him. I grabbed my coat, and we went for a walk. I can't remember many of the words he spoke that day, due to being overwhelmed by his relapse. I do remember him saying, "I'm sorry, son; I know you are disappointed in me. I don't know how I got here, but I will get it together."

After he spoke those words, Dad gave me a hug and then asked me a question that has haunted me to this day.

"Can I borrow $10?" and offered some lame excuse of why he needed it.

We both just stared at each other. All speech failed me momentarily, as I attempted to dissect what I heard. My dad had just asked me to give him money so he could get high. He had been so careful with all of his previous relapses, ensuring I would not see him in that condition. That time he let his guard down; he asked his son for drug money. I knew he had hit rock bottom, and he knew that I knew.

"Dad, I don't have it," I sadly answered.

"I understand," he said and walked away with his head down.

How devastating to me—my hero, my dad had fallen to that depth. He went to Pint's house the day after I left and allowed her to take him to treatment. She was that wind beneath his wings; he was the wind beneath mine. But, he had crash-landed again.

I Need a Favor

The challenges Dad faced really troubled me, and to make matters worse, my mother wasn't faring much better. It was my second semester junior year, the money Ant and Ty gave me had run out, and I was in between jobs at school and barely scraping by financially. It started to affect me at school, especially my Army ROTC responsibilities. I missed class, PT (Physical Training Exercise), and skipped battalion assignments. One day, Captain Terry invited me into his office.

"Take a seat, Jemal. I haven't seen you around in the past couple of weeks, so I figured something must be wrong. You're not your usual jovial self; your brow is pretty tight, and you look like a walking zombie. So, tell me what's going on, Gibson?"

Wow! He read right into me. Was it that obvious? I tried to find the words to start making up excuses; instead, tears started flowing. As much as I tried to hold them back—especially in front of Captain Terry, my Army ROTC professor—I just couldn't. How embarrassing! I was supposed to be high charging, high speed, and squared away, yet there I was crying in his office. I had not broken down like that since my first day at FAMU, two and a half-years earlier, when Dr. Flamer saved me during my admissions fiasco. On both occasions, I seemed at the end of my rope—tired mentally, emotionally, and physically.

"Gibson, I know I'm one of your professors, but since we are also Alpha brothers and Masonic brothers, for the next thirty minutes, just talk to me as your brother."

So I did—quite candidly, as a matter of fact. I told him my plight, including the past and recent drug issues with my parents, my financial challenges, everything. I felt so relieved once I finished. Having my life tucked away and not revealing to anyone who I really was or where I really came from left me totally drained at times.

As I finished my story, Captain Terry looked at me with great empathy. "I never knew that about you. You should be so proud of how far you have come. I realize your parents' situation is difficult, but that's why you have to do well here in school, so you can make a difference in their lives." He fumbled around in his wallet while speaking, then pulled out some crisp "Benjamins."

"Here, this is $400. Hopefully, it will relieve some of your pressures so you can focus on your classes. Pay me back whenever you can. I will not hold the absences from my class against you, either, but you've got to start coming again."

I was floored at the extreme generosity of Captain Terry. With so many pressing needs, I couldn't even fix my lips to say "no" to the gift, so I took the money. "Captain Terry, I can't thank you enough. This was extremely kind, and I will pay you back as soon as I'm able. Equally important, thank you for taking care of the absences; I won't miss another class."

We stood, shook hands with the Alpha secret grip, then the Masonic secret grip, and then we exchanged a brief hug. As I walked out of his office, I thought about the beauty of small colleges. The teachers can more easily get to know you as a person, not just an ID. If my dad had it his way, I would have transferred to Notre Dame or some other prestigious school for what he thought would be a better and more "rounded" education. Not only did I not want to transfer, it wasn't even feasible. How would I pay for it? Would my credits transfer? There were lots of unanswered questions, so I never gave it much thought, even though Dad talked about it quite often.

A couple of weeks had passed, and I was back to my old self: High Speed-No Drag-Gibson. The money helped pay some bills, leaving a little extra to eat. I continued to feel so indebted to Captain Terry.

One day after class, Captain Terry asked me to come in his office. I figured he wanted an update. "How's it going?" he asked, ushering me in through his door and closing it behind me.

"A lot better sir! Once again, I can't tell you how good it was to get some of that off my chest. Your financial support gave me a little breathing room, so I really appreciate it."

"That's good to hear. Everyone needs a little help every now and then. Speaking of which, I need a favor." Captain Terry offered me a seat and he got comfortable in his chair behind his desk.

"No problem Captain Terry. What can I do for you?" I eagerly replied, as I sat on the edge of my chair facing him. I thought about how anxious I'd been to actually pay him back his money. Perhaps the favor would be a great opportunity to show him my gratitude until the money was there to give him.

"I am thinking about going into business with a guy. As a matter of fact, there are a couple of us in this thing together. But we have a problem. We think this guy is gay. So, I was wondering if you could come by my place tomorrow. We are having a little gathering, and he will be there. I would like you to give me your opinion of him and maybe tell me if he is gay. Can you do that for me?"

I sat back in my chair. My mind started racing a hundred miles per hour as my street senses kicked in. I needed a little more clarification on the whole thing. "Captain Terry, you can't tell if he's gay?"

"Not really," he replied.

"What about your other partners? Can't they tell either?"

"One says he thinks he is, and the other doesn't know."

"Who all is going to be at your gathering?"

"Just a few guys from around campus," he said very evasively.

"Can you tell who some of them are?" I pried.

"Jeff Simon, Fred Smith, Shawn Riley…"

Ding, ding, ding. That was enough for my intuition! I didn't know any of the other names, but I knew Shawn Riley. He was my Masonic brother, and every time I saw him he would give the secret grip, then a hug. The only problem was his hug came on a little too tight and a lot too long. Then he would keep his arm around my neck while talking to me. I'd have to pry him off every time. It got so uncomfortable that I stopped giving him the secret grip. I asked another brother if he had the same experience, and he confirmed my suspicion by saying, "Yes, Shawn is gay."

Even though at the time, I was very naïve about alternative lifestyles, I was no homophobe either. I've always respected a person for who they are and for how they treat me and others—which, by my standards, has nothing to do with their sexual preference. Right away, though, I knew that Shawn's actions toward me were definitely crossing that "respect" line, since I gave him no previous indication that I would be okay with him hanging on me like that.

So, I couldn't believe what I was piecing together from Captain Terry's conversation. Was *he* gay? Was he trying to set me up? Captain Terry had a wife and kids; although, I had heard that he was getting a divorce. I never met his family and barely knew him, so I didn't want to pass judgment. He didn't look feminine, he didn't act feminine, but I was finding out—even in my naivety—that not all gay men are effeminate.

"Gibson, can you do that for me?" he asked again, breaking my train of thought.

"Captain Terry, I don't think so. I don't have radar for detecting gay men. If you think he's gay, then he probably is. If you're not sure, then one of the other guys at your gathering can give you that information,"

"But Gibson, I need you to do it. I trust your judgment; that's why I am coming to you with this," he said in a very stern, but anxious way.

"I don't know Captain Terry." What does *his* trust in my judgment matter, if I just told him I wouldn't trust *my own* judgment in detecting gay men? I sensed some desperation in his voice that was unsettling. I didn't like where that whole conversation headed.

"Come on Gibson, we are brothers. I just gave you some money; I hooked you up on your absences. I looked out for you. You can't do this one thing for me?"

Bingo! That was it! He *was* setting me up—and using his "supposed goodwill" act in his manipulative scheme. He wanted me at his house to see if I would be comfortable in a room full of gay men, perhaps before putting the move on me. But at that moment, that wasn't even the part that hurt me most. It was the fact that he had preyed upon me at a time when I was most vulnerable and down. He stepped in to help me with his loan of $400, only to turn around and use that very act of kindness to make me do him a favor. I was really hurt by that breach of respect. I had thought he was sincere; I thought he really cared. But apparently, he only cared about taking advantage of me.

"I'm sorry, Captain Terry, I can't do it. I'll get your money back to you as soon as possible. Good luck with your situation." I got up and walked out. I didn't even ask if I could be excused.

I found a job as a waiter. Getting good tips every day allowed me to pay back Captain Terry within a few weeks. After that, I rarely spoke to him unless I had to. I think that he knew that I was on to him. There was also nothing he could do to me for disobeying any request from him, because he probably feared me exposing him. As the weeks and months went by, I observed Captain Terry hanging with a few of the gay men on the yard.

My street senses had served me well, but the incident changed me. Unfortunately, I started to second guess all acts of kindness. In the back of my mind, I wondered the motive behind someone's kindness. What was in it for them? What did they want from me?

That lesson with Captain Terry also taught me to be mindful of what I am taking from people. I had seen my dad get caught up with people who gave him things or did things for him and then had particular expectations of what was required from him in order to "balance the scale," so to speak. That person was using his or her façade of kindness to create a scale or a specific measurement of "payback."

Sometimes, I believe the lesson made me too cynical at a young age; however, I have to believe it did more help than harm. It helped me to distinguish conditional love from *un*conditional love, and at that point in my college career, I decided a healthy dose of skepticism in order to get to those realizations certainly couldn't hurt.

General Gibson

By the Spring of 1990, it was safe to say I fell in love with the Army. I could get the maximum score on the Physical Training (PT) test, and I loved being in the woods on field training exercises (FTX). I simply loved everything about ROTC. My roommate, Rick Fair, an Army Ranger, had formerly been a Ranger Instructor. I idolized him as a high speed, smart guy who endured several life-changing experiences. Being a little older allowed him to share with me valuable insights on how to become a responsible young man.

Rick started training a few of us to see if we could earn a Ranger School slot, instead of going to Advanced Camp. All ROTC Cadets went to Advanced Camp during the summer prior to their senior year to demonstrate capabilities and readiness for the Army. Unfortunately, that year they gave all of the Ranger School slots to West Point cadets—at least that's what we were told. So, off to Advanced Camp at Fort Riley we went, home of the Big Red I.

At Advanced Camp, I felt right at home, especially after training so hard for the PT test and the STRACtrac lanes (Strategic Army Corps tactical movements). Because of the leadership positions I held with Pershing Rifles, I had confidence in my leadership skills, as well. My platoon consisted of a lot of guys with prior service time under their belts, so they really knew their stuff. While we performed well as a team, we stayed in competition mode at all times. I really had my work cut out for me because those guys were squared away.

A couple of the guys, besides Rick, who were really squared away were

Dion Lyons, my best friend and double fraternity brother (Pershing Rifle and Alpha) from FAMU and Greer, one of Rick's Ranger instructor buddies from another school. Greer sculpted his body into a lean and hard form, with muscles like they were cut from steel. He bore a "sweet" Airborne Ranger tattoo, which became the inspiration behind my tattoo. I went toe to toe, competing in every way with them—albeit in friendly fashion. I wanted to make my qualifications known throughout that camp. The best score one could achieve—a score of five—remained a goal on my success list for almost a year. By camp's end, I was in a zone. I excelled at everything: the PT test, STRACtrac lanes, and Basic Rifle Marksmanship.

I also became the "go to" cadet for cadence in the camp. On long road marches, I provided the rhythmic words and tempo that kept us marching in beat for miles. I guess that came from my dad, the vocalist, flowing from me. One day, the entire Advance Camp class, consisting of a couple hundred cadets, assembled in the auditorium for a briefing from a General. Greer, who headed the event, received orders from one of the training officers to get the auditorium fired up before the General made his entrance. There began a rippling of whispers throughout the auditorium, requesting my rhythmic leadership. "Where's Gib? Where's Gib?"

As word finally reached me that I was being summoned, I initially feared being reprimanded for something. Instead, I felt honored when Greer said "Gib, I need you to get this place rocking."

"No problem, Brother," came my quick response. I swiftly proceeded to the stage and started off with, "Way down in the valley."

The entire audience repeated, "Way down in the valley."

"I heard a mighty roar."

It echoed back at me, "I heard a mighty roar."

"It was a mighty, mighty Alpha."

It repeated once more, "It was a mighty, mighty Alpha."

"Using Bravo as a toy."

"Using Bravo as a toy," rolled through the room.

I rocked that stage for ten or fifteen minutes—one cadence after another. For the first time in my life, I felt what my dad must have experienced each time he performed in front of an audience—people applauding and cheering in expressive approval and love for him and his music.

As the General approached the stage, I hopped off and let Greer take over. After we saluted the General and took our seats, the General said with a smile, "I could hear you guys clear outside the building. That's the loudest I've ever heard it in here!"

A great sense of pride washed over me for helping to fire up my peers. I got a "five" grade at camp, just as I affirmed on my success list. One of my training officers said he could not believe I was born and raised in the city because of the way I mastered the woods and understood tactical missions. He also said I fared better out there than anyone he had ever seen.

That year, FAMU got the most five's out of any HBCU in the country, ranking us among the top schools at Advanced Camp. My "room doom," Rick Fair, along with Dion Lyons got five's, as well. Rick earned the Battalion Commander distinction. Even though I wanted that Battalion Commander spot, Rick was better suited for the position and certainly wiser. It was best he had it anyway, since I mainly sought it for the honor more so than the responsibility.

Dion, who was already Airborne, achieved Battalion Executive Officer, and I was granted Battalion S3 in charge of the battalion training and readiness of Battalion. We held the three most important positions in the battalion. The whole experience proved critical in my life, in that it gave me confidence to succeed in the military. At that moment, I knew I could be a General.

The deal became sealed in my heart when retired Colonel Bernard Hendricks, the Vice President of Student Activities at FAMU, recited an Army Creed to our ROTC Rattler Battalion. He said it with such vigor and passion you could sense his sincerity in every spoken word. An inspirational man even during small talk, it was fitting that Colonel Hendricks be the one who truly connected my heart and soul to the military that day.

Apple, Inc.

In my fourth year at FAMU, in the Fall of 1990, I ranked as a junior since I started at the School of Business and Industry (SBI) during my sophomore year instead of as a freshman. I could have caught up by taking classes in the summers, but I decided to do a couple of internships, one in the summer of 1991, and the other in the summer of 1992. Internships were not required for ROTC cadets since that time usually consisted of Junior Camp one summer and Advanced Camp the next. However, my own strategy included securing a solid business background for myself early on, in case my military career ended earlier than planned.

Even though my strategy meant graduation would be delayed by almost a year and a half, I was okay with that. After all, it seemed more important to get my future plans right than to rush them. The internship process simulated job-hunting, so it needed my full and immediate attention. In other words, initiative and a sense of urgency were essential if I wanted to secure a good internship. If I performed well during my summer with that company, then they would most likely offer me a job, so it made sense to intern only with a company I liked. I discovered some of the best internship programs were with Pfizer Inc., Arthur Andersen, LLP, Goldman Sachs, Corning Inc., and a few other major corporations. Those companies paid well, and I heard the interns had a great time—two qualities I highly regarded in my search.

To secure an interview with one of those Fortune 100 companies, they first arranged interview days on campus, and those days would be posted on the bulletin board in the SBI building. Only a limited number of spots were available, so you had to hang around like a vulture, just waiting for the schedules to be posted. I did just that and signed up for two interviews, one with Corning, Inc. and the other with Apple, Inc.

The year I signed up happened to be the first year Apple, Inc. participated in FAMU's internship program. Historically, they accepted Stanford, UC Berkley, and Harvard-type students only, but they finally decided to include FAMU. Also, their internships were offered exclusively to MBA students. Not aware of their selectivity, I put my name on the board for an interview. My interview with John Lipscomb of Apple ranked as one of the toughest I'd ever experienced. He grilled me with question after question and apparently liked what he heard since they selected me for the program. Only after hiring me did they discover my non-MBA status. SBI wanted Apple to rescind their decision and hire an actual MBA student instead of me. However, being quite happy with their decision, Apple refused.

Securing the internship meant I had competed with some of the best MBA students at SBI and won—as a junior! I felt vindicated since in the beginning, SBI denied me entry into their school as a freshman, due to my test scores. Then, when I finally got in as a sophomore, I did not own a suit nor could I afford one. Because I violated SBI's strict suit wearing policy for its students, I ran the risk of receiving a bad grade from one of my professors.

One day, as I entered the SBI building, I noticed pieces of paper plastered on almost every door, elevator, and stairwell inside that read, "Jemal Gibson, please report to the office." I got to the office and discovered my dad had called and told them how unfair they were for jeopardizing my grades because I didn't wear a suit. I assumed he also told them I couldn't afford one. Of course that embarrassed me, but more importantly, I received approval to wear my Class A military uniform on "suit day," until I could buy one. After some of those and other struggles, what a sweet victory to then be chosen for one of the more sought after internships in the program, and for Apple to refuse to recant their decision to hire me against SBI's wishes.

Working at Apple's corporate office in Cupertino, California opened my eyes to many new opportunities. I remember landing in San Francisco on May 5th or Cinco de Mayo. Chalk it up to my naiveté or just plain ignorance, but I never knew what the celebration was about. I decided to hang out and enjoy the big party and soon realized it involved numerous ethnic groups far beyond Hispanics. I truly stumbled upon a great party!

Another pleasant surprise came in the form of my corporate wear for the summer. SBI taught us to dress to impress, including the do's and don'ts of business attire. There at Apple, all that training went out the window because no one wore suits. You might see a guy in cut-off shorts, a t-shirt, and a spiked hairdo making a hundred thousand dollars. My whole team wore jeans, polo shirts, and other casual clothing, whereas there I sat in a suit with suspenders. It took me a whole week to become comfortable going to work in casual clothes. Apple's dress code philosophy wanted you to focus on your creativity, not whether or not your shirt matched your tie or if your pantyhose had a run.

My manager, Rene Schaumburg, contributed to my phenomenal Apple experience, as well. Her meticulous work ethic ranked second to none. I never met anyone more thorough. She set the bar for me and showed me what hard work and its results looked like in the corporate world. Her influence began to help me immediately as I tackled my first assignment—be among the team that worked on developing a budgeting program. That required me to learn about the Macintosh (Apple's computer system) through a self-study program the first couple of weeks there. I would leave work and go to a lab and spend hours and hours learning about Mac's. That training took my learning curve "vertical" instantly. I fell in love with Apple, thanks to their great technology and free-spirited people.

Apple's Black Network organization gave me my first introduction to social networks. I met Baron Cox there, and he became a godsend to my little sister, Eboni and me, when I brought her to live with me in California my first summer there. I wanted to help her escape the roughness of Chicago's West Side for a moment, while at the same time expose her to life outside of the ghetto, giving her greater things to aspire to.

It occurred to me to bring Ebi out to California after attending her eighth grade graduation at Michelle Clark Middle School where I listened to the speech of her fellow classmate and Valedictorian. As that young girl spoke, I wondered what her future would include. Her intelligence was revealed in her impressive speech, but as she stood there pregnant at age thirteen or fourteen, I realized just how difficult it was (and probably always will be) to escape the social patterns in poor black neighborhoods. Although it would not be impossible for her to succeed, it saddened me to know that her journey had certainly been negatively altered. It definitely reaffirmed my need to assist my sister, hoping she would discover possibilities for her young life other than early motherhood.

I enjoyed the time I had Ebi under my care. I enrolled her in the same day camp as Baron Cox's daughter. It required almost twenty-five percent of my paycheck while my rent took up over fifty percent of it. Every now and then, Baron helped me out financially. After sharing some of my struggles with him, he encouraged me to stay in California, work for Apple full-time, and take custody of my sister. I researched the idea, but too many things made the decision complicated; transferring my college credits, my ROTC commitment, and getting my mother to go along with it were just some of the potential obstacles. Besides, I had to consider the possibility that if I started working full-time, going to school at night, and taking full care of my sister, I would not finish college at all. So, I decided to just make the most of our one summer together.

My sister and I delighted in talking and laughing about a lot of things throughout our months together. For example, after watching Wesley Snipes in *Jungle Fever*, she would always do that dance like Gator to get money from me. In fact, she still tries to do it to this day! My love for her grew so much that summer, as I wanted to protect her innocence and precious spirit. Ebi had not yet been corrupted by the streets with drugs, sex, or gangs, and I wanted to keep it that way. Her California stay really paid off, as she took in more of the Bay Area sights than I did, due to her many day camp field trips to the museum, zoo, bridge, and other landmarks. On the contrary, I visited very few tourist attractions, as I worked my tail off, going into work early, staying late, and volunteering around the office every chance available.

I enjoyed my job and it showed in the positive feedback I received from my manager. Still, imagine my surprise when Apple requested me again the following summer. FAMU discouraged them (or any company, for that matter) from picking the same student twice because they wanted us to experience the culture of different companies, which they felt would make us more marketable. But, Apple insisted on having me, and I definitely wanted to go back. So I did. Since I spent most of my first summer in California with my sister, I set out to explore more of the beautiful West Coast for myself that second time around.

I had a little more disposable cash the second summer as well, so I bought my first car—a 1973 convertible MG, which cost me $500. I proudly recognized that being able to buy my first car without help from anyone was a true sign of my independence and budding success. I looked kind of good in that car, too, as I matured into early adulthood. With an already slim, muscular build that had developed over my years of playing sports, the disciplined regimen of my ROTC training allowed me to keep my physique, and apparently, it was attractive to women.

My level of maturity really became evident to me when one day, Sherry, one of the vice presidents from another department, asked me out on a date. Sherry was fine, sophisticated, and I assumed in her mid-thirties. I, on the other hand, had barely turned twenty-one. She took me to the Paul Masson Mountain winery— a favorite to locals and tourists alike. Located in the magnificently encompassing Santa Cruz Mountains, it struck me as one of the most beautiful places I had ever seen. As we pulled up to the entrance, I spotted limousines, Mercedes, Porches, and many other luxury cars all lined up. It told me a lot about the caliber of people inside.

Sherry had packed a small picnic basket full of finger foods, and we settled down on the mountainside to enjoy one of the many concert series held there throughout the year. As we ate, drank wine, and talked, it all seemed so surreal—like a movie set, perhaps. A short while later, the concert began. Staged in an amphitheater built into the mountains, the featured artists were the Neville Brothers. The stars were out, the music was off the chain, and my date looked hot. Everything seemed perfect, except for the fact that I was scared. I didn't know what to do. I had never been on a date with someone of Sherry's maturity level, so I tried hard to not seem immature or overly excited. As a young man not used to being wined and dined, I didn't want to disappoint her in the end by taking advantage of her, so I decided to end the evening with a short, gentle kiss.

Reflecting on that evening, I had to chuckle at the prospect of Sherry perhaps feeling like most men do after paying for an extravagant evening out with a beautiful girl, and the girl offers little or nothing in return. As the comedian, D.L Hughley, would say, "Do you know what side of the menu that is?" alluding to the premise that ordering from the expensive side of a menu guarantees physical action that is definitely more than a kiss. Obviously, I did not have a clue, so I chose innocence in the face of greater sophistication.

A Different Ballgame

In my fifth year at FAMU, the future dominated my thoughts. I had major decisions to make. Do I go straight into the Army? Get an educational delay and receive my MBA? Most of the guys in ROTC and SBI had received their delay and acceptance into FAMU's MBA program long before. My desire to secure my financial future complicated my decision making process, especially after making great money with Apple that summer.

I waited tables as one of my part-time jobs during the school year. Its flexibility worked well with my class schedule and social life. While I earned great tips and still managed to have time to date, I needed to make some *real* money. One day, while talking on the phone with my dad, he shared something with me—wisdom I'll never forget.

"Mal," he began, "you are playing in a different ball game than your friends. You can't fail because you don't have anywhere to come back to. You must play the game differently. You don't want to be the guy who is nickel and diming and playing girls at your age while other cats are hunkering down, hitting the books, and setting themselves up to make big money later.

"Those same girls who you were hanging with back then won't want to be with you," he continued, showing me a possible future scenario. "They will be with the guys who were squares and nerds back then but are making big paper now. And, where will you be? Do you want to be one of those cats? Then, stop hanging around, wasting your time with women now. If you want to make some money, then you need to start thinking about what it will take to make some money while getting the best grades you can."

His words rattled my core and woke me up. He truly made me see what could happen long-term if I gave in to the short-term instant gratification so many people seek. My dad put things together in a logical way that made sense to me. It's no wonder every person he touched in his life, especially me, loved him so much. He articulated wisdom beyond his earthly years. It pained me, however, to see how incorporating those same teachings and knowledge into his own life presented such a challenge for him.

His challenge demonstrated another one of Dad's own lessons: "Do as I say, not as I do." I realize that rule may be contrary to today's leadership philosophy. My father studied many great principles and spiritual laws to which he did not always adhere. He cautioned: "Don't use me as an excuse or a crutch. Just because I can't or don't apply the principle doesn't mean it isn't right or worth applying." Dad loved boxing and used Angelo Dundee, one of the greatest boxing coaches who ever lived, to illustrate his point.

"Angelo Dundee coached two of the greatest boxers who ever lived— Muhammad Ali and Sugar Ray Leonard," he said. "They could have easily dismissed Angelo's coaching and training advice, considering he never boxed professionally. Instead, they chose to listen to the principles, advice, and coaching, and as a result, became world famous champions. So Mal, let me be your Angelo Dundee. Never get caught up in whether *I* am doing it or not."

He prepared me to go beyond *his* limits by sharing his knowledge. Too many times people place those they respect on a pedestal, only to crucify those same people when they display fallible human qualities. Where is the compassion for our fellow man? Those times when we fall from grace don't mean the principles aren't right, and it certainly doesn't mean we should be stoned like they did Stephen in the Bible, though crazy literalists who would advocate this are still among us.

This acknowledgement of how we are all flawed as human beings was especially true in the case of my parents. I recognized that my parents were imperfect people, doing the best they could with what they knew, for the betterment of themselves and their offspring. I had to take into consideration where they were in their life's journey, in terms of their knowledge and resources, and where they had been in their past, also having struggled through difficult childhoods. Only with this awareness could I so easily respect them for all the brave steps they took along the paths of their lives.

My father's advice on the strength of principles became invaluable and life-affirming guidance for me. It caused me to strive to apply the principles others shared, regardless of whether they were successful in applying those principles. It taught me to be empathetic, compassionate, and forgiving toward those who make mistakes. After all, the root meaning of the word "sin" is simply "to miss the mark."

As usual, my father made so much sense. I could not afford to fail. I needed to focus on success and my future, instead of distractions like women and other non-productive activities. I stopped seeing Jian that very day. Incredible, beautiful, sexy, a phenomenal communicator, and probably the smartest woman I had ever been around, I could see she was the kind of woman my father spoke about so wisely. I needed to get my act together so I could provide the kind of life Jian, or someone like her, deserved.

Call it what you like, serendipity or divine order, but later that same day, I ran into Mario "Rio" Shirley at the registrar's office while working at another one of my part-time campus gigs. He informed me that he, Norris Sumrall, and Gary Lewis were thinking about opening a record store. All of us knew each other from ROTC, and Mario and I participated on the drill team together. Without knowing all the details—the how, when, and with what—I instantly said I wanted in on it. It didn't matter that *I* never owned a CD or a CD player. Other people did, so we certainly had our market, and we were on our way to becoming business owners.

In Record Time

Plans immediately got underway between Rio, Norris, Gary, and me to put together the hottest record store in town. We worked through the concept, and soon Rio and I drafted a business plan. At the same time, we all looked for a location. We found the perfect spot on South Adams Street. You could easily walk to it from campus, and how fortunate that it sat directly across the street from *Faces*, one of the hottest nightclubs in the city. Thanks to Norris and Gary, we bypassed institutional financing and they personally bankrolled the entire operation.

We each brought knowledge to the table about the kinds of music we liked to listen to, figuring it would be what our customers wanted as well. I loved a different kind of music than perhaps most of my classmates listened to, so I figured I would be able to add value or exposure to other genres we would come across. The music I loved was the same kind of music my dad loved—jazz.

My dad challenged me with this question one day, "Why would you want to sit and watch other people do their job on TV (i.e. movie stars and sports stars), when you could be doing things to better yourself?" That question led me to forego TV watching throughout college. Instead, I primarily listened to music and inspirational teaching tapes that Dad made for me before I left for college. I studied, ate, and meditated to a few cassettes featuring Wes Montgomery, Miles Davis, John Coltrane, and other jazz greats. While my friends knew every word to songs by Eric B. and Rakim, NWA, Luke, and 2 Live Crew, all I knew were the hooks and the beats.

The guys and I moved quickly in finishing out our store in preparation for ordering inventory. Mario and I went to St. Petersburg to pick up shelves, racks, and other equipment from his cousin, Mike Atwater. Mike, who already owned several record stores in the St. Petersburg/Tampa Bay area, provided us with items and guidance. Actually, Rio's entire family was instrumental in getting our store off the ground. His mother, Mrs. Hildergarde, his stepfather Larry, and his sister, Tracy, all invested. Mario's brother, Scootie, also worked for us and helped us keep things afloat.

We invested wisely in our first round of carefully selected inventory: approximately two thousand dollars' worth of recordings. The new CD's and tapes were promptly delivered, and we stacked them all on the shelves along with tons of used CD's, mainly from Norris's personal collection. We labored hard and fast to get everything in place. Finally, we could stand back and give an approving nod at our very own "Ups N Downs Music & More."

Unfortunately, that inventory came the day *before* the "burglar" bars were installed on the windows and doors. We poured our life's savings into that store, and we certainly didn't want to lose it all to someone else's "smash and grab" opportunity. Therefore, Rio and I decided to spend the night in the store as our own security. Both armed, we slept on the floor "aiming" to protect our livelihood.

Rio took his "aiming" duties literally, as I happened to wake up at one point in the middle of the night to find Rio's gun pointed straight at my face. My first instincts were to yell, "You idiot!" I quickly decided against that, just in case I startled him, which would cause an instinctive reaction to pull on his trigger. So, after easing slowly away from the barrel of his gun, I yelled, "You idiot! What the hell you doin' with your gun pointed at my face, Rio?"

He simply said, "Oh, my bad, yo'," and fell back to sleep.

Talk about a close call with sleepwalking! Once my heart stopped pounding at a hundred beats per second, I just looked at Rio and smiled. That night solidified our brotherhood even more. Always friends, since the first time we met in 1987, Rio and I had traveled the country together for FAMU's Pershing Rifle Drill Team. However, standing together that night—ready to protect our future at all costs—bonded us as brothers. We've been that way ever since.

As students from FAMU and owners of Tallahassee's only black-owned record store, we received an overwhelming amount of attention. Our grand opening of Ups N Downs record store was spectacular! Hundreds of people attended. We rented a stage and Clay D, a famous MC from Florida, rocked the microphone! Soon, our local fame earned us perks: we got into clubs free of charge, promoted concerts and lots of parties, and the most fun of all was that people treated us like little rock stars. It felt like more than Warhol's predicted "15 minutes of fame" for each of us.

The store's cozy environment developed out of Norris' talented design concept. Several girls from campus—Kim Mcommon, Tiffany Sipple, and Angie Slack—worked for us to help bring that concept to life. Scott "Dog" Parker cemented our lifelong friendship by acting as an honorary partner to us and contributing also to the ambiance of the store with his huge fish tank. It coordinated well with the couch and DJ listening area.

We had it going on, but as with many small businesses, we had our challenges, as well. For instance, we didn't have the best bookkeeping system. Most days, when we looked at the sales, the list read: "Dr. Dre's *The Chronic;* Mint Condition's *Pretty Brown Eyes; Mario's lunch;* Dr. Dre's *The Chronic; Jemal $5 dollars"* and so forth. It's funny now, but back then we engaged in heated debates over how we used the register as an allowance for whatever we wanted to do for the day. Some days, the books showed as many personal entries as sales entries. Consequently, Norris and Gary left the business for personal reasons, so Rio and I ran it alone for many months.

Investors and would-be partners maintained an interest in our store, including my little brother, Monty Brock. Monty was actually the little brother of Mike Brock, my Alpha line brother, best friend, and a fellow Chicagoan. One day, Monty surprised me by offering to invest in our store. I had just hopped in my car after closing the store, and he approached me, showed me a stack of bills, and made his offer.

Some years prior, Monty had gotten into a lot of trouble in Chicago, so Mike petitioned his mom to let him come down to live with us in Florida. I committed to taking care of him, as well. Mike secured a job for him at a clothing store, and because we all wore the same size, Monty borrowed our clothes to get him started at his new job. In fact, he borrowed our best stuff and established a pretty cool image for himself. For awhile, Monty's life ran quite well.

Unfortunately though, Monty started meeting not-so-good people and drifted away from the positive environment we took care to establish for him. In short, he started selling drugs. I remained unaware of this until he offered to invest in the store. I looked at him, bewildered, and asked, "Where did you get that money to invest in a store?"

"I hooked up with some guys here; we been doing some things, and I've made a little money," he explained. "I've made a few runs to Miami. It's cool."

"Monty, that is not cool," I said. "You don't know these cats down here. You are an outsider. You might be the set-up guy. They don't know you. In Chicago Heights, you might have some clout, respect, or support because people have known you since you were a little boy. They know your dad, your mom, and your brothers. They are less likely to hurt you because of those lifelong affiliations. But, you don't know these guys, and they don't know or care about you." I knew he heard me, even though he got a little restless with me preaching to him.

"Run and get me something to eat," he said.

I laughed and said, "Monty, I'm not one of your do-boys. I love you, li'l bro. Be careful out here. Remember what I said."

"A'ight, love you, too," he said.

I drove off extremely disappointed, mostly in myself. I had not spent a lot of time with him and hadn't realized he had drifted so quickly. I felt at that moment that I let him, Mike, and their family down. I did not want Monty to do what he did, and I didn't want him to blow his money, either. I realized even though we needed investors, allowing him to put his money into the record store would only create legal problems for us with him and whomever he was working with. I had to turn him down.

Another investor, my Alpha line brother, Corey Brown, expressed an interest in the store. Corey also grew up on the West Side of Chicago and attended Whitney Young. Initially, he offered to buy the store outright. We entertained the idea but decided to cut him in as a partner instead. Finally, we grew into a sustainable business, and things felt good.

Pass Me By, Please

As a full-time student at FAMU, I continued to manage Ups N Downs. Because of my successful summer internships with Apple, they offered me a full time position in Atlanta, as a Systems Engineer. It was really cool. I made more money than some of my professors! Apple allowed me to go to class in Tallahassee on Mondays and Fridays then Tuesday, Wednesday, and Thursday I would go to work in Atlanta. On campus, I promoted concerts and parties, and my popularity had DJ's calling out my name at the clubs. The financial success allowed me to buy my second car, a Saab 900s, and rent two places—an apartment in Tallahassee and a room in a house in Atlanta, owned by my KDU Brother, Marc Christmas.

I never stopped to question how I could handle everything because the natural high of living "the dream life" provided the necessary adrenaline to keep me going strong. My dad had always told me I needed to play in a different ball game than all those around me. I could not afford to fail. I had nothing to fall back on like most of them—no home with my old bedroom to go to; no family financially fit to bail me out; no solid backup plan; no backup plan at all, actually. *I* was it—*I* represented my only plan. So far, so good though, since I arrived in Tallahassee with just twenty dollars to my name and within five years had acquired quite a bit! Life was great!

That "different ball game" mindset also kept me from living at "The Ranch," a large house with five or six bedrooms that the KDU crew rented. I would've loved living with those I considered my best friends, those I knew and trusted better than anyone else in my life. Instead, I passed on that opportunity, mainly because of the pressure I might have faced to engage in an occasional smoke or drink, while kicking back and having fun with them. That is not to say that kind of activity happened frequently (quite honestly, I had no idea how much my friends smoked or drank), but any amount of it presented more pressure than I cared to handle.

Every now and then, I did manage to hang out with the fellas. One such occasion was to celebrate Jeff Beasley and Heather's upcoming wedding. The two had been dating for a while and really loved each other. When Heather got pregnant, Jeff, with a strong sense of family, did the moral thing and decided to marry her. Seeing that Heather came from a good family with a solid stake in the community (her uncle was FAMU's President, Dr. Frederick Humphries), I would say that Jeff's decision proved wise, as well as moral. Being connected to that family would open doors for Jeff that otherwise remained closed. It pleased me to know he received a "free pass" from the ghetto that only his poor judgment could revoke.

The guys really packed the apartment being used for Jeff's bachelor party! It seemed like all of the Who's Who on the yard showed up: Alphas, Kappa's, Que's, as well as the "just cool" fellas. Even Mr. Beasley, Jeff's dad—or "Pops" as we lovingly called him—joined the fun. Wise in his years, Pops reminded me of Ant's father, Donald. Both men always had a knack for relating their life experiences to our young lives. They delighted in all our successes and, in doing so, reminded us of our great potential. That time, like every other, Pops immediately told me he was happy and proud of me for my involvement with the record store and for working at Apple. Ironically, Pops and my dad were friends before Jeff and me. Pops started a magazine in Chicago, and my dad was once on the front cover, which I thought was really cool and made it an even more interesting connection.

Based on my upbringing, he knew those accomplishments meant even larger, yet-to-be-fulfilled dreams were on the horizon. The joy in his eyes shone almost as brightly and sincerely as it would have in my own father's eyes. Pops' encouragement gave me such a deep sense of pride. I don't think he could ever realize his impact—even though I've told him as best I can.

As with any typical bachelor party, all the guys got fired up, sounding like a bunch of sea lions during mating season as we anxiously awaited the strippers. I delighted in just seeing everyone, since my hectic travel schedule kept me from spending much time with them. Seeing lots of liquor and smelling weed in the air, I also figured joints would be passed around, and everyone—even the non-weed smokers—would be expected to take a puff. I could count on one hand the number of times I had taken a "puff." With Jeff's wedding being a special occasion, I decided ahead of time it would be OK if I took one. Right, wrong or indifferent, somehow I had rationalized one puff from 'peer pressure' was not the same as 'joy smoking.' Of course, that thinking was more wrong than either right or indifferent, but I tried to never get comfortable even with a puff. The fellas would tease me, as it looked like I was putting a scorpion up to my lips and tried to inhale as little as possible. "Puffs" and "drags" were definitely differentiated, in my mind and in practice.

Shortly after arriving at the party, I started noticing a few of my friends not hanging around anymore. As I scanned the room on my way to release my beer-filled bladder, it seemed more and more of them went missing. When I encountered a locked bathroom door, I stepped back and stood to the side, waiting for its occupant to come out. When the door opened, imagine my surprise to see not one but about ten guys standing around in the bathroom! At first, I didn't know what to think. No billowing weed smoke contained within and no lone stripper hidden among them, so my mind couldn't register the attraction in that cramped room.

James, a Kappa, said, "Mal come on in." So, I reluctantly walked in. A few of my KDU crew stood around, as well as some Alpha's, Kappa's, and other guys from around the campus. Most of those guys were very popular and known for being smart, coming from affluent families, or being real ladies' men. As I stood there shoulder to shoulder, I wondered, "What in the hell is everyone doing in here?"

Suddenly, one of the guys standing in the tub turned around with a plate. On that plate, I observed white powder, and my heart sank. Cocaine! John, who held the plate, carved a section out, put what looked like a rolled up dollar bill to his nose and snorted it. I could not believe my eyes. Of course, I knew this occurred all the time; after all, I came from that environment, but I only expected that kind of stuff to be happening back in the 'hood' and in the projects, not here among scholars and kids in college trying to do something with their lives.

I was sixteen the first time I ever saw someone snort coke. While playing basketball for Whitney Young, a bunch of us players decided to chill at Tony's house before one of our home games because he lived near the school. As I sat on his couch, he came over and snorted something off of a mirror, right over me. Some of it sprinkled down on me, and then whatever else he held dropped. I yelled, "Tony, what the hell are you doing?" as I brushed that stuff off me.

"Damn!" he fussed as he scurried to scoop it up.

I asked again, "Man, what are you doing?"

He replied, "We always get high before the game; it makes you play better. You should try it."

"You must be crazy!" I retorted, "I'm not doing that. Besides, you don't even play; you sit on the bench!"

The rest of the fellas started laughing, "Yeah man, you sit on the bench!" they taunted.

I could not believe it. Not surprisingly, Tony never made anything of himself. He and his best friend, Pete, one of the stars on our team who received both an academic and sports scholarship, ended up strung out on drugs a few years later. I saw Pete get on the bus one day when I was visiting home from college, and it greatly disheartened me. He looked worn down, dirty, smelly, and high. Almost unrecognizable to me, I didn't speak to him. Not that I purposely ignored him, but I guess you could say witnessing his painful state rendered me speechless. Pete—handsome, smart, and athletically talented—had so much promise in high school. His parents appeared supportive, too, since they came to most of our games. I could not believe how his life turned out. My mind ventured back to that day at Tony's and how I'd thought then that those guys were headed down the wrong road. At Jeff's bachelor's party, that same thought occurred.

The plate continued to circulate among those I cherished as my best friends and others that I knew very well. Each person carved out a small section and snorted it. I grew nervous, since they obviously only invited me in that bathroom based on our implied circle of trust. The lump in my throat swelled with each passing moment, as I racked my brain for an excuse to say, "No," when the plate came to me. I kept thinking if I didn't partake, the guys crammed in that tiny bathroom would know I held a secret of theirs. That might cause them to suspect I would compromise our trust if ever a question arose about their drug use. I felt trapped, like a captive bird flapping its wings at the edge of the cage, yearning to fly though the bars and escape. In my case, though, the only thing flapping was my mind.

Judging by the conversation and the skill with which they handled that plate and rolled up dollar bill, I quickly assessed they had all done coke before. Next person; then, the next person; then, finally the guy to my right cut his section and snorted. "Oh God, help me please. Give me the courage to say, 'No,' and not cave in to the pressure. Please don't let me start down this slippery slope."

The guy on my right passed the white powder-dusted plate to me with several thin lines left on it. Just as I reached for the plate, a voice behind me said, "He's good."

It was Trace, one of my best friends. The guy to my left looked at me and asked, "Oh, you don't want any?"

Before I could answer, Trace stated again, "Naw, he's good."

Anyone studying me could easily see my nervousness and discomfort. I hoped they were all too high to recognize it or care. I looked at Trace as if he had saved my life—in that moment, he actually had! I can't imagine what I would have done without his intervention.

Trace knew some of my background and the predicament that bathroom scene placed me in. He knew some of what my mom and my dad suffered through, and to some extent, how I had been affected by their circumstances. He understood why I usually hesitated and tried to weasel my way out of taking a few pulls on a joint, even when just the fellas passed one around. Trace knew me; he knew my dilemma and saved my life that day.

I walked out of that bathroom and straight out of the apartment. I met up with everyone the next day at Dr. Humphries' house, in preparation for the wedding, without a word ever spoken about the night before. The wedding played out beautifully. Most of our KDU crew participated in the ceremony. We will always remember it as a particularly special affair, since it was the first wedding of someone in our crew.

Everything Happens In Threes

Things started to slip again at the record store and tensions began to build. Profits sank and didn't provide sufficient funds to purchase enough inventory. The business ran on our own personal funds, and we knew we could not sustain that for long. We received a great opportunity to promote an after-party with the Alphas and the AKA's. The party took place after a concert with Luke, Poison Clan, Common Sense (now just Common), and a couple of other artists. We needed the publicity, something to jumpstart the store's brand.

At the concert, I sat with my KDU brothers, Tony Hall and Eddie Buck. The concert appeared to be 'hot,' but we found ourselves in a very somber mood. We received word that night that Big Tone, one of our KDU brothers, had committed suicide back in Chicago. It caught us all off-guard. Big Tone, a hard-core dude, could knock you out with one punch. Equally, his gregarious nature made him a lot of fun.

The thought of him taking his own life did not sit well with us. All during the concert, we dissected the situation and could not make heads or tails of it. It was reported by the neighborhood gossips that Big Tone started selling drugs. He grew up on Chicago's West Side, right off of Cicero Avenue and the Eisenhower Expressway, just a few blocks from Tee's and a few blocks from where I lived. Drugs and gangs ruled that area, and while I didn't feel shock over his involvement, I did feel bitterly disappointed.

Without all the facts, a conspiracy theory developed around his "suicide."

Most people didn't think he could do it, and the police reported he shot himself in the head with his left hand. Many in law enforcement will attest it is unusual for someone who is right-handed to shoot himself with his left hand. It's an awkward trigger squeeze, making it not impossible, but very unlikely. Aware of the scandalous nature of the area, I found it more plausible that Big Tone suffered through an execution. Needless to say, I remember very little about the concert and left early to go the Avant Garde Club to get ready for the after-party.

Soon, the partygoers packed in and grooved to the sounds of Vince Adams, the DJ. Vince and I played ball together at Whitney Young and are considered "ism's"—meaning we carry the same pledge number (number 15) but pledged different years with our fraternity, Alpha Phi Alpha. He truly created the "House" movement at FAMU because no other DJ played it until he started rocking it at the Chicago Club parties. He now travels all around the country and internationally as one of the hottest DJ's on the circuit.

The party became too "live." Lots of people crowded the door, and they started pushing and shoving to get inside the club. Vince yelled over the microphone, "All brothers to the door." Normally that meant a mad rush of guys to the door. When I got there, I saw only a few other brothers, but still they had managed to push the crowd back.

Corey Brown stood outside the door, looking to his right. Straight ahead, I noticed a guy seemingly focused on Corey while being restrained by his friends. Finally, he broke loose and lunged at Corey, so I reached out to block him. Corey, not seeing any of that, turned around to go back into the club while pushing those nearby back inside.

"Bang!! Bang!!"

Someone started shooting! I stood out on the stairs while the guy I protected Corey from disappeared into the crowd and began shooting. I remember a pole stood in the middle of the stairway, and thought I hit it because my knee was aching. When I looked down, I saw a hole in my jeans with blood pouring out.

Oh God! He shot me! I started to fall back into the club when more shots rang out.

'Bang, Bang, Bang Bang!'

At that point things moved in slow motion. As I fell backward, I looked all over my body for additional wounds. I scanned for more blood. I remember thinking this was the moment I was going to die. I just knew I had been shot more times and not realized or felt it due to shock.

My line brothers, Ray Matthews and Corey Pressley, caught me.

"Jemal's been shot!" Ray yelled. "Jemal's been shot!"

Finally, I realized I only had one wound. Thank you, God, just one gunshot wound! But now my attention turned toward that wound. My knee felt like someone hit it with a sledgehammer! The pain radiated through every part of my body. My breath came fast and shallow, and the movements around me felt blurred and chaotic. My friends picked me up and put me on a table. Then the table started to wobble from the crowd forming around me, jostling for position. I begged them to quickly move me off the table. Corey and Ray took me to a less crowded area by the bathroom.

In the short time between the shooting and my bloody entrance back into the club, the party crowd moved from frightened to hysterical. My girlfriend at the time, Sarah Smith, stood crying, along with the majority of girls at the party. All of my fraternity brothers stood around and looked down on me with confused, sorrowful faces.

Mike Bouldin crouched in front of me, and Mike Brock kneeled to my right. I could hear people saying all kinds of crazy stuff.

"He's passing out!"

"He's bleeding badly!"

"Put a tourniquet on him! Lift his head! Raise his feet!"

All of it became too much! I knew I could lose my leg because the maniac shot me in my knee, but I also knew if someone put a tourniquet on me, I almost surely would lose it because of lack of blood to the area. My words were stifled by the fear and shock that ruled my body. In its place, thoughts of death riddled my mind while the blood oozed non-stop.

"Do not put a tourniquet on me," I said.

Several people echoed it, "No tourniquet."

The environment remained chaotic, which made me more uncomfortable. Suddenly, Edwin Hawkins, another "ism" and a police officer, showed up. I felt immediate relief as he controlled the crowd, moved people away from me, and reassured me. The paramedics arrived and started to work on me right away.

Mike Brock stayed with me the whole time. He had found his older brother dead just two years prior, and I knew seeing me like that was difficult for him. Mike's brother had developed a drug problem along with a few other issues. It became too much for him, and he shot himself in the head. Unfortunately, Mike found his body. I can't imagine the images Mike carries in his head, but I know they get to him every now and then. Because Mike and I pledged together, lived together, and suffered family tragedies together, we were bonded and connected in significant ways. I hoped I did not cause him additional pain. If I did, he never let me know, and he never left my side. Once he got a glimpse of the bullet wound, he finally cracked, "Oh, that little thing; you'll be alright."

I thought to myself, "Gunshots don't need big gaping wounds to threaten someone's life." I felt a little angry with him, but eventually recognized his attempt at humor to try to lessen my stress.

Finally, the paramedics secured my leg, placed me on a gurney, and rolled me out of the nightclub. Once outside, I saw two ambulances and someone else on a gurney. The gunman shot someone else in the melee. They loaded me into the ambulance and sped toward the hospital. As I sat there, the paramedics checked my vitals and kept talking to me to make sure I didn't black out. I remember telling them, "All the times I've been near shots fired on the streets and all the fights I've been in while living in Chicago, to be shot at college when I'm trying to better myself is pretty crazy."

As the frenzy settled a bit, I realized that the sirens weren't going, and

I inquired, "Guys, why aren't the sirens on?"

One of them said, "Since we have you stabilized, the protocol is to turn them off."

I laughingly asked, "Can I at least get the sirens like they do in the movies?" They laughed.

We finally got to the hospital, and people worked frantically going through all the necessary routines. They fired questions at me and at each other:

"What's your name?" "Where is the bullet?" "Is there an exit wound?" "Does he need blood?" "What's his pressure?"

At one point, it felt more chaotic than being at the club on the floor, but at least it was controlled chaos.

They finally got me prepped for surgery. Unfortunately, the bullet had not exited and had instead lodged in my knee. While I waited for the on-call orthopedic surgeon to arrive at the hospital, I began thinking about what my life would be like with one leg. No one told me they would have to amputate my leg, but my mind went there anyway. I ran, played basketball, and had plans to become an Army Officer. All that seemed to be over.

While not perfect, I tried my entire life to live right. I stayed away from gangs, drugs, and other illegal activity. I excelled as an honor student with a great future ahead of me, and now I felt afraid that it could all change. Eventually, the thought of losing my leg became too much for me, and I tried to think about something else.

My next thought—thank God, I'm not dead. The other bullets had hit the door right at chest and head level.

In 1993, it was rare for the average person to own a cell phone, and most of them were big and bulky. But because of my high tech job at Apple, I had a relatively small NEC phone which was still in my pocket. While I waited, in excruciating pain, I decided to call my father to tell him about the shooting.

"Dad."

"Hey Mal."

"I've been shot," I said quickly.

"What?" he said.

"I've been shot, Dad."

"What?"

I realized he could hear me, but shock took over his ability to process. I scrambled to dismiss the extent of the injury, so he wouldn't worry. I didn't give him any other information. I just remember telling him I would call him back to explain it all. What's funny is that even though Dad and I took different paths in our lives, we shared a few similar experiences. The jealous boyfriend of a woman he once dated had shot him. Fortunately, the bullet just grazed his stomach, but he wore a permanent scar. No wonder he told me to "lay off the women."

The doctor finally arrived and performed the surgery right there in the emergency room. The pain medicine finally began to work, so I experienced less pain.

"Do you want general anesthesia or local," the doctor asked.

"What's the difference, Doc?" I asked.

"With general anesthesia, I put you asleep versus a local where I numb the area," he replied.

"So I can watch you take the bullet out?" I asked.

"Yes."

"I'd rather watch," I said firmly.

"Ok."

He stuck his finger in the wound. "It's stuck on their really good," he said. "This is going to be a little difficult."

He then ordered additional equipment from the nurse. He used one instrument after another trying to get the bullet out. Even though he numbed the area, the pressure of all the pulling and pushing was very uncomfortable. He finally took some surgical pliers and wiggled and wiggled until he finally yanked it out.

"Wow," he exclaimed, "A .38 caliber. Son, you are extremely lucky. It looks like this didn't have a solid impact upon firing. If it had, as close as you say he was to you, this would have torn your leg up, and we would have had to amputate."

"Thank God," I sighed. "I was so scared, Doc. I mean, I was really, really scared. I thought you were going to have cut my leg off. Thank you, God!! Can I see the bullet?"

Doc passed me the bullet, and I examined it. It seemed rather small, but I understood bullet size didn't necessarily determine what kind of damage would result.

"Can I have it, Doc?"

"Unfortunately, you can't," he said. "The police will need it for the investigation. You need to get some rest. You're a lucky young man tonight. Just relax for a while. We will need to observe you for a few hours before we let you go."

I was fine with that. I started thinking about my luck. Yes, I just got shot, and I couldn't change that, but it could have been a lot worse. As I lay there, many people came in and out of the room to see me. The staff told me my friends packed the entire waiting room. I dozed off and on and remember snatches of people coming in and out, recanting the sequence of events from their perspective. I was just glad to be alive.

The next couple of weeks became my personal hell on earth. Intense pain moved in as a constant companion. It felt as if my leg was going to fall off. I didn't know at the time, but I should have asked the doctor for more medicine. As I look back on it, I am puzzled why the doctor only gave me Ibuprofen in 800mg doses. That's what I take today for a headache!

After a couple of weeks, my mother finally came to Florida to take care of me. It was her first time traveling to Florida since I had started school. I knew no one could take better care of me than my mother, so I did not discourage her when she said she wanted to come. She couldn't hide her discouragement, knowing something like this had happened while I attended school, not out on the streets I was from. She wanted me to sue, but that would've meant suing my own fraternity and sister sorority. I couldn't do that, although I admit to being disappointed in the lack of support I received from both of those groups. After my shooting, I barely received a Get Well card, let alone anyone coming over to help dress the wound or tend to me.

My mother's hope for getting out of the Chicago ghetto lay with me; therefore, my brush with death because of senseless violence did not sit well with her. I understood her feelings. Her life was hard, and I opened a path to make it a little easier. If the shooter had aimed a few inches higher, or if the door had not blocked the other four bullets...

I bore the pain well with the loving support of my mother. After two weeks, when I became strong enough to get around on crutches, she went back home, and I continued to struggle with debilitating pain.

I traveled to Panama City with my Pershing Rifle Line Brother (LB), Ron "Newk" Newsome, to get away for a couple of days. Panama City is a beautiful beach town on the Gulf of Mexico. We loved going there because it of its close proximity to FAMU—less than ninety minutes away. The water there—a clear, calming blue—relaxed me, and I hoped it would help me put the shooting into perspective.

Newk and his mother inspired me. A loving and affectionate person, I always called her, 'Mom." Although Newk's father died when Newk was young, his mother raised him in a positive way. I enjoyed seeing them interact together. Their relationship grew out of friendship and respect for each other. The beauty of their relationship inspired me to develop the same type of relationship with my mother.

One evening, Newk said, "LB, you still in a lot of pain? I know what might make some of the pain go away."

He pulled out a joint and said, "This might help. At least that's what they say on TV." We both laughed. With the exception of a few pulls or "puffs" with the fellas, I resisted smoking all my life, but the pain overwhelmed any qualms that lingered in that particular moment. Newk knew I didn't smoke, and he had never offered weed to me before; however, at that point, we both knew I would use it for medicinal purposes.

There are mixed emotions and mixed results about whether marijuana works to relieve pain, but I can attest—it works! I stayed pain-free for several hours for the first time since the night at the club. After eating a couple of boxes of fries from Grady's in Panama City, I slept very well.

I still feared I would start a habit and continued to believe I might have a genetic predisposition to drugs and alcohol because of both of my parents. I did not smoke anymore that weekend. Well, one more time and another time with Mario's brother, Kirk, a week later. That's it. They say people get paranoid when they are high on weed. Because of my family background, my paranoia began at conception, not practice or application! That was the last time I ever smoked weed in my life.

When I returned home, I threw myself into my classes. Graduation loomed, and I had missed weeks of class. Most of my teachers were sympathetic to my issue; however, my biology teacher acted as the exception. Luckily, a classmate helped me get through it.

Early one morning, Sarah, my girlfriend, got a page from Stacey, Mike Brock's wife. Apparently, Stacey had been trying to call me all morning, but I kept the telephone ringers off in my apartment—a bad habit I picked up from my father. He never liked to hear the phone ring. I only knew a call came in by the sound of the answering machine springing to life. Sarah called Stacey back and immediately started screaming, "Oh, my God! Oh, my God!"

I jumped up terrified. "What's wrong?" I said.

"It's Monty; he's been killed, and Mike is in jail," she wailed.

"What? Monty? What? What happened? What happened to Monty? Why is Mike in jail?"

The questions and tears tumbled out as my mind dissolved into emotional chaos. Monty's dead! Before I knew it, we dressed and headed to the jail to get Mike out. The rest of the day became a jumbled mess of images and words, which I still cannot clearly decipher.

I don't remember if we got Mike out of jail, or if they had released him before we arrived. I don't even remember seeing him. I do remember I ended up at the record store with the shades down, lights off, and Boyz II Men, *"It's So Hard to Say Goodbye"* blasting on repeat.

The loss of someone who was that close to me, the first loss of this kind, became too much. Yes, Big Tone was my boy, but I hadn't seen him in years. Monty was my brother, and I was responsible for him. I melted down completely, drinking two 40 ounces of Olde English malt liquor in the process. I also wrestled with tremendous guilt: I let him down; I let Monty down. His family let him come to Florida, knowing Mike and I could guide him. Mike... damn, I just remembered Mike. How could I be so selfish? Only a couple years apart, the brothers could pass for twins at first glance and now Monty... Monty's dead. Mike lost Skip his older brother only two years earlier because of drug issues and now Monty. Damn!!

A lot of people came by the store, but I didn't let anyone in. I didn't even go to the door. Reggie, the owner of the store next door, called the police when he heard the music blasting, and I wouldn't answer the door. He assumed something was wrong. I did open the door for the police. I explained the situation, told them my little brother died, and that I was grieving. They said something like, "Be careful." I closed the door and went back to drinking and crying, and wondered in agony how Monty died.

Another knock at the door. I thought it was the police again, but it was Mike. I let him in, and we hugged and cried for a few minutes, and then finally I asked, "Mike, what in the hell happened?"

He told me Monty played pool with a couple of people and when he put on his coat to leave, he realized someone had stolen the money out of his coat pocket. He assumed one of the guys he had been hanging out with took it, so he went looking for him. Monty found the guy getting out of a cab over by the Krispy Kreme on Tennessee Avenue, where Mike and I used to go. When Monty reached in to pull him out, the guy shot him in the neck. He fell to the ground, bleeding profusely. One of Monty's friends standing nearby saw the whole thing and rushed to his side with a Bible. While waiting for the paramedics to arrive, she read the 23rd Psalm to him, and he repeated it with her:

"The Lord is my shepherd, I shall not want. He maketh me to lie down in green pastures; he leadeth me beside the still waters; he restoreth my soul. Yea, though I walk through the valley of the shadow of death, I will fear no evil, for Thou art with me...and, I will dwell in the house of the Lord forever."

And then he died.

The image of Monty lying in the middle of the street, bleeding to death, mouthing the most well-known of the Psalms, burned through my brain. I used to live in the apartment complex just a few hundred yards away from where he died. I could easily visualize every detail of those surroundings: the motel on the corner, the Krispy Kreme on the opposite corner, the bushes, the trees, the signs... I wished the image away, but it wouldn't leave. I replayed it over and over in my head like a tape loop.

Pain overwhelmed me, but I could only imagine the immeasurable amount of pain Mike dealt with for years. Mike explained that Monty told his girlfriend if she ever had to answer police questions to say Monty was Mike Brock. When she arrived at the hospital to identify the body, she told them Monty was Mike Brock. When the police called Mike, he went to the hospital to identify the body and told them the body was his brother, Monty.

Things became chaotic and confusing at that moment because the police had previously issued a warrant for Monty's arrest. When Mike tried to explain the difference between him and his brother, they couldn't discern the truth, so they took Mike to the police station. While his brother lay dead in a hospital, Mike sat in jail trying to prove his identity.

I could see the despair in Mike's eyes. He usually refrained from becoming emotional and stayed quite calm and unresponsive in the most difficult of circumstances. However, the pain of losing another brother and the confusion of the moment left him bewildered and devastated. I couldn't do anything for him. I cried for Mike. I cried for Monty. I cried for me. I truly cried a river that day.

The family held Monty's funeral a week later. Mike broke down and passed out during the services due to hyperventilation or an asthma attack. They never confirmed exactly what happened, but I chalked it all up to being completely overwhelmed emotionally. At the funeral, I still walked with crutches, still healing from my own gunshot wound.

People asked, "Why are so many of our young black men involved in such violence?" No one could answer. I reflected back on the past couple of weeks: a good friend supposedly killed himself; someone shot me, and my best friend's little brother was shot and killed. They say everything happens in threes. A few short months later, Mike's father died. So, maybe fours...

Thou Shalt Not Kill

After the shooting, a few people would stop by every now and then to check on me. Female friends as well as ex-girlfriends wanted to stop by but Sarah, my girlfriend at the time, wouldn't hear of it. While I understood her hesitation, her schedule didn't allow her to be there as much as I needed her. Trivial things (like tending to pledges from her sorority) took precedence over my needs. Some nights she didn't stop to check on me until very late in the evening. Usually, until she showed up, I managed to take care of myself. With difficulty, I hopped around to get food, take my meds, change my dressing, and do anything else I needed to do. Fortunately, my mother had come to the rescue earlier. Maybe I didn't communicate my needs well, and maybe Sarah didn't realize how much I needed her. Whatever the case, I decided to end our relationship once I healed.

We had been together for over a year, so the breakup would hurt us both deeply because our lives were intertwined in so many ways. Our best friends were married, and when they started a family, they named us godparents of their baby girl, Tylar. We had already decided Sarah would come live with me after she graduated, and we made other plans for the future, as well. However, after thinking it all through, our future plans wouldn't be the only problem I anticipated with the breakup.

Sarah's personality had become another complication. She had always been a rather emotional and clingy person. In the beginning, that worked well for my ego since I loved feeling needed. With the inner scars of an abandoned child, I felt good having someone to love and hold, and having her love me back added to those good feelings. Yes, emotional and clingy—the very things I felt I loved about her were the traits I knew would make matters worse when we broke up.

My father advised me to be completely open with women. He said, "Every time you lie, you lose a bit of your manhood. If you lie, manipulate, or are less than open, you squirm and shrink as a man and as a human being." Well, I took his advice literally.

When the day came, I called her over. I opted for a direct, face-to-face discussion. When she arrived, I went right into it, no preamble or introduction, just wham, right in her face!

"You were extremely selfish by not paying more attention to me after I was shot," I started. "I needed you, but you showed me your true character. It's a stark contradiction to your clingy yet loving nature, which was starting to wear on me anyway. But, when I needed you to be clingy, you were out doing your own thing."

Rightfully, Sarah started crying.

"I'm sorry," she said. "I thought you were OK. I checked on you in the daytime after class. I didn't know that you needed me!"

"How could you not know that I needed you?" I asked incredulously. "I'd been shot! Maybe you weren't even out with the girls; maybe you were messing around with someone else.

"Jemal, I didn't know," she started again, but I didn't care to hear any more excuses.

"You didn't know I needed you?" I yelled, tears rolling down my face. "What I need is a 'foxhole buddy' and you have shown me that you are not able to be that person. I can't depend on you, and I can't trust you. So, it's over!"

I really loved her, but I really did not feel I could depend on or trust her anymore. She took it extremely hard. She cried so hard, I thought she would to pass out.

"Please, please don't do this!" she screamed. "I promise I will be better; I promise!"

I wanted to give in; I really wanted to, but I could not move past lying in the house by myself for days respecting her wishes by not allowing other women who wanted to help me come and visit. The overwhelming pain and loneliness drove me to a kind of insane place in my mind. I felt abandoned by her, and I just could not forgive her for the neglect I felt.

She cried non-stop for over an hour. Eventually it got so bad, I couldn't stand it anymore. I just left her, in anguish, alone in my apartment. I went to my record store to take care of a few things.

I hobbled on crutches into the store and began putting up inventory. I don't know how much time passed before Sarah came into the store with tears streaming down her face. She weakly handed me a bottle. I recognized it as one of my prescriptions. Prior to getting shot, I had started getting headaches. Likely, my crazy schedule took more of a toll on me than I wanted to admit. Instead of slowing down, I went to the doctor and he prescribed Verapimil.

Looking into Sarah's distraught and oddly dazed face, I realized the bottle was empty. "What happened to the pills?" I asked hesitantly.

"I took them," she said. "If I can't have you, I don't want to live anymore."

"What?!" I screamed. "Why did you do that? Sarah, why did you do that?"

I watched as Sarah's body fell in slow motion to the floor. I didn't know if the medication or the extreme emotions that racked her caused her to fall.

"Sarah, get up baby; we have to go the doctor," I pleaded. "Come on baby, get up."

I lifted her off the ground and instantly felt waves of pain radiating up and through my leg. The pain became background noise to the immediate horror of reality. My girlfriend had just taken an entire bottle of prescription drugs. Guilt washed over me as my mind skipped ahead to her funeral.

As I carried my poisoned girlfriend out of the store and hoisted her into my car, my thoughts went to what I learned from studying metaphysics. "Thou shalt not kill" had two meanings. It meant not only literally killing someone, but also killing someone's self-esteem—rendering them emotionally dead. Did I kill

Sarah? Did I kill her self-esteem by taking away her will to live?

Driving to the hospital, I pushed away those thoughts in favor of calling Sarah's best friend, Stacy.

"Stacy, you need to meet me at me the hospital; Sarah just tried to kill herself!"

Stacy's loud, screechy voice went up two octaves and almost blew out my eardrum through the phone.

"What happened?" she screamed. "What did she do? What did you do to her?"

The latter question shook me to my core, and I could only respond in a panicked, pleading voice "Stacy, just please meet me at the hospital. Please!"

I hung up, called Mike, and begged him to meet me there.

Turning briefly to look at Sarah, I saw her take a turn for the worse. She zoned in and out of consciousness and occasionally whimpered, "I love you," followed by a moan and silence. When we arrived at the hospital, she was non-responsive. Through surging tears, I guided the car to the emergency room entrance, jumped out, and hobbled around to the passenger side. I snatched Sarah out of the car and carried her into the hospital. Pain threatened to consume me. I didn't want to lose her, but the physical exertion of carrying her with my as yet unhealed leg made every step unbearable. My heart broke, and my leg felt like it was being ripped off.

Finally, I reached help. I yelled to the lady behind the desk as I held out my empty prescription bottle, "She just took all of the pills!" The woman sprinted from behind the counter, took the bottle, and yelled for help.

Within seconds, people rushed out and threw Sarah up on a gurney and took off with her through the double doors to care rooms on the other side. I hobbled after them, desperately trying to stay with her. As they took her vitals, one of the doctors asked me a bunch of questions.

"What's her name?"

"Sarah," I responded.

"Can you tell me exactly what happened?"

"Yes, sir," I sobbed. "We had an argument, and I broke up with her. I left my apartment, and later she came to my record store with the empty bottle, saying she took all the medicine."

"Whose prescription is it?"

"It's mine," I replied.

"Do you have heart problems?"

"Excuse me, sir? Heart problems?"

"Yes, heart problems. This medicine is used for people who have heart conditions, high blood pressure."

"No sir, I don't have heart problems, I was taking them for..." I trailed off when suddenly the activity in the room grew more intense. I looked to the doctor in the hope he could tell me what it all meant.

"Her blood pressure is starting to drop; we are going to have to pump her stomach."

One of the nurses started yelling, "Sarah! Sarah! Can you hear me?"

Another barked at me, "Sir, you're going to have to wait outside!" as she shoved me toward the double doors.

My feet moved automatically, but my mind stayed behind in the room with my girlfriend. In the hallway, I heard them yelling, "Sarah! Sarah!" I limped down the hall, tears falling until the weight of it all became too much, and I doubled over, collapsing on the floor along the wall. I just sat there as I screamed inside my mind over and over again, "What have I done? What have I done?"

A few minutes later, Stacy and Mike showed up separately, and I told them the whole story. I felt so ashamed. I second-guessed everything I did; maybe I could have waited or maybe I could have said what I said in a different way. Did I really not love her anymore, or was I just mad about how she treated me?

I knew she loved me, but recently, life had increased in intensity. Someone shot me; Monty died; Sarah became pregnant with our child and decided to have an abortion. I needed to know she would live. I walked up to the front desk, determined to find out.

"Ma'am, how is Sarah doing?"

"They are still working on her," the nurse replied. "Based on my understanding of the situation and hospital protocol, since this was an attempted suicide, and you are a principle figure in the issue, we will not be able to give you information. Should she pull through, we will not be able to release her to you and she will have to stay overnight for supervision."

"But Ma'am..." I started.

"I'm sorry, sir," she said abruptly, "That's just our protocol. Is there someone else we can contact?"

"Yes ma'am; she's here now. Stacy, please come up here."

Stacey became the chief person in charge of making decisions for Sarah. Wow! How did we arrive here?

Finally, the doctor came out, and my heart raced as we all walked up to him. He directed his update to Stacy:

"Sarah is fine. We had to force her to drink a chalky substance to neutralize the medicine in her stomach, which was difficult because she was in and out. Then, we had to pump the stomach..."

As the doctor talked, I kind of zoned in and out. Relief, regret, remorse, and pain washed over me, making it impossible to pay close attention. I heard the words I needed to hear, "She is going to be OK."

We all left the hospital, and I went home. My head ached, my leg throbbed, and emotionally I felt drained. I could not believe what just happened. Sarah—so smart, so beautiful. Sarah—the Jane Kennedy of campus. Sarah—who loved me so dearly. That is the same Sarah who had just tried to kill herself.

I caused this, and I still didn't know what I felt. Do I love her? Do I still want to be with her? What would her parents think of me? What would her friends think? I never answered those questions. When the hospital released her the next day, we picked up again like nothing ever happened.

We broke up for good almost a year later while I was attending the Infantry

Officer Basic Course in Fort Benning, Georgia. I made it seem as if the problem lay with me, not her. It is how I handled most of my break-ups after that incident. Almost losing her because of my unfiltered honesty left me scarred. I couldn't allow myself to be as honest or transparent as I wanted to be in my subsequent relationships, so I backed out or "cowarded" my way out of them. I never wanted to confront anyone with a laundry list of faults or accusations again.

I realized finding something wrong with me that made the relationship impossible to continue made for an easier break-up. A lot of people cannot handle someone else's honesty, and perhaps I have never learned or trusted myself enough to end a relationship with tactful, direct honesty. I simply never wanted to kill someone's self-esteem again. One brush with that was enough.

That's My Son!

I managed to pull all my loose ends together and graduate from FAMU in the spring of 1993. It pleased me greatly that four influential women who helped raise and mold me—my mother, Aunt Bob, Aunt Betty and my grandmother—attended my graduation, along with some of my cousins. They all traveled from Chicago for that joyous occasion, which served as a celebratory event for them, as much for me. My grandmother suffered from vascular dementia, which is similar to Alzheimer's, but caused by a stroke, so she couldn't fully comprehend the purpose of the occasion. Nor was she aware of how much it meant to me having her there.

My graduation festivities consisted of two ceremonies: first, the standard diploma ceremony, requiring the traditional cap and gown, and then the ROTC commissioning ceremony, to which I had to wear my Class A uniform. As I sat for hours looking for people, I tried to store at least one point into my memory bank from the speaker's commencement speech—a hectic day indeed.

During my first ceremony, as I emerged from that sea of green and black attire and approached the stage, it occurred to me that this was a life-changing moment for the Wilson family. Dating back to my great-grandparents, who picked cotton in Wedowee, Alabama, we could count the number of college graduates on one hand and none were men. As I walked across the stage, I heard many of my friends cheering and yelling my name.

Modestly speaking, I did have a lot of friends, and I was pretty popular, but it still overwhelmed me to hear the loud applause. I wondered if some part of my friends' jubilation for me stemmed from the shooting just a couple of months prior. To see me up there with diploma in hand did put a lot of things in perspective, considering what could have been the outcome. I took it all in and cherished the moment.

Several hours later, as I once again sat in that auditorium, this time waiting to walk across the stage for my commissioning, I reflected upon my entire life: my family; growing up in the projects; the many schools I attended; the drugs; the pain; the love; and my dad, who couldn't make it there for a reason I never knew. I wanted to stop the clock and continue reflecting, yet the moments all seemed to flash by so fast. Just then, a solution came to mind as a way to savor the moment— a slow cadence march across the stage.

My slow cadence march (death march) was one of the best on the drill team. My plan called for movements that were crisp and sharp (as was usual), but slow enough to allow me to bask in the full glory of the moment. Before I knew it, they called my name. I slowly marched across that stage, contemplating segments of my life's journey with each step I snapped forth. Thoughts swirled in my mind, yet I remained conscious of the audience, which began to murmur.

Next, a slow crescendo of cheering and clapping swept across that crowd. By the time I got to my Colonel, the cheers and applause came forth steadily. I did a right face slowly and snapped into position. For my salute, I brought my right arm up slowly, deliberately, and tightly. When I snapped my arm into a full salute, the entire Civic Center erupted! Talk about magical!

More amazing was seeing my family out of the corner of my eye, standing, cheering, and crying. Even my grandmother rooted for me. I wondered if, even for a moment, she knew what was happening. The little boy she once claimed as her son, who was loved by many but almost lost in the struggle, had finally made it. I like to think she was lucid in that moment.

As I turned and walked off the stage, people screamed my name from every direction. Folks high-fived and jumped up and down like they had just seen

Michael Jordan do one of his incredible dunks. That audience helped create an extraordinarily triumphant moment for me—one I'll never forget. But more gratifying was the fact that those special women—who looked on with broad smiles at a young man graduating from a top university with honors—could say with pride, "That's my son!"

A Higher Standard

After graduation, I reported to Fort Benning, Georgia for Infantry Officer Basic Course (IOBC). There are many divisions in the Army, and they each serve a unique purpose. Most of my fellow ROTC Famuans focused on support divisions like finance, supply, logistics, and intelligence, areas that allowed them to put their degrees to use. Then there was combat arms division for those directly involved in combat. Some of these guys rode in tanks, flew in planes, or shot artillery rounds. I, on the other hand, wanted to confront the enemy with no barriers between us. I didn't want to be in a two-ton tank, be a mile away shooting artillery rounds, or flying above the fight. I wanted to be right in the thick of it. Infantry, otherwise known as the Queen of Battle, is Army's foot soldier division. We patrolled the jungles, mountains, and desert on foot and confronted the enemy face-to-face. Maybe that was the 'hood' coming out in me. We fought face-to-face without million dollar equipment.

Nevertheless, while I was there, I learned principles of leadership and tactical skills like land navigation, weapons training, tactical movement, and assaults. Not knowing what to expect caused more intimidation than the curriculum itself. My training company accommodated 110 officers from all over the world: West Point, College ROTC grads, Congo, Central Africa Republic, Iraq, Saudi Arabia, and many other locations.

Aside from the U.S. Army's objectives set forth in that training session, I had my own personal mission to accomplish, as well. Just as I had graduated at the top of the class in my Advanced Camp, I wanted to do the same at IOBC. Therefore, that goal went on my success list.

My platoon turned out to be one of the livelier units around. Out of the six African-Americans in the course, four of us were in the same platoon and on the same squad. Clinton Gilder and Michael Giles were two of the funniest guys I had ever met. Giles came from North Carolina and Gilder from Alabama. At about six-foot-three with a muscular build, Gilder bore a striking resemblance to Isaiah Thomas, that is, until you heard his southern accent. We all bonded very quickly, mainly because we not only resided in the same platoon, but we stood next to each other in formation. This occurred because they customarily organized us alphabetically. Therefore, we became known as the three "G's"—Gibson, Gilder, and Giles.

I have many fond memories of IOBC because of those guys. One of the funniest ones involved Gilder, who I'm not even sure wanted infantry, since he didn't seem to like all the field exercises. We had been in the field for almost a week, and it was pretty cold. All we had to eat were MRE's (shrink-wrapped Meals Ready to Eat), and I could tell Gilder was getting quite fed up with the food, not to mention feeling a little homesick.

I, on the other hand, loved MRE's! They weren't exactly "ready to eat" as their name implied. For instance, the dry-packaged pork patty required water added to it in order to eat it properly. Skipping that important step caused it to absorb fluid in your stomach resulting in major cramps, a consequence that those who forgot to add water suffered every time. The "gourmet" came out in me as I experimented with my MRE's, adding crackers, applesauce, and other things besides water. In fact, I discovered that orange Kool-Aid® made it taste like Chinese orange chicken. I believe that every soldier who has spent considerable time in the field gets good at being a "field chef."

One day, they surprised us with a hot meal. The guys were pretty fired up about that, as a hot meal on a cold rainy day functioned as a huge motivator. I volunteered to serve because servers always got a little extra. As the lined formed,

I saw my buddy, Gilder. I knew I had to hook him up with the best portions I could dish out. After scanning the serving pans, I spotted the biggest quarter piece of baked chicken and set it aside for him. Gilder approached me, and I could see the pleading in his eyes, "Please hook me up, Gib."

When I placed that large piece of chicken on his plate, you should have seen his reaction. You would've thought he just won a million dollar lottery; it was priceless! He looked at the chicken, looked at me, looked at the chicken. I would almost swear that a tear fell down his cheek. He raised the plate to his face and kissed it slowly like it was the last kiss he would experience, ever so tender and passionate. A big smile broke across my face. I didn't know whether to laugh at him or cry with him in his expressive gratitude. We all ate well that night. I actually hooked all my boys up, including Gilder, with a few extras in their meals.

While in training, I felt blessed that my leaders selected me as a sponsor for several African soldiers, but primarily Gerard Mackfoy, an extremely intelligent soldier from the Central Africa Republic. As his primary sponsor, I ensured that Mackfoy understood all aspects of infantry training, as well as our American culture. As one might suspect, I ended up learning much more from him than what he learned from me.

Mackfoy hailed from a very wealthy family and spoke five languages (French, English, Spanish, his mother's native language, and his father's native language). His father worked in the banking industry and, if I remember correctly, had six wives. Through those unions, Mackfoy had over fifty brothers and sisters! Naturally, I had heard about cultures that supported men having multiple wives, but never before had I actually known anyone personally living it. That custom made me wonder if the opposite scenario existed anywhere in the world—women with multiple husbands. After contemplating the male ego, which seems quite similar across cultures, I pretty much answered my own question.

Sometimes at night, instead of talking about ambush tactics, Mackfoy would share about his family back in Africa. He had one wife and a fiancée and admitted he could have as many wives as he could afford to take care of. He had prepared his dowry offering to his fiancée's family, which would consist of money, cattle, and other items of value. He would often say to me, "Gibson, I don't know how you Americans do it. How could you only have one wife? You brag of a culture of monogamy and many speak ill of my culture of polygamy. What I notice is that most Americans have affairs and, in many cases, marry several times in their lifetime. So, you engage in a serial polygamy. In the end, you marry three times, and I marry three times; but in the end, I have all of my wives, and you die alone."

His viewpoint seemed so profound to me, not to mention that his observations were accurate! Many Americans engaged in multiple relationships while supposedly committed to one person. Many Americans also died alone after a lifetime of three wives (or maybe *because* of three wives)—crazy! For a while, Mackfoy's conversations made me wish I lived somewhere in Africa. He made life sound so reasonable, wonderful, and rosy. However, with the situations on the ground in many African nations being anything but rosy, my romantic meanderings sobered pretty quickly. I appreciated America all the more, and my understanding and appreciation have grown every time I have traveled to another country, or gotten to know someone from another culture.

As we progressed through the training, I outperformed most of my peers on every graded event. According to the leader's board, I alternated between the number one and number two spots with Lt. Garcia as my greatest competitor. Garcia failed a few major events like land navigation and basic rifle marksmanship, resulting in his having to perform re-takes. Although he scored relatively high on his re-takes, we figured that in the end, the fact that he required re-takes would hurt his chances of being the Honor Graduate.

We had a couple of grueling events like the twelve-mile road march. As a timed event, we were expected to finish in less than three hours, carrying a forty pound ruck sack and a weapon. At the beginning of that important event, we started running in big groups, but the packs got smaller and smaller as our distance increased. Before I knew it, I ended up by myself with one or two guys in front of me and the rest behind. Jogging along at a good pace, I suddenly caught a cramp in my hamstring. I remember yelling out in agony in the coolness of that night air. I then heard a distant voice yell, "You OK?"

I responded, while puffing through breaths, "Yeah, I'm good."

Actually, I wasn't good, but I couldn't stop. We were being timed, so I couldn't afford to stop. I kept up a light trot hoping that the cramp would go away. Eventually, it did dissipate, only to reappear in my other leg and then in both legs at the same time. Finally, I downgraded to a slow walk, yet I endured and would not stop. I kept going that beautiful night. You could see the moon, the stars, and silhouettes of soldiers moving; certainly, it was too beautiful of an atmosphere to be in such pain. A few more guys passed me while I worked though the cramps. I kept chanting, "Pain is for lesser creatures," and "Pain is weakness leaving the body," along with a few prayers of, "God, please don't let me fall out!" Fortunately, the cramps went away, and I finished among the top five guys in the company of approximately 110 soldiers.

That same endurance and perseverance that heightened in me at IOBC carried over into Corporate America. I've gone to work while suffering with Bells Palsy, an illness that causes the facial muscles to weaken or become paralyzed temporarily. Drooling throughout the day and shocking my cheek during breaks became occasional occurrences. I've held conference calls while experiencing back spasms and accidentally yelling out in pain on the phone but continuing with the call anyway.

Sometimes though, I had to remind myself that there is a distinct difference between the military and Corporate America when it comes to perseverance. While the display of pain and agony is accepted in the military as a normal part of one's performance, it's usually a little unsettling and uncomfortable for people to witness in the workplace. In other words, although a person is expected to compete to his or her highest ability in Corporate America, nobody wants to see the painful process; they just want to be part of the glorious achievements. So, whatever ailments and disadvantages life hands us, we'd better quickly learn to "suck it up and deal with it" to stay in the game.

My African-American IOBC captain, Captain Jones, came down very hard on me all the time. Sometimes, I felt his motive was simply my race. I know that some black leaders feel they need to be harder on us because they are preparing us for the difficulties of the real world. But, there are times when that philosophy can go too far, and the hardness becomes unfair practice, at which point, the results turn disadvantageous.

I'm not a whiner who's always playing the "race card" when speaking about unfairness; however, the unfair treatment toward me at IOBC became obvious to others, as well. I outperformed Garcia in almost every graded event. I received top scores on my first tries; whereas, he re-took several of his events in order to achieve high marks. Nevertheless, Garcia graduated number one, and I graduated number two in our platoon. I admit I felt very disappointed but had to just accept the results.

Missing that number one spot meant that I could not choose my first assignment; however, graduating in the top 10% placed me on the Commandant's list, and receiving special recognition for sponsoring the soldiers from Africa was rewarding in its own right. Being a top military graduate was another major achievement and one that put me farther away from the ghetto of Chicago.

Right around that same time, I met a young lady named Celeste from Detroit. She was really cool, quite eclectic, and extremely funny. After dating for a short period, we got engaged. I fell in love with the concept of establishing a family and thought she would be a very loving and nurturing mother to the children I had always hoped to have. I thought the world of Celeste and her family; they were all extremely close, and I wanted to create that same kind of life for myself. I yearned for such a life because my own nuclear family experiences had always been so erratic and disjointed.

My dad adamantly objected to the idea of marriage for me at that young age. He felt I had a lot more living to do before I settled down. In short, I took my dad's advice and ended the relationship with Celeste. I know it really broke her heart as much as it broke mine. My dad "hit the nail on the head" regarding most things, so I complied with his judgment in that matter. As usual, his advice benefited me, so I harbor no regrets about that decision. The cause and effect nature of our choices and their consequences has been made to clear to me in so many ways.

So, back to focusing on what I *could* accomplish—I proudly attended the U.S. Army's Airborne school. Gilder and I went together and had a blast. Physical training (PT) proved fairly easy with the most difficult part being PLF's (Parachute Landing Falls). A few days of those will keep the entire body nice and sore. On second thought, I'm not sure about the "nice" part, but definitely "sore!"

My first jump felt incredibly surreal. I obviously knew we were going to jump out of the plane, but when the guys stood up and started shuffling toward the door, all I heard was the jump master saying, "Go, go, go!" The guys went— one by one—quickly! I'm not quite sure why I became so dumbfounded, but it suddenly dawned on me that those guys were leaving the plane without any way of getting back on, and I would soon be joining them! No do-overs; no "wait a minute;" no "I forgot something." They were simply gone. I got simply nervous.

As I shuffled my way toward the door behind the others, the jumpmaster said, "Go!" I jumped without hesitation. My riser was attached to a static line and opened my shoot immediately. It was the most incredible feeling ever. I traveled downward in complete silence. Birds flew by, the sun shone brightly, and the clouds hovered in puffy formations. I sensed complete peace. Every now and then, I would hear someone yell out something. I could hear them as if they were floating right next to me, even though they floated hundreds of yards away.

As I descended slowly to the ground, I knew in my heart Infantry was what I wanted to do. Even though lots of people who were *not* Infantry went to Airborne school, I knew I would be able to jump all the time because I *was* Infantry. I was also thankful that I chose Infantry because it paralleled my father's experiences. Although his paratrooper jumps in Vietnam were full of danger, he and I shared that love of "falling through the sky." He always said it brought reality to the many dreams of being able to fly that he had experienced since childhood.

At that instant, coming out of an airplane, unchained from earth and allowing our bodies to be totally free and unburdened, we felt truly at one with our spirit. That was yet another element that bound us as father and son.

I graduated from Airborne school with no fanfare. I received "blood wings" from my older Pershing Rifle and Alpha Phi Alpha fraternity brother, Andre Batson. Blood wings happens when the person pinning you punches the Airborne wings with two metal pins in the back into your chest, as opposed to pinning the clips through the back of your shirt. They had outlawed that piercing practice because of injuries, but people found a way to do it anyway. Andre was my mentor when I made Junior Lieutenant, but our roots ran deeper. We both were FAMU alums, Pershing Rifles, and Alphas. Yes, we were deeply connected, so he made sure I got the Blood Wings. Hoorahhhh! I later bestowed the same honor on my younger cousin, Duke!! Hoorahhh!!

After Airborne, I prepared for the U.S. Army's Ranger School. Ranger School is one of the Armed Forces' most elite Special Operations units, consisting of sixty-one-plus days of intense combat leadership training, oriented to small-unit tactics. Airborne School and Ranger school are the only two entities that accept members from other branches, i.e. Marines (Navy Seals), Air Force (Para Rescuers), and so forth. I approached that training course with great excitement and anticipation, in spite of its disheartening failure rates. Statistics show the graduation rate has fluctuated between 50–56% in recent years, slightly up from past years. Still, out of that percentage, only 20% of the graduates made it through all the phases without having to repeat a phase.[12] There are four (technically five) phases. As long as a soldier doesn't fail all the phases completely, they get recycled and can re-do the failed phase.

My first week there was the Assessment Phase. It started out looking like a scene from the movies; it was raining harder than I had ever seen it rain. Even that "cats and dogs" cliché couldn't describe that rain. Although we were supposed to be outside by six o'clock in the morning, anyone arriving at that time was considered late already. The Ranger Instructors (RI's) found a way to fail all "lateniks" in the first week.

I showed up that first day at four o'clock A.M. with Lt. Hogan, another Alpha fraternity brother I met on the base. By the time we got there, believe it or not, some guys were already in formation. There were no instructors, no direction, so you just jumped into formation, dropped your gear, and stood at parade rest (arms folded behind your back). It continued to rain. More guys showed up. Whispering started among the formation, speculating who would be the first to go. I don't know how they knew that, but they were right, at least from some of the faces I could remember.

When those gates opened a couple hours later, promptly at six o'clock, you would've thought the charge on Hamburger Hill ensued. The instructors ran out screaming, yelling, and kicking our stuff. Then the "smoking" commenced—push-ups, flutter kicks, sit-ups, and every other exercise you could imagine. The rain soaked to our bones, while we lay in puddles, yelling cadence. And to think that was only the beginning of two months of near hell!

The PT (physical test) came shortly thereafter. Generally, PT for guys going to Ranger School is nothing difficult. It consisted of a two-mile run and a certain number of sit ups and push ups, based on your age. I usually maxed the test, which meant I got the highest score possible, completing the two-mile run in less than eleven minutes, eighty-five push-ups in two minutes, and ninety-two sit-ups in two minutes. Of course, there was no resting on my knees while doing push-ups, nor any lying on my back while doing sit-ups. Normally, it would be a piece of cake for me, but I was so worn out after getting smoked for almost an hour that my arms were like rubber bands, and my stomach stayed in knots.

At that point, I didn't care if I maxed; I just wanted to pass, and I did. We lost about 20% of the class that day. The rest of the week consisted of other mandatory tests we were required to pass, in order to officially start Ranger School. Land navigation, swim test (which is where we lost most of the brothers— I don't know why most black folks can't swim), and a few other tests. That phase concluded with a forced road march to where the Jungle Phase would start.

Those who made the road march were considered Ranger students. We lost a lot of guys in the road march. Fortunately, I didn't get any cramps, so there I was, ready to start Ranger School. There were four phases left: Jungle, Mountain, Desert, and Swamp. Each lasted close to two weeks, and each had its own inherent challenges and perils.

The Jungle Phase in Dahlonega, Georgia was filled with thick bush and was extremely difficult for maneuvering land navigation. The Mountain Phase, conducted in the Appalachians, was where we lost a lot of people who failed knot tying. Knot tying proved one of the most important skills needed because of the need to carry people and equipment in the mountains. The weirdest thing about the Mountain Phase is that we were given a safety briefing directed primarily toward the black Ranger students. They told us not to get lost because the people up in those mountains aren't so friendly and tend to be not too fond of black people. We were told to always have a buddy and never stray off-course. Of course, that warning made me rather nervous. But, what seemed even more strange was after we finished a mission in the mountains, people literally came out of nowhere, right on our objective, and collected the casings from our M16's, M249's, M60's, and other weaponry.

Rumor had it that those mountain people repacked our ammunition for their own weapons. That didn't sound right for many reasons; nonetheless, that was the word around camp. Why would they need weapons like ours? Maybe it was part of the conspiracy theory that we heard in college that some people were preparing for a time when there would be some internal struggle in the United States between blacks and whites, South against North again, or a rebellion against the government.

I always believed those stories to be a pretty far-fetched notion; however, some years later, the DEA raided warehouses around the country where caches of large weapon supplies were stored. Later, officials determined that those warehouses were owned by white supremacist groups. Unfortunately today, the number of militias and hate groups is on the rise, now that we have a black

President. How sad to think of the depths of hatred people harbor for no other reason than the color of one's skin. As my dad's favorite expression goes when he was responding to things he knew were far beyond his control, "Oh well…"

The Desert Phase of Ranger School was brutal. We were far outside of El Paso, Texas—hot, dry, flat El Paso, Texas. The sand felt like hot coals during the day and ice cubes at night. It became difficult to navigate due to a lack of landmarks close enough to check your azimuth, unless you used a distant city light or a star. And, we won't even talk about all the rattlesnakes that continually crossed our paths.

The Swamp Phase became the worst phase of all for me. Their demonstration of how to wrestle a alligator made me rather nervous. The waters were infested with them. We would see them as we paddled down the river, and when it was time to get out of the zodiac (rubber raft), you could see the whites of everyone's eyes opened as wide as saucers. Nothing proved more frightening than performing a river-crossing at night. I imagined my mother getting a letter saying I died in a training incident—no specifics given to indicate that I had been eaten by a alligator. To my knowledge, it had never happened before. That became the one place in all my military competitions where I had no desire to be first.

Overall, I performed well, passing six out of seven patrols, which for Ranger School remained extremely difficult to do. Because of the tremendously arduous missions and scope of leadership responsibilities, it is almost impossible for people on the outside to imagine how heavily the cards are stacked against a person successfully completing that training. You could get failed for anything at all. That's exactly what most Ranger Instructors were looking for, too—anything, any little thing. Just one small weakness and bam, you were gone.

The one patrol I failed was really a bogus failure. It happened in the desert. I was in command of our defensive position, and my RI (Ranger Instructor) asked me how far out my LP/OP (Listening Post and Observation Post) was. I reported: 125 meters. He walked the distance and discovered they were out about 135 meters. No one else failed a patrol for something like that. But what could

I say? I gave an incorrect measurement, which perhaps in a real situation, could have ended up being highly detrimental. There were at least a hundred other things to be coordinated, inspected, and prepped to make that a success. My mission was tight except for those ten meters.

Interestingly, that same RI tried to get me kicked out for a weapon missing a firing pin, and the weapon wasn't even mine. We had to clean weapons after every mission, and someone took my weapon out of a pile by mistake. Many of us were in the same situation, but were told to just clean our buddy's weapon and find our own later. So, after I took that other person's weapon apart, I took it to the RI and reported that it was missing the firing pin. He chewed me up one side and down the other. He elevated the situation to the OIC (Officer in Command). Once I explained the circumstance, the OIC dismissed it as quickly as I could get my last word out. So, am I wrong to assume it a coincidence that after the weapon incident that same RI failed me for the ten meter discrepancy?

I strove to be the Honor Graduate, knowing a perfect record would put me in good contention. In addition, my peer evaluations were great, which meant the guys really valued my leadership and work ethic. Peer evaluations were a tricky thing. Every cycle, the guy with the lowest peer evaluation generally got recycled. That usually happened for one or two reasons: either they were actual slackers and deserved the low markings, or other guys banded together to support each other and ambush someone else—sort of like they do on that "Survivor" reality show.

Not only was I blessed to have gotten good peer evaluations, but apparently most of the RI's also thought highly of me. In every phase, they would put someone in charge of the platoon, the company, or the battalion. They would do that prior to or after completing a patrol. If your group showed up late for anything, didn't complete assignments thoroughly, or had low motivation, they generally fired you. People got fired every day. They pegged me as one to be selected for battalion commander during the Swamp Phase, our last one.

Getting selected for the last mission in Swamp Phase generally meant those individuals were deemed as the most squared-away soldiers. That translated to possible Honor Grad designation. Many of the guys speculated that being chosen for that honor came down to me and another Ranger buddy in my Platoon, Captain Morgan. He was squared away, but he failed land navigation in the assessment phase and had to re-take it. However, he had perfect patrols. I thought my patrol failure and his land navigation failure would make us even. Some said I would surely get the Honor Grad designation. Others said Morgan would get it.

It turned out that Morgan got assigned to lead the last mission. So, now he needed to pass it. It would have been easy for me to sabotage his mission, but it wasn't in my nature and certainly not part of my character. However, I needed to have a great night. I had to execute my assignment flawlessly. Ranger Morgan had a great plan, and he asked me to help him execute certain parts, which I did. We finally started our last assault on the objective. Since it was the last objective, they spared no expense with the pyrotechnics and ammunition. Guys were getting picked off left and right. The opposition seemed to be everywhere; there were explosions on all sides, smoke, loud gunfire, and mass confusion. It was crazy. But I fought on just like our Ranger Creed says: "Though, I be the lone survivor."

The opposition killed everyone in our battalion except for two people, me and my Ranger buddy, Rudy. As we charged the objective and moved up the hill, everyone had to sit and watch while we maneuvered our way to the top. Now we were taking them out left and right. Rudy laid down suppressive fire on the right side. I moved to the next tree. "Ready—go." Rudy opened up firing while I maneuvered. "I'm set. I'll clear the left. You move. Go!" Although outnumbered, it appeared that we took twenty or thirty of them down. We were finally killed, but we got an ovation from everyone who watched the last push. I felt total elation having accomplished that.

Even though I was technically dead, I received the honor that would have been given to a fallen soldier who fought to the bitter end. Not only that, I thought my performance would surely put me in good standing for Honor Grad. Ranger Morgan got a "go" for the patrol, so he finished 7-0, and I finished 6-1. When we got back to Dahlonaga, where it all started and where it would finally culminate with our graduation ceremony, I was still Battalion commander in charge of all of our operations and movement until Ranger School was over, or I got fired.

Obviously, I had never been in that position before, but the word was that the Battalion commander at the end was usually the Honor Grad. A couple days later, they brought us together to make the announcement. As the commander talked about how hard everyone worked, he also talked about how prestigious the Honor Grad award was. I sat on pins and needles! With all of the training I completed in ROTC and being one of the only guys to select Infantry, that distinction would certainly set my career on the right path.

Finally, the announcement for Honor Grad came: "Ranger Morgan!" My heart dropped to my stomach. Once again, I suffered such disappointment. I couldn't show it in front of the guys because that wouldn't be leadership-like behavior. After the initial announcements were made and the direction given for graduation practice, they dismissed the formation. We hung around talking, and Ranger Morgan came up to me.

Before he could say anything, I congratulated him, "Well done, brother."

His first words to me were, "You should have gotten Honor Grad, Ranger Gibson."

It was comforting and noble of him to say that. He certainly didn't tell the RI's, but I didn't expect him to. Both of us displayed honorable gestures toward each other because we highly respected one another.

Unfortunately for me, that created another example from the Army that I was not good enough to be first, even though my performance was the best of the group. As I look back on it, I realize that I could have had better performances to even further distinguish myself. I'm sure I could have worked just a little harder. But, I started learning an important lesson in life—sometimes the most talented are not always first. Nonetheless, at that point in time, it really impacted my view of the Army.

My body hurt pretty badly due to the old gunshot wound in my knee and a parachute malfunction that had torn my shoulder out, so I needed a lot of physical therapy. It finally got to the point where I took 2400 milligrams of Motrin everyday—well beyond the prescribed limits—just to cope with all the pain. Eventually, I realized that I might not be able to handle the duty of being in the Infantry, so the Army gave me some options: I could either be discharged with a medical disability or go to another branch like Finance or Intelligence. I figured if I couldn't do what I loved, I would rather get out. I knew I could make more money in the civilian sector, anyway. So, I honorably discharged with medical disability, and my military career was over.

Selling Point

I reached the sunset on my time in the Army. I felt a little nervous because the military can be a security blanket. Some people thought it crazy to leave, but I didn't feel that way at all. If I could not do what I loved—jumping out of planes, tracking through the woods, hunting people down, blowing stuff up— then I would find something else to love. I wanted my life to have purpose and meaning.

It was the latter part of 1994 and I, being thankful for the preparation and business skills I learned at FAMU, set out on a new chapter in my life. My resume writing skills were pretty decent, and several recruiters worked on my behalf. At that time, it seemed Corporate America was starving for Junior Military Officers (JMO). I secured several interviews with companies in logistics, operations, and sales.

Pilon Inc., the world's largest research-based pharmaceutical company, appealed to me most. I became familiar with the company through SBI at FAMU. Many of my friends, who held careers in marketing, finance, or human resources, had interned with them during college. I remembered how they spoke positively of the company and their internships. So, when the recruiter asked me if wanted to interview with them, I didn't have to think twice.

The position available involved sales, and I had cultivated plenty of experience selling everything from clothes, tires, rims, and other items at the flea market in Chicago, doing telemarketing while in high school, and working with the sales team at Apple. I didn't realize how much pharmaceutical sales differed from the other things I had worked on previously. In fact, I had never heard of the occupation before, and I didn't have the ability to research the company in that short period of time, given the lack of widespread Internet access at the time. I just didn't have much time to prepare for the interview. I still lived in Fort Benning, Georgia and drove a couple hours north to the interview location in Atlanta.

I met with my first Pilon interviewer, Steve Smith, an ex-military and human resource professional, who made me feel very comfortable. I believed I did well on the interview, even down to the task of selling the clock on the desk, at Steve's request. I had participated in many interviews before that one and had answered all kinds of interesting questions; however, I had never run into that one before. Nevertheless, I sold the clock, based on the way I sold 15-inch rims at the flea market. Steve appeared impressed and forwarded me on to the next interview.

An elderly man awaited me with a stoic countenance that could fool even World Series Poker champion, Chris Moneymaker. Also a military veteran, his heroic service in Vietnam had earned him a silver star. After about two hours of a very tough meeting, I could not ascertain if I impressed him enough, that is, until he concluded the interview by saying he'd like to send me onto the next round. I guess I must have done okay.

Bob Rainer, the District Manager for Tampa, Florida, headed the next interview. I could tell I impressed him after the first few minutes, even though the interview lasted about two hours. Afterwards, he shook my hand, smiled, and said he would be in touch with me after a few days. I traveled back to Fort Benning and waited for the call.

I received a call, not with an offer, but for a field ride with a pharmaceutical representative in the Atlanta area. I became slightly disappointed by the long and tedious process, but quickly realized part of the interviewing process involved making sure applicants knew and understood the job requirements. The process also allowed the company another opportunity to assess each potential employee.

I decided I would do whatever was necessary to get that job. I rode in the field with Jonathon Koushouty, also an ex-military person. I couldn't believe all the guys with military service who worked for Pilon. I felt right at home. Jonathon really impressed me with the job, and being with him that day sealed my commitment to working for Pilon. I just knew I could do a great job selling pharmaceuticals.

After the field ride, I drove back to Fort Benning to again wait for Bob's call. He called about two days later and said he wanted to bring me on the team. He offered me $39,000 a year as a starting salary, along with a $7,000 signing bonus, a company car, moving package, and terrific benefits. It almost tripled my salary as an officer in the Army! I felt ecstatic and very relieved. Knowing a job waited for me before my honorable discharge helped to settle my nerves. The starting salary also represented more money than anyone in my family had ever made.

I started at Pilon a few weeks after my discharge from the Army in January, 1995. My nature required me to "be all that I could be," with or without a slogan to inspire me. Instead of doing home study, Pilon asked me to go to Atlanta, stay in a hotel and study there. I received several boxes full of modules, each with over one hundred pages. The material needed to be read within two weeks. Every other day, I traveled to the regional office and took a quiz. I received a hundred percent on almost every quiz.

At one point, they must have thought I cheated because I did so well; therefore, my trainer, John Hamrick, made up a new quiz one day. I received one hundred percent on that one, as well. I took studying seriously. I approached it just like I did while in school. I shut most people out for a few weeks and scheduled time to read both day and night. I worked out, ate well, and meditated and prayed every day. It was perfect.

Then, the live training started in the office. That training involved more quizzes and selling skills, as well. I learned how to give icebreakers, features, benefits, and probes; I mastered how to handle objections and how to close the deal. I can only describe the information and training process as incredible. The clinical education I received empowered me. It felt like I had trained to be a doctor in just a few months, at least in a few specialty disease areas.

Developing my sales skills taught me how to communicate with people, especially doctors. Those skills were transferable to anyone I needed to communicate with in any way. I studied each detail the company gave, every word on every page. I wrote out exactly what I wanted to say. When I delivered a presentation, it included impact, empathy, and clinical information. John Hamrick did a heck of a job preparing me. He made me one bad dude with a great flair for sales!

Soon, the time came to go to New York and learn from the trainers at headquarters. That meant more quizzes, more details, and videotaped presentations. Once again, I focused on being the best. I wanted to beat everyone in class. The company gave two awards at the completion of all of the training: "Best Communicator" and "Most Technical," which used the highest accumulated test scores. I won both awards in my class of over forty trainees. I reflected on my experience in the military where I barely missed the top spots I competed for and realized that at Pilon I felt fully rewarded for my efforts and performance. My goal was to be the best. I knew I would love working for this company.

The Power of Visualization

Equally as important as loving my work was how I loved my friends—namely, Mario Shirley, or "Rio" as we all called him. As one of my best friends at FAMU and record store partner, Rio and I became inseparable. Actually, his entire family, who lived in St. Petersburg (St. Pete, as the locals called it) treated me like one of their own. He had three brothers: Kirk (Lacey), Frankie, and Scootie (Alvin), as well as one sister, Tracy. His parents and siblings had all invested in our record store—financially or otherwise.

Rio's parents remained as interested in my achievements beyond school as when I attended school and ran the record store. They expressed how proud they were of me that I got a good job. I actually heard that kind of "good job" comment often, while launching from the military into the real world. Black people, especially our elders, really do like to note the successes of young black men and women. Perfect strangers within our communities would tell us how proud they were of us, "G'on boy, you got you a good job! Company car, expense account, making good money... I am so proud of you!" I love that about our people, and I loved hearing it. It truly cheered me on to do even better.

Rio had lots of extended family in St. Pete, as well. The most notable were his cousins, the Atwaters, a huge family of at least ten children; with each of them having several children, their crew continually grew. Soon after meeting them, the Atwaters took me under their wings, introducing me around town as their 'Cuz.' One of the sons, Mike Atwater, had been an instrumental figure in the opening of our record store in Tallahassee.

I suppose I possessed an adoptive demeanor with a lot of families who enjoyed having me around. I enjoyed the Atwaters and appreciated their gesture, since I had longed for that kind of stability all my life. With Rio's family as such an "ideal family away from home," imagine my elation to find out my newly assigned territory with Pilon, Inc. would be St. Pete!

I started house-hunting. I knew visualization worked, so I started envisioning myself sitting in the back of my new house, looking at the waves, and watching the sunrise. I held that image and others like it, bringing them to life in my head. I looked at a few houses, but none really appealed to me. Finally, I met with two middle-aged ladies at a house on 22nd Avenue, in a community called Tropical Shores. It ranked way up there as one of the coolest houses I had ever seen, not to mention that it was positioned right on the Gulf of Mexico! You could walk out into the back yard about twenty feet, and dive into the Gulf, right off your own sea wall. The entire back portion of the house consisted of windows, so you could see that water from any room. You could also see the downtown areas of both Tampa and St. Pete.

The landscaping all around had as much appeal as the water out back. A grapefruit tree, an orange tree, and a banana tree graced the back yard. Sage, planted against the side of the ranch style house, emitted the sweetest aroma in every breeze. As though all those perks weren't enough, just perpendicular to the property sat a beach. I knew right away, this house was it—just what I had visualized!

The two ladies who showed me the house were long-time friends. One of them, Barbara, owned it with her husband, who was out of town on business. Barbara said they had lots of people view it, but they wanted to make the best decision regarding who to rent it to. At that moment, I found myself applying all the charm, selling skills, and life experiences I had in me; I poured them out. We sat, and I chatted with them about my life (not *all* the details); I told them about where I had lived, all the places I worked, and my military career. I hoped to show them my level of maturity, while also connecting with them personally.

As it turned out, Barbara's husband worked in sales for Wang Laboratories, a big competitor of Apple, Inc. where I had worked. So, her easy-going personality and knowledge of her husband's job got our conversation going in that direction. We talked about the computer industry, from its good moments to its many challenges.

At that time Apple, Inc. had almost fallen off the map, with the wave of other companies making computers readily available through large retailers. Apple, Inc. stood firm with its concept of forcing people to come to its own stores, not other retailers—a strategy that almost put the company out of business. Their superior technology allowed them to hold on to their market share in the education sector. Plus, they eventually altered their game plan and moved their stores to prime shopping malls and districts across the country. Then along came the iPod, which really put the company back on the map. Fortunately for Apple, Inc., they emerged quite well after their difficult period.

Those women also liked my army officer status. Perhaps they saw *An Officer and a Gentleman*, a highly acclaimed film in the 1980s, or maybe women really do relate favorably to men in uniform. I merely used the military information to indicate my accountability and trustworthiness.

But, once I told them I worked in the pharmaceutical industry, the conversation really charged up. They both took Paxil and often felt tired and groggy. I shared with them my company's product for depression, Zolo, which had distinct advantages over Paxil (i.e. less sedating and fewer interactions with over-the-counter medicines such as cold remedies). I suggested that they ask their doctors to change their prescriptions to Zolo.

We spent hours talking until they had another appointment. However, before I left, I made sure to close—a soft close, as I had learned in sales training. I told Barbara they could count on me to take good care of the house and that I would really enjoy living there just as much as they had. I asked her to please consider me and that I looked forward to hearing back from her soon.

Lastly, I wished them well with their health issues, in case we didn't have a chance to talk again.

That afternoon gave me a personal opportunity to apply all the communication and selling skills I had learned in my Pilon, Inc. training. Two hours later, Barbara called me and said I could rent the house. I immediately catapulted to Cloud Nine! I worked for a great company with great pay and, on top of that, I had just secured an awesome house on the Gulf of Mexico. No doubt, I experienced heaven on earth that day!

Work Hard, Play Hard

Rio's birthday coincided with my move to St. Pete, so I threw him a party that very first weekend in my new residence. As a matter of fact, he and I partied every weekend we were both in town, from April through September. That summer, Norris Sumrall and Scott Parker moved down to St. Pete, as well, so the Ups N Downs crew reunited. We enjoyed some of the best times of our lives during that period. As an inseparable force, we "turned St. Pete out" on many weekends.

Friends would come down just to hang out with us for the weekend and would not want to go back. We had "eat what you catch" parties at my house. If you didn't catch any fish, crab, or conch, you wouldn't eat unless you grabbed something from Popeye's chicken restaurant. We would go to the Attic Night Club and have a 'Squirrel fest'. The Squirrel was a dance that has managed to last in Florida, like the Electric Slide has prevailed all over the country. After the Attic, we would go to the all-night reggae spot on Central Avenue. After that, we'd take a dip in the Gulf of Mexico at three o'clock in the morning at St. Pete's beach. We partied like there was no tomorrow—that is, until one time when there almost *wasn't* a tomorrow for me, Rio, and Scott.

Scott lived on the Tampa side and taught at a local high school. Incredibly smart, Scott graduated from FAMU with a Masters in Pharmacology. Although his teaching pay paled in comparison to what he could've earned in the pharmaceutical field, he loved teaching, and his students loved him. Sometimes he would invite me to talk to his students. I enjoyed doing that because those kids needed to see a positive black male who had escaped a challenging environment similar to theirs. They needed to be shown living proof of it instead of just reading about it.

Anyway, one night Rio, Scott, and I partied at Club Atlanta in Tampa. Being very irresponsible that night, we drank ourselves to the point of not being able to make it home to St. Pete. Instead, we got in the car and swerved our way to Scott's—a much closer destination. What transpired next has notoriously been dubbed our "Dumb, Dumber, and Dumbest" episode.

Being a fairly cool night for Tampa, Scott lit the kerosene heater, and we all went to sleep. I fell asleep on the couch. At one point, I woke up in middle of the night and noticed how warm and good it felt. I looked at the heater, and saw a little fire under the pot. I thought, "Hmm, how nice, that kerosene heater is really kicking. I might need to buy one of those." I drifted back to sleep.

Scott slept in his bedroom. At one point in the middle of the night, he also woke up. He went to the restroom and noticed smoke. However, it never registered in his head the oddity of that smoke, so he just cracked the window in his bedroom and went back to sleep.

Rio woke up the next morning and came and got me off the couch. I looked at him and asked, "What the hell is on your face?" With his black covered face and stone-white teeth, he looked like Buckwheat from the old comedy series, *The Little Rascals*.

He asked, "What the hell you laughin' at?"

I said, "Your face, Buckwheat! Why is it so black?"

As I sat up on the couch, Rio reported, "Damn, look at the couch!" My body had created a tan silhouette against the newly blackened couch. He said, "Your face is black, too."

We rushed to the bathroom to look at ourselves, but couldn't see the mirror. Soot covered it entirely. We yelled for Scott, who came out of his room and started laughing, "What the hell is wrong with ya'll?"

All three of us quickly headed toward the front door, realizing that perhaps we needed to release whatever had darkly clouded everything inside. Not until then did we notice that everything had turned black—the walls, the floor, the furniture—absolutely everything!

As soon as Scott opened the door, a gust of wind rushed out of the house, except this gust was pitch black smoke. We walked out the door and looked back at the house. From the looks of the smoke bellowing out, you would have thought the house was actually on fire. All of sudden my chest felt heavy, and I coughed up black phlegm. Our entire bodies from head to toe were black.

Scott called the fire department. They got there rather quickly, rushing into the house to check the source. One fireman asked about the kerosene heater and how it burned up. That's when the "Dumb, Dumber, and Dumbest" story came out. Mario was dumb because he never woke up; Scott was dumber because he saw the smoke and just cracked his window, and the dumbest was me because I saw the actual fire and thought kerosene heaters worked that way, and I went back to sleep.

We laughed so hard, talking about each other and spitting up a ton of soot. The firefighters got a big kick out of us cracking on each other, but then they turned serious when telling us how close we came to dying. Had we stayed in the house a little longer, we all could have died of smoke inhalation. They suggested we go to the hospital to get our lungs checked out, in case of unforeseen damage.

For that next minute or so, you could see the fear on all of our faces as we contemplated the seriousness of the matter. Suddenly, I pointed to Rio and quipped, in pure Buckwheat style, "O-Tay!"

We started cracking up, laughing uproariously again. Looking back on that, all I can say is, "Thank God." As they say, "He takes care of babies and fools." Apparently, we were fools worth saving that night.

Just like Ant

As a Pharmaceutical Representative (rep) for Pilon, Inc., I worked extremely hard. I made more calls than the average rep, which at that time totaled eight calls per day. I would make at least ten calls and sometimes as many as fourteen or fifteen. I produced that type of volume with ease because I loved my work. Pushing myself to work harder than the other reps certainly paid off, judging by my excellent reviews.

Pilon, Inc. required their managers to do "field rides" with the reps. When doing so, they would perform a written evaluation. My manager Bob would write things like, "Jemal is a first-round draft pick," or "Jemal's selling skills are awesome, and his technical knowledge is excellent." He once told me I performed better than any sales rep he had ever seen, given my tenure. I believe my work ethic represented a combination of what I learned throughout Pilon Inc.'s training and what I gleaned from the streets.

Ironically, selling drugs on the street and selling drugs legally have many similarities. A drug dealer works a certain area and so does a pharmaceutical or drug rep. A drug dealer gives samples and so does a drug rep. A drug dealer compares his product to the competition and claims its superiority; the drug rep does the same. The longer a drug dealer stays out to sell on a given day, the more drugs he sells, and the more money he makes. The more visits a drug rep makes each day to doctor's offices, the more drugs he sells, and the more money he makes.

The jobs were eerily similar in operation, but totally paradoxical in principle. Drug dealers destroy lives with their products; a drug rep helps people heal and live healthier, happier lives. I truly felt good and so connected to life and its goodness. Yes, I sold drugs, but within a system that had a positive impact on the people to whom those drugs were administered.

There were days when I would be calling on doctors and leaving samples, and I would imagine my brother quite possibly selling drugs, doing the same thing as me, at that very moment. Both of us were basically in the same profession in different parts of the country. I had become just like Ant, with the exception that one of us destroyed lives, while the other one helped to save them.

All That Glitters. . .

By my mid-twenties, I must admit, I had had more than several love interests. Not surprisingly, though, my youthfulness and immaturity negated any ability on my part to appreciate the true value of those relationships, especially the one I had with Serena. I believe I really made a mistake by not exploring a deeper relationship with her. At the time, our relationship appeared "too good to be true," so I senselessly ended it, afraid she would leave me one day anyway. That time—and rarely ever since then—I allowed fear to lead my decision-making.

My father always told me one day I would meet a woman who would hurt me as much as I hurt some of them. While I never intentionally "hurt" women, I understood his point, based on the familiar axioms, "You reap what you sow" and "What goes around, comes around." I guess the way I ended things with Serena, no warning or valid explanation, justified the necessity to take heed of Dad's advice.

By St. Pete's standards, I easily became one of their most eligible bachelors. As a newcomer to the city, news of my status traveled pretty quickly: single, rather good looking, nice house, and a very decent paying job. On that note, the number of women trying to "holla' at me" got quite challenging. I turned down many proposals from women for dates and for sex. One dejected woman even spread a rumor that I was gay. The lengths people will go to and the slander they will commit just to protect their own ego or pride really amazes me.

Not too long after that, someone broke into my house and stole everything.

I mean everything—sheets off the bed, dirty clothes, opened liquor—everything! The fellas swore the rumor-monger girl did it, but the police never found the perpetrator. That moment proved very difficult for me, mainly because I had ascended to a certain level in my lifestyle. In my mind, that level represented a point beyond where my personal belongings would be stolen. The burglary reminded me of Village Green in Peoria and took me back to the basement apartment on Menard Street in Chicago.

Why would someone do that? I tried to think of any similarities between those past and current home violations. I remembered in Village Green my mother got mad at me when I informed Jerry of our travel plans. She told me to never tell people we were going out of town. Sure enough, the weekend we visited Chicago, someone broke in, stole all our valuables, and totally trashed the house. After a few minutes of reflecting, while standing in my empty Florida home, it dawned on me. I had left a message on my answering machine that said I would be out of town for six days, and sure enough, the burglary happened.

At that point, I made a firm commitment to myself to never alert anyone—directly or indirectly—of when I would be out of town. Later, my family and friends would complain that they never knew where I was. I realized that at times I might be a little obsessive in not informing those I loved, but I preferred to deal with their complaints rather than risk someone ever taking my worldly possessions again.

Nevertheless, there I stood contemplating the arduous task of starting all over with buying household goods. The co-worker, Stephanie McNeal Brown, who happened to be married to my college friend, Harry Brown, came to my rescue. She brought me a pillow, some sheets, and a few other items to get me by. The following day, I went to their house for dinner, since I didn't have any pots and pans. While there, I happened upon a picture of a beautiful, young, light-skinned woman with hazel eyes. I inquired about her.

"Oh, that's Yvonne. She's a doctor finishing her residency at the University of Tennessee in Memphis." Stephanie continued, "You would like her. She's cute, smart, comes from a nice family..."

"Hey, hook it up for me!" I responded, having heard enough wonderful attributes.

Yvonne and I first conversed on the phone during my drive to Pilon's Zirex product launch in Orlando, in February, 1996. After talking for a couple of hours on that one call, I could tell I would enjoy getting to know her. Our interconnected professions made me think a relationship could be good for both of us.

I arrived at the launch unprepared for the magnitude of the whole production. During the day, intense learning sessions taught us about the clinical and pharmacological aspects of Zirex. We also covered the competition and practicing our detail. In the evening, the partying began! Food and liquor galore was flowing with a live band and dancing throughout the night. The event simply blew me away!

One thing about the pharmaceutical industry was that there appeared to be no shortage of beautiful people. The launch resembled an Ebony Fashion Fair runway or a photo shoot for Elle magazine. Not to leave the men out, the women also reported an abundance of handsome men. Now, if you imagine lots of hot women, lots of hot guys, and lots of liquor, you might deduce that lots of wild things happened. Yes, my first product launch introduced me to the real concept of "work hard and play hard," and with each product launch or national meeting from that point on, I required no refresher course.

Yvonne and I carried on a long distance relationship over the next 6 months. It progressed to the point where we began talking about marriage. Normally, since we both had budding careers, the decision of where to live—St. Pete or Memphis—would have presented an issue. However, as timing would have it, trouble brewed between my manager at Pilon, Inc. and me, so I started looking for employment elsewhere. A good friend and FAMU grad, Craig Glover, who worked for Clarke-Smith Pharmaceutical, told me they were hiring and that he could help me get to Memphis. Shortly thereafter, I started with Clarke-Smith in Memphis.

Yvonne and I got married, and I thought she was everything I ever wanted in a woman; she was smart, extremely beautiful, and caring. We were even featured in a newlywed issue of JET magazine the small, digest-sized weekly that is mainly marketed to African-American readers. It covers topics like fashion and beauty tips, entertainment news, dating advice, political coverage, health tips and diet guides.[13] That article was all fine and good for the outside appearance of our relationship. But one thing I didn't count on…Yvonne had an anger management issue on the inside. Did I give her some reasons to be angry? Like any husband, I'm sure I did, but nothing that justified the kind of physical and emotional abuse she unleashed on a regular basis. I left the marriage after just a few months.

Our masculine culture conditions men to think that as the *physically* stronger partner, we should be able to take abuse from a woman in stride or "just deal with it." But, since when is it acceptable to be repeatedly hit with fists and flying objects? Why should it be okay for someone to tell you out of spite, "Now, I know why your parents abandoned you"? I saw nothing right with that type of behavior. I had come too far to marry someone who acted like they grew up in the projects and didn't know any better. I realized that it would have taken just one push on my part or a bump on Yvonne's head, and I would be in jail. She wasn't worth throwing my life away because of her agitated behaviors.

We tried counseling, but even in counseling she tried to justify her violence because of something I did and never anything that related to her. I may have spent extra money or helped my cousin go to college or didn't get to some of the chores, like putting up blinds in the living room at the very moment she asked. Simple things would escalate to physical or emotional abuse administered by her, and she would never take responsibility for any of it.

Well, I realized Yvonne needed another type of man. I guess she thought that any man would be crazy to leave her since she was a physician, a beauty queen, and had millionaire parents. After we finally settled the divorce, I allowed her to take the land we purchased together, which had appreciated quite nicely, as a gesture to apologize for what I may have put her through. Besides, her parents had spent a tremendous amount of money on the wedding, so perhaps in giving her the land I indirectly repaid them for their involvement with me. Since the divorce, Yvonne and I have never spoken again, but I have always hoped for the best for her.

Two Wrongs Don't Make A Right

Let me back up to St. Pete for a moment to elaborate on how things went sour with Pilon, Inc. As I mentioned before, I worked harder than ever there, and my performance reviews reflected that. Our quotas, however, were getting more difficult to maintain due to the medical industry's managed care. In 1996, the St. Pete market displayed a larger percentage of "managed lives" with Humana and Cigna being the major players. Pilon did not believe in contracting with those companies to get our drugs on a formulary list—meaning the drugs would be on a plan-approved list. Instead, they thought the doctors who had Humana and Cigna would write our products anyway, and if they didn't, Pilon thought it could make up the business elsewhere.

Needless to say, the strategy didn't work, and my numbers were low. I stayed above quota for Zolo (used to treat depression) and Procar XL (used to treat high blood pressure) because they were available on Cigna. I fell below quota for Norva (used to treat high blood pressure) and Gluco XL (used to treat diabetes) because neither of those drugs were formulary. Other areas in Florida seemed less affected by managed care, so they continued doing fairly well. More and more areas started feeling the pressure; however, none were as bad as my territory. I continued making as many calls as I could, but since the physicians' hands were tied, I wouldn't leave as many samples. Even the samples I did leave would still be there when I returned weeks later for a follow-up visit.

One day in April, my manager, Bob, rode with me for his typical field ride.

We experienced what I considered a good day, as usual. He said great things about me, and my coaching form reflected such. On that particular visit, he told me the old calendar system I used should be updated to a newer one, such as a Franklin planner. He approved for me to expense it, so I bought a nice planner, transferred my upcoming appointments, and threw away my old planner. Two weeks later he called asking me to meet with him. I said, "Sure."

We met at the Marriott Tampa Airport Hotel. After a few pleasantries, Bob plowed right into his real reason for being there. "I have a concern about your work activity and performance. Do you have anything you want to say?"

I'm thinking to myself, "What in the hell is this guy talking about? He asked me to meet, doesn't tell me the purpose of the meeting, and then drops a bombshell question like this?" I didn't know what he was referring to, let alone did I have an apt response. So I said, "The reason my territory is not performing well is due to managed care and my key brands not being on formulary."

"Is that all you have to say?" he questioned.

"Yes," I curtly replied.

He then asked me about my work activity. "Tell me about a normal work day."

"A normal work day? Why is he asking this?" Questions raced in my head. So once again, I went along with it and ran down a typical day for him. Finally, the meat of the matter revealed itself. He started with what sounded like accusations spewed by a prosecuting attorney toward a suspect on the stand.

"Well, I have here twenty-one days of no work activity for you, Jemal, and that concerns me. Can you tell me where you were on the following days?" He then rattled off several random dates, and of course, I could not recall them off the top of my head. Furthermore, because he had advised me to get a new calendar system, I no longer carried my old calendar showing old appointments, nor did I transfer old dates to a new calendar.

I finally told him, "I don't recall any specifics about any of those dates at the moment. And, since I don't have my old calendar, I have no reference to fall back on.

But I can assure you that I do not have twenty-one days of no work activity. I guarantee I work harder than most reps doing the job."

I knew this to be true because most reps worked only from 10 in the morning until 2 in the afternoon. I would have already made a few calls in the morning by the time they even got to their storage units to pick up their product samples. While some reps left the field early to pick up their kids from school, I didn't have kids, so I kept working. While some reps left early to go play golf, I didn't play, and instead, kept working. I didn't want to squeal on anyone, but I knew I worked harder than most of them. It didn't matter how many calls I made; I was not going to get over the market dynamics of managed care and our refusal to do business with them.

"Nevertheless," Bob said, "let's put this behind us and move forward. I just want to make sure that you are giving it all you've got."

I reassured him that he was getting my very best. I left that meeting feeling very disappointed and uncomfortable. What was his motive? Was he really concerned about performance? Was he using me as a scapegoat since the district was not performing well? Why were there so many days of no activity?

When I got home, I looked for my old calendar but it was long gone; I had thrown it away after transferring my appointments going forward. As I sat back in my chair, I noticed my wall calendar. Yes! There, marked on that calendar, were twenty of the twenty-one so-called "no activity days," full of appointments and activities.

Five days were for a convention in Orlando; three days were for a convention in Clearwater; two days time were given to recover from the burglary at my home; three days sick during which my manager brought me Imodium, soup, and juices (so he could confirm my illness); four were vacation days, and the final three days, I was working with other peers in the territory. Just one day I couldn't account for—I felt relieved! I pulled all the information together to share with him the next time we rode together. We never got to ride together again.

A week later, Bob called and said he wanted to meet about the issue.

He stated that upon further review, my explanation was unacceptable and that I had to go on a performance plan. All of this, of course, before he allowed me to verify my twenty "found" days. I decided to call Bob's boss, Todd, to discuss Bob's unfair treatment. I shared with Todd my dissatisfaction in how Bob was managing me in this situation and asked him to attend the upcoming meeting with Bob and me.

A few days later, they both came to town, and we met at the same Marriott Tampa Airport Hotel. It relieved me to know I had someone who would be neutral and objective in the whole situation. I had never had the opportunity to share with Bob about the unexcused days, but I brought all the information with me for the meeting. I also prepared a detailed analysis to show the impact and penetration of managed care into my territory and how to improve performance considering the circumstances. Lastly, I brought along all of the positively noted coaching forms and written communication I had received from Bob.

After the salutations, we got right down to business. Bob pulled out a Performance Improvement Plan and gave a copy to Todd and me. It was a pretty aggressive Performance Improvement Plan, with the next step being termination. At that point, I discerned some bullsh*t going down. It incensed me even more that Todd, who I had called to provide an objective opinion, seemed more in cahoots with Bob. His body language gave me the feeling that he was perfectly comfortable with the document, and he exhibited a sense of support for Bob.

I read the document; it listed the days absent, my performance, and lack of impact with customers as observed in field rides. So, I buckled up and prepared to share my point of view. I showed the information regarding the calendar and how I accounted for twenty of the twenty-one days. I also stated how I didn't appreciate the process of informing me about the issue without the opportunity to even prepare any rebuttal material. I made a commitment at that time, should I ever become a manager, that I would never surprise my people with performance management discussions.

Next, I presented them the analysis of the territory, documenting the steady decline in business over the past two years. I reminded Bob of our interview, during which he told me that the area I interviewed for ranked as a top-producing territory. That turned out to be a lie. Furthermore, the guy who left prior to me did so because of the territory dynamics. So, I got snowed.

Lastly, as it related to my impact in the field, I told them both how it was quite surprising to hold such a meeting with me when my coaching forms as recent as four weeks prior told a different story. I passed them a copy and said, "Every form you look at, one after another, says Jemal's communication skills are outstanding. Jemal uses his detail piece like no other. Jemal has terrific clinical knowledge. Jemal is the best rep I have ever worked with at his tenure. Every form for the past year has nothing but glowing comments about my impact."

After they both held all the supporting documents, I stared back and forth at each of them and asked, "At what point was impact starting to be an issue? Based on the information I've shared, it is no way indicative of a performance plan. Quite frankly, it's more a question of the real purpose and integrity of these claims of yours."

Todd sat with lips pursed tight and his jawbone clenched. I could tell he suppressed a look of embarrassment and disappointment in Bob. My information and evidence was overwhelming and irrefutable. Todd stood up from his chair and said, "Can you give us a minute?"

He motioned for Bob to step outside with him. They were gone for about twenty minutes. I wondered if Todd would continue to stick with Bob throughout this fiasco.

It amazes me how people do stick together even when they are wrong—and in Bob's case, dead wrong. I tried to decide if corporate politics dominated that situation or good old racism. In my mind, it didn't matter; neither was acceptable to me. Two wrongs don't make it right. Period! I began thinking back to a time in grade school dealing with racism with Coach Frank, and having to put up with the racial tendencies of my teammate, Jeff Rail. Unfortunately, those weren't the only times I had experienced this insidious reality.

Years prior, while attending FAMU, I worked at Ryan's Family Steakhouse in Tallahassee. One day, a fight broke out between a white guy and a couple of black guys. The white guy's girlfriend had told him that the black guys, who were talking amongst themselves, used foul language. The white guy went up to the only two black guys he saw and said, "You should have better manners than to talk like that around a lady."

Based on my recollection, the white guy and his girlfriend appeared to be around the same age as the black guys. Both fit the typical stereotype that one would claim about the other. The tall white guy sported blonde hair cut in a mullet style and wore his sleeves cut to the shoulder of a plaid shirt and cowboy boots. The black guys had on loud, light-colored T-shirts of light blue, orange, and green that matched the candy-colored cars they parked in the lot. Gold teeth topped their ensemble.

So, after the white guy made his comment, the black guys responded with, "F**k you."

Then white guy called out, " F**k you, niggers."

Next thing you know, the white guy's lip was split open and bleeding. The punch came so fast, I didn't even see it! I stood on the other side of the buffet and saw the white guy pull out a Rambo-like knife about twelve inches long, shiny, and very sharp looking. Unfortunately, what he didn't know was that the two black guys were there with six or seven other guys at a different part of the buffet. A yell came, "Hootie Hooo!" Some sort of trouble call I assumed. Before you knew it, they started beating up the white guy; I mean, they were whuppin' his ass. They punched, kicked, and stomped him down. Then some other white patrons jumped to the white guy's defense; it was a rather futile attempt because the black guys started beating them, too.

I quickly ran back behind the register and watched these black guys kick the asses of everyone in the restaurant who dared to jump in. They threw some serious haymakers in addition to ketchup, mustard, A-1 steak-sauce bottles, plates, glasses, chairs, tables; they wrecked the place! They finally worked their way to the exit, ran to their cars, and sped off, just as the police pulled up.

I came out from behind the register, and the restaurant looked like a tornado had gone through it. People were bleeding, crying, and yelling racial epithets. It wasn't my fight, and the way they whupped ass, it didn't need to be, but I started getting angry from all the racial slurs I had heard.

Finally, the straw that broke the camel's back came as an injured father spoke. He appeared to be with his injured son; their wives held both of them. "Damn niggers," he spewed in the direction of the parking lot. "Let them out of their caves, and this is how they act."

At that point, I lost it, and got in their face. "What, what did you say? What did you say?"

The police quickly ran over and started to pull me away. The only thing I could think of to say was, "We don't come from caves! Go read your history books, assholes."

"Sir, if you don't quiet down, we're going to take you to jail," the policeman said to me.

That whole thing was absolutely crazy. Why would *I* go to jail for responding to a racist comment? They walked me back to where my manager stood and asked me if I knew what happened. I told them the whole story—everything.

One police officer said, "Well, we haven't seen a knife."

They asked my manager if he saw a knife, and my manger went and got a steak knife and handed it to the police. I told the police that knife came from the restaurant and was not the knife the white guy had wielded. I assured the police he had a long Rambo-like knife, at least 12 inches long. Thank goodness they believed me and searched the place. In doing so, they found the exact knife I described—in my manager's office.

It turned out that my manager had taken the knife from the white guy and had hidden it. The police arrested him with charges related to interfering with an investigation or something to that effect. As they led my manager off, he stared at me with a "you're fired" look in his eye. Getting fired for telling the truth happens more than we know in our "land of the free and home of the brave," and it's unfortunate when race is part of the equation.

Then, as with the Pilon incident, I questioned and bemoaned how people can stick together and cover up for someone else's wrongdoing. Even though I was right, I jeopardized my job for doing the right thing. The next day the paper read, "Race Riot at Ryan's." Nice alliteration, but I quit that week, not only fearing my manager would fire me, but also realizing I did not want to work for such an obvious racist.

Unfortunately, I had that same feeling again while Bob and Todd stood in the hall having their private conversation. Once again, I sensed my job in jeopardy, but I really didn't want to work for racists, or people who stick together when they are wrong instead of being truthful and honest.

When they re-entered the room, Todd spoke, "Thank you for providing your perspective on these issues. We have taken them into consideration, and we are going to remove the portion about the days absent and the issue about the impact in the field. However, we have decided to leave the information about your performance as is, which we believe is still unacceptable. We will downgrade the Performance Improvement Plan to an Immediate Action Plan. Any questions?"

"Yes sir," I replied. "I have only been in the job for a little over fifteen months of which almost four of them have been training. Everyone told me it takes at least eighteen months before a rep starts to have real impact on a territory, so why am I being assessed at fifteen months when all supporting documents showed that I was doing a great job and that trends were improving, despite the market dynamics?"

"It's our belief, considering how successful this territory used to be, that you should have been able to move this territory more than you have. So, we are going to put you on this plan. There are no consequences to it. We are just going to put a plan in place for you to follow." Todd refused to back down from Bob's asinine claims.

"That's fine, but I am not signing this document," I said. "It does not reflect the truth, and if you've had to alter it because of false information and accusations, why would you continue with a plan?"

Todd just repeated his previous statement, as if it were scripted. And, I refused to sign. The meeting adjourned with no real course of action or follow-up.

Very soon after, I made my move away from Pilon, landing a position with Clarke-Smith in Memphis, where Yvonne and I married. I later found out Pilon terminated Bob, the untruthful manager.

The word about Bob was that at least two or three lawsuits were brought against him for discrimination and policy violations. What really shocked me was that it took that many lawsuits for Pilon to finally act against him. He later went to another company that Pilon eventually bought, and they refused to bring him onboard.

The Ultimate Bachelor Pad

By most people's standards, a failed marriage is a misfortune. However, my misfortune immediately turned worthwhile because it paved the way for a lifelong dream of mine: an opportunity to live with my dad. At the time of my divorce, Dad lived in Indianapolis. He had been clean and sober for almost six years, his singing career was on the upswing, and he modeled on the side.

I called Dad on the phone and told him the news; I had requested and received a transfer to Indianapolis! I sensed his genuine joy through the phone. Like me, he had also dreamt of us living together. Finally, he would be with his true pride and joy—24/7. It had been fifteen years since we had last lived together in that tiny studio apartment in Hyde Park. Even then, my stay lasted no more than a month which made it feel more like a visit than actually living together. The time I lived with him as a baby doesn't count in my book, since I don't remember our interactions. I got excited on that phone call, as well, knowing the consistent communication I longed to have with my dad and the ability to tap into his wisdom, intuition, and all-around mental and spiritual wealth would soon be a reality.

Anyone who came into my dad's life benefited—psychologically, sociologically, spiritually, or often in all three ways. The wisdom and knowledge he so selflessly shared came as a result of years spent in recovery, his Masters degree in Psychology, intuitive thinking, and hanging out with people he befriended along the way. One such close friend of Dad's was multi-millionaire,

John Asarath, also of Indianapolis. Dad bragged about him all the time. He would show me what I could have if I had the same desire as John and practiced the same kind of discipline.

Dad and John shared many enlightening conversations and great moments together. I joined in with them on one of those great moments when John invited us, as his guests, to a seminar Bob Proctor and he were hosting in Las Vegas. Bob Proctor was an international motivational speaker, life coach, and self-help author, and he and John were friends. What I paid for Dad's and my airfare and hotel proved miniscule compared to the priceless learning experiences I encountered while there. I met a billionaire, lots of multi-millionaires, and many more people who aspired to accumulate more wealth than they'd ever known before. The seminar exposed me to masterminding, visualization exercises, and so much more.

So many people at that seminar complimented Dad and me on our beautiful and special relationship. I had to agree with them that we coveted the most unconditional love two human beings could have for each other, and it showed. How fitting that the most significant person in my life shared with me such a life-changing experience that weekend. And boy, did it change me. In fact, it changed me just to *see* so many millionaires in one place.

Some of the people at that seminar earned their millionaire status from very simple businesses such as nail products, cotton swabs, and toilet paper. Many step-by-step examples were given of how to become a millionaire. The most important step that I remembered turned out to be a simple one as well—believe that you already are a millionaire. All my previous readings from Napoleon Hill to Eric Butterworth to Les Brown culminated at that moment. The thought of conceiving, believing, and achieving resonated with me. I always heard a lot of people speak about it, and as I said, I read about it, but never before had I seen the results in real life. No doubt, that seminar showed me a complete manifestation of wealth, love, and success that I was destined for.

When we returned from Vegas, Dad and I started our house hunt.

With both of our incomes, we could afford a very nice one. Most of the ones we looked at followed the traditional floor plan of a big master suite, with the other bedrooms of much smaller proportion. Of course, Dad loved all of them, having demanded the master suite no matter which house we chose. House after house he would exclaim, "Mal, this is it!"

I would counter, "No, it ain't. Cool for you, but not cool for me."

I reiterated to Dad we needed to find the "ultimate bachelor pad"—a place where we coexisted as *roommates*, not father and son. In other words, my bedroom had to be just as cool as his. He finally understood, and we found the perfect house in Fishers, Indiana. It had 3600 square feet of living space, which included a finished basement. Two huge bedrooms and a bathroom graced the second level, with the master suite on the main floor. We decided the whole upstairs would be my space, and Dad got the master suite and basement. The perfect bachelor pad, indeed!

Next, came time to "hook it up." We hired a painter to paint all the rooms. We set up our fish tanks, birdcages, beds with mirrors all around, plants and trees, and nice furniture throughout. The place was tight!! Thanks to our military training, we were both neat freaks, so the house stayed clean. If either of us left any dishes in the sink, twenty-five push-ups per dish paid for the crime. While push-ups remained infrequent, teasing each other, while one of us knocked out fifty or seventy-five push-ups at a time really added to our fun style of living. We had a weight room in the basement and worked out together most days. My muscles grew significantly with dad encouraging me, and he got into great shape, too.

Dad had an insatiable appetite for reading and could hold an intelligent conversation about almost any topic. In my desire to emulate him, I developed that same insatiable appetite, sometimes gobbling up a book in just one day. At times we would buy the same books, read them at the same speed, and then discuss the book's take-aways. In order to improve our diction, we wrote words on 3x5 cards with their definitions on the backside. While driving, we used the opportunity to quiz each other on those words. It was as if we stayed on a crash course to be the best we could be in every aspect of our lives.

Then came the women…as two fairly handsome, pretty smart and charming men, with great bodies and sincere personalities, dating never presented itself as a problem. Keep in mind, I'm speaking modestly; if my dad told the story, he would not be modest at all about how great we looked, nor about how many women we attracted! Dad definitely knew how to promote himself!

Sometimes, Dad and I double-dated. Once in awhile, we even found ourselves engaged in intimate moments simultaneously. We would bump into each other in the kitchen, swap adventures, laugh, get some water, hug, and then head back to our own domains. During those times, I'd almost have to pinch myself, as I thought, "This is my Dad! How cool is that?"

I realize most young adults raised all their lives by both parents in the same household cannot fathom that scenario as cool by any means. Because my parents divorced when I was a baby, I never really saw my parents as "a couple." Therefore, becoming a friend to my dad and doing friend-like things with him simply felt natural. Actually, most of my friends, regardless of whether they'd been raised by one parent or both, admired my relationship with my dad.

Most young boys, when separated from a father they adore and look up to, dream about spending time together. Living with Dad awakened an amazing and symbiotic relationship that readily and sublimely filled the void left from my childhood—a time where I missed him deeply and painfully and cried for his presence incessantly. Our bachelor pad represented so much more than a nice home; it became our piece of heaven on earth, and for me, a real childhood dream come true.

Love Again

One day, I called on Dr. Khari, an endocrinologist who also owned a research company, to encourage him to use our new drug, Relon. As I waited for him to finish with a patient, one of the most beautiful women I had ever seen walked into the hallway. She stood there for a minute talking to someone, laughed at something said during their exchange, and then disappeared through another door. For several long moments thereafter, I maintained a vision of her standing in that same spot, with her beautiful dark skin and hair that could easily belong to a "Dark and Lovely" hair products model. Her smile mesmerized me nearly into a trance.

I decided to stay put and watch for her return. Instead, Dr. Khari came, so I detailed him on Relon, finding it hard to focus on my own words. Instead of looking directly at the doctor, my eyes kept darting toward the door down the hall, waiting for the beauty queen to walk back through it. Unfortunately, she never did. I even waited a few extra minutes after the doctor left, playing around with the samples in the sample closet and attempting to look busy. She never came back. I would have stayed the whole day if I could just have seen her again, but I had a lot of calls to make. With much regret, I left.

Days went by, and I could hardly wait for Dr. Khari to come up in my call cycle again. The following week, my counterpart, Sally Black, was scheduled to deliver samples to Dr. Khari. Sally, a very attractive and sweet divorced mother of two boys, worked extremely hard, making her an awesome partner. She called me one day to tell me she couldn't get to Dr. Khari's and asked if I could take the samples to him. Before she finished her sentence, I turned my car around and excitedly drove in the direction of the doctor's office.

I arrived at the office, checked in, and waited near the sample closet. As I stood at the closet, I kept my eye on the door that led to the research part of the building. I felt sort of like a lion sitting in the tall grass waiting for a lone gazelle to inch closer before jumping out for the attack. What can I say? Most of us men are hunters by nature!

Funny how I stood prepared to attack without a single game plan of what to do once I seized my prey. Having just recently emerged from my divorce, I stayed clear of serious relationships, so that certainly couldn't be my objective for meeting that beauty queen. On the other hand, with the HIV/AIDS epidemic on the rise, casual dating had lost its appeal with me, as well. Therefore, I guess my intentions during that timeframe fell somewhere in the middle; I was looking for a consistent and monogamous companion.

Finally, the woman I longed to see again came out and walked down the hall toward me. She strolled right past me and didn't say a word. I thought, "Damn, she could've at least given a brother a little eye contact." I guess I had to share some of the blame, since I could've spoken to her first. That is, if her dark, beautiful, flawless, and smooth skin had not rendered me speechless. Her hair was whipped again—that told me she really took care of herself. She turned the corner. Fortunately, a little convex mirror hung down from the ceiling in the corner, in order to view oncoming traffic. Through that mirror, I noticed that she went into the restroom. I was determined not to let her pass by again without me saying something.

So, I continued to wait patiently, watching the door though the mirror. Suddenly the door cracked open, and before I knew it, I had jumped around the corner and extended my hand and said, "I don't believe we've met."

She replied, "I don't believe we have."

Although she didn't speak it, I got the sister-girl look of, "Boy, excuse me;

can I at least get out of the bathroom?"

If I could have turned red at that moment, I would have, as I found myself literally standing in the ladies' restroom with one foot across the threshold. Reacting to her look, I took a step back, but I didn't withdraw my hand. "I am Jemal Gibson."

She shook my hand and said, "I am Lisa Twitty."

As I retreated to give her some space, I started talking. "I am new in the city, originally from Chicago, but just moved here from Memphis."

She rather nonchalantly answered, "You'll like it here."

Her tone didn't exactly imply that she was prepared to roll out the city's welcome wagon, but I continued anyway, "Maybe one day you can show me your city."

She said, "Yeah, I could do that. You just missed my Super Bowl party. It was really nice. But, maybe one day we can get together."

Great, it started going in the direction I'd hoped, so why slow down? "How about tonight?"

Her eyes widened, and she snapped her head back slightly, unprepared for my forwardness considering the fact we had only met two minutes beforehand— awkwardly in the doorway of the ladies' restroom, at that. I sold for a living; so closing became second nature to me. At that moment, my best product was me, so I closed "me." Sometimes I could be very bashful and other times very bullish. I knew the moment did not call for bashful.

Lisa responded, "Well, let me check my calendar," still looking somewhat surprised.

On that note, I gave her my number and said, "I look forward to your call."

When I left the office, I felt like jumping and clicking my heels, as I felt like I'd "macked" her down. As the day progressed, I waited for her call. It got later and later in the afternoon and then early evening arrived. I began second-guessing those "macking" skills of mine. Just then, my phone rang, and I grabbed it in a hurry. "Good evening," I said in a deep baritone voice.

"Hello, may I speak to Jemal?" the caller inquired.

"This is he. Who is this?" I replied, already knowing who it was.

"It's Lisa. It looks like my schedule is free, so we can get together tonight."

"Yes!!" I said in my mind. "Around seven?" I asked.

"That's fine," she replied.

After getting her address and directions, I hung up the phone with an ear to ear grin on my face. I believe that grin remained all the way back to my house. I later picked Lisa up. She wore some tight jeans, and they made her look even finer!

I knew the date with her would be a lot of fun. We went to Champs Sports Bar and Grill. After that first date, we ended up spending almost every day together for the next couple of months. In fact, I chuckled over my dad's slight jealousy over my time spent with Lisa.

"Going out with *that girl* again?" he would ask.

"Yep," I would say. I couldn't pinpoint what warranted such feelings on his part, since at that time, he dated someone and they spent a lot of time together, too.

Every now and then, he would ask me, "What do you see in her?"

I would say, "Lisa is beautiful. In a way, she's beautiful like my mother."

"No she ain't!" Dad yelled back, "*Evelyn* is beautiful!"

He implied that Lisa wasn't. That's when I knew his comments came from a place of envy or resentment because Lisa would be considered beautiful by almost anyone's standards. But I understood what spawned those emotions from my dad. Sometimes when he enjoyed continuous dates leaving me home alone night after night, I remembered feeling resentment toward the woman who was taking his attention away from me. Of course, it made me happy to see him enjoying his life, and I certainly didn't expect him to slow down on my account, yet that feeling of mine emerged well before I realized its presence. Dad and I had a unique bond with each other that we knew no woman could match, so there were moments for both of us when we felt jealousy about the way time was being spent, as if it would run out before we had enough of it with each other.

Even though I enjoyed Lisa's companionship immensely, the voice of my divorce counselor kept ringing in my ears: "You should not marry the first person you date after your divorce. That 'next' person is generally just satisfying some needs that your spouse did not fulfill. These rebound marriages usually end with a higher divorce rate." I didn't know if that held up statistically, but he said it, so I took it to heart and remained dead set against making that mistake.

On the other hand, Lisa began to tell everyone that she had met her future husband—her soul mate. I didn't feel a need to discourage her from saying that, but by the same token, I hadn't made any measures to publicly classify or de-classify our relationship. Internally though, I knew the odds were stacked in favor of her being "the one" for several reasons: her beauty astounded me, our intimacy ranked off the charts, and very importantly, I really enjoyed her family.

I had never been around a family like Lisa's. The McBradys, on her dad's side, celebrated every birthday and holiday together. Also, on most Sundays, everyone gathered at Ma's house for dinner. Ma was Lisa's grandmother on her father's side. Also on birthdays, everyone brought a gift and a covered dish. It must've felt like Christmas all over again for the birthday person, and with all the food, it felt like multiple Thanksgiving Days throughout the year for the entire family. Even though her father had not raised Lisa, she remained extremely close to his side of the family, which seemed unusual to me.

Unfortunately, her father had spent a large part of her life in jail for murder. Like my father, he also became a victim to drugs early in his life. Lisa's cousin and his wife were murdered in front of their kids—allegedly due to drugs. Her uncle was murdered, also allegedly due to drugs. I could go on and on about her family's tragedies because of drugs. In a strange way, it drew me closer to her, seeing how her family's challenges mirrored mine. I felt she could relate to my family's issues, unlike my ex-wife, who harbored great disdain for just about everyone in my family—including me.

I started to fall for Lisa—hard. The aspect that sealed the deal occurred late one night when I went to her house. I had gone to see Dad sing earlier that evening and didn't arrive at her place until two in the morning. As I entered, she asked, "Are you hungry?"

I said, "Yes."

Within fifteen minutes, she brought to her bedroom a steak, baked potato, and a salad. That floored me! I expected maybe a turkey sandwich and some chips—not a full, hot meal!

I asked her, "Did you cook that earlier today?"

She said, "No, I just made it."

"You're lying," I said half joking, half serious.

She said, "It doesn't take long to fry a steak. I microwaved the potato and cut up the salad. It was nothing."

"This is a trap!" I told myself. "No woman is going to repeatedly wake up in the middle of the night and at two A.M. cook a steak, baked potato, and salad for a brother. OK, I'll try it again." So another night, shortly after I came in late, I got another equally sophisticated meal. "Yep, a trap," I laughed as I ate the meal, looking at her thinking, "You ain't slick."

So, I continued to ask for meals at unusual times, and it never failed— a meal always came right up. I finally learned that she loved to cook and was never opposed to preparing food for me. Never before had any woman taken care of me like that. So, I fell deeper and deeper in love, against that divorce counselor's supposed better judgment.

While in Indianapolis, I received a promotion as a trainer for new hires. My position worked side by side with a training team responsible for product knowledge and selling skills training. I rapidly honed my skills in this role, giving me the opportunity to speak in front of large groups. I not only trained them on the technical aspects of our job but also managed to sneak in a few of what I consider "life principles." I felt so comfortable in front of the groups, inspiring them to achieve their best, both personally and professionally.

Based on my good performance, in September, 1998, I received yet another promotion. This time, it was as District Manager in Cleveland, Ohio. As a District Manager, I would be responsible for tens of millions of dollars in sales with approximately twelve sales reps working for me. It was my responsibility to teach them how to sell and how to find and maximize business opportunities.

That brought an end to the bachelor pad era and the end of a fulfilled childhood dream. It was bittersweet for both Dad and me. I suppose I can liken it somewhat to a kid leaving home for college—you know it's in his best interest to go, but you also know you're going to miss him terribly. Nevertheless, the many special moments and experiences Dad and I shared had been incredibly precious and life-enhancing for both of us. I felt as though I earned my Master's degree in "life" sciences while living there.

That promotion also meant I would be leaving Lisa in Indianapolis. At that time, we had dated for almost a year. In December of that year, we traveled on a cruise with my family. We all had a blast eating, drinking, and partying for seven days straight. A few weeks later, Lisa found out she was pregnant. From the very moment she told me, I knew we would have the baby and raise it together. I had always said that I would stay with any woman who got pregnant by me if we kept the baby. I didn't want to have a lot of kids with several different women.

Un-wed pregnancies had been an issue in my entire family, with many of my young female relatives giving birth to children by different men, who themselves had other children by different women. I could never be judgmental of someone in that position; however, I speak accurately when I say it adds such a strain to sibling relationships. On certain holidays, one sibling may go to be with his or her other parent, while the other sibling goes to be with their other parent. They miss the true togetherness of holidays or summertime moments together.

In some worse case scenarios, one of the siblings may not have another parent who is involved with them. Imagine then, how much less significant they feel when their sibling does get the proper attention and love from a non-custodial parent, in addition to their custodial parent. I promised myself I would not contribute to such dynamics, but instead would help break that cycle within my family. I knew I would have to stand by that vow, regardless of my own personal readiness or happiness.

So, Lisa moved with me to Cleveland where we had our first child, Iman—truly my "# 1 princess." I named her Iman because her name means faith. Just as my father had faith in me to be something special, I have faith that she, too, will achieve extra special things in her life. Her middle name is Eboni, after my sister. My sister and I made a pact that my firstborn would have her name and that her first-born would have my name. And, so it was.

Baby Iman looked like me, but with my mother's beautiful caramel-brown eyes. My world changed from the moment she entered into it. I always loved people, life, and especially children, but I learned the true meaning of *unconditional* love with Iman. She depended on me for food, shelter, love, affection, everything; you name it, I was the provider. I felt that responsibility to love and protect her lay with no one else but me. Her birth allowed me to understand how some parents could say they would die to allow their children to live. Certainly, if I was prepared to die, I would be prepared to make any other sacrifice for her, as well, to have a stable, loving upbringing. After all, that is the very least every child on earth should have. I determined in my heart that my child would have the best of everything.

I Am My Brother's Keeper. . .

It was December, 1999. With the holiday season fast approaching, my brother, Anthony, kept coming to my mind. I hadn't talked to him in quite awhile; it had probably been six months, which was extremely unusual. As a matter of fact, I had no idea where he even lived. The last time we spoke, he lived back in Chicago. The time before that he had just moved to Pine Bluff, Arkansas, back in 1994. I had just started working for Pilon in Atlanta and inherited a company car. Since I didn't need two cars, and since Ant aspired to a fresh, new start away from his life of drugs in Peoria, I loaned him my Saab.

Actually, Ant had no choice but to start fresh somewhere else. Word on the street indicated that he and our 'cousin,' Ty, had screwed over some big time drug dealer in Peoria, and they both went into hiding. Our other 'cousin,' Kenny, offered his home in Pine Bluff as a place where Ant could live while getting his life back on the right track. In light of all that, I figured the least I could do was help him out with temporary transportation.

Before handing the car over to Ant, there were some mental hurdles I had to overcome. For instance: What if he gets into an accident? What if he does something illegal and the car is in my name? I thought about a dozen scenarios stemming back to me being the responsible party should anything happen. So, I decided to transfer the car into his name, clearing my conscience regarding all those scenarios. When I told Ant about the car, I made it clear that I might need it back if somehow my new job did not work out. Of course, he didn't have a problem with that, so he came to Atlanta and got my car.

A couple of weeks later, I tried to reach Ant, but he never answered my calls. He didn't return my messages for awhile, either. When we finally spoke, I immediately asked, "Ant, how is my car?"

"Aww, bruh, I had to put it in the shop," he reluctantly replied.

"What was wrong with it, Ant?"

"The ignition went bad."

I did experience problems with the ignition before he took it, so that explanation seemed plausible. In Saabs, the ignition is between the seats on the floor, and you could easily spill a drink into it. That 1989 Saab, the second car I paid for in college with my own money, was my favorite. While in college, most of my friends' vehicles were purchased for them by their parents. For example, Greg Calhoun, owner of a chain of supermarkets in Alabama and the father of one of my Alpha line brothers, bought his son a 325 BMW with a gold plated inscription: "Especially for Malcolm..." Of course, I don't knock their good fortune, especially since Malcolm let me drive it when I needed wheels. Nonetheless, I was proud of my major accomplishment of buying my first car on my own.

I called my brother again a week or so later, and he said the car remained in the shop. I called him a few times after that, and he went back to not answering my calls. I decided to drive to Pine Bluff and pay a surprise visit to Ant and check on my car.

When I arrived in Pine Bluff, I called him and announced my arrival. He seemed to be very excited at the prospect of me being there. He told me where to come pick him up. That could only mean one thing, and it wasn't good news.

When we met up, I gave him a hug and then right away asked, "Where is my car, Ant?"

He started off with his usual defensive act. When he discovered that didn't fly with me anymore, he just blurted it out, "You know, I sold that car!"

"What?!" I just knew I heard him wrong.

"You know, I sold that car," he repeated.

"What the hell are you talking about? What do you mean, you sold *my* car, Ant?"

My heart sank. I could not believe my brother treated me like a regular cat on the street, someone he would take advantage of without blinking. I didn't think he would ever stoop that low with me. We stood there staring at each other for a long time, not saying a word. My eyes filled up with tears, as rage-filled thoughts raced all around my mind.

"How could you?" "You're my big brother!" "That car belonged to me!" "I worked hard to buy that car!"

After a few minutes, we got in my company car and started driving. I'll be damned if we didn't drive past a house that had *my* car sitting in the yard! I just looked at my brother in disgust. His drug habit had affected me personally for the first time. I vowed right then it would be the last time. Of course, it wasn't.

Now, fast forward to December, 1999; I'm in Cleveland wondering what's going on in Ant's life. I called my sister, Eboni, to get the latest scoop and, as I suspected by his absence, he had relapsed back to selling and using drugs. She told me he held a spot on the corner of Cicero and Gladys Avenues in Chicago.

I knew that spot well. As kids, we used to go to the liquor store there to get candy. How ironic that we went to the liquor store to get candy. I suppose the habit of going there would make it easy for the transition to a 40 ounce bottle of beer or some other liquor of choice at an age way too early. Nevertheless, we saw drug dealers hanging out there regularly. How difficult to imagine my brother there because the guys I recall on that corner always looked very young, hard, ruthless, and hopeless. None of those descriptions fit Ant; none of those things defined who my brother was to me.

Next, I asked Eboni when she had last seen him. "A few weeks ago," she reported, "he slept outside my apartment door in the hallway one night. I'll let him sleep in the hallway, but not in the house because things turned up missing the last time he was here."

I could hear the sadness in her voice, having to make her brother sleep in the hallway. But, I totally understood. She had two young sons, Marvell and Markell. Like any conscientious mother, she didn't want her boys to see their uncle like that. She continued to give me all the sad news about our brother. She told me how bad he looked and how much weight he had lost. "He got beat up in front of the house and Mommy saw the guys do it."

"My goodness, what happened?" I asked.

"It had something to do with him using the drugs he should've been selling, and you know, they *will* get their money or get you. Mommy ran out and told them to stop and they told her he was lucky they knew her; otherwise, they said they would have killed him."

"Damn. He's going to get himself killed."

That one thought kept coming to my mind. The irony of that moment was that in a few weeks, I would win the award for selling the most drugs in our region at Clarke-Smith, and my brother could be killed selling drugs on the street. What a paradox to watch unfold, except I didn't want to watch my brother's half of it.

I called my mother, and of course, she re-told the story about him getting beat up. "Ma, why didn't you call and tell me?"

"I didn't want you to worry," she answered, regrettably.

I hated when she did that. Lots of times things happened that I wouldn't hear about until days, weeks, or months later.

"So where is Anthony now?" I asked.

"Somewhere in Madison, Wisconsin."

"What is he doing up there?" I asked.

"He's supposed to be working, but the last call I got from him was from a homeless shelter. At least that's what the Caller ID said."

"So have you talked to him?"

"Not in a couple of weeks," she replied.

"Give me the number, Ma."

I thought about my brother's three children; Keysha and Tocki were sixteen-years-old, and Anthony, Jr. was eight. While I had not spent a lot of time around them, I knew the whole situation hurt them deeply. The girls loved their daddy's "dirty drawers" (as the saying goes), like too many inner city children whose father's absence looms larger than his presence. The mixture of adoration and fantasy is more than a notion. That adoration is viscerally impressed upon a child's being because the desire for the missing parent is so great. Well, my desire was for my brother to be a better father. But, first he had to be a better person to himself.

I called the shelter and inquired about an Anthony Holloway staying there. The person who answered the phone said, "Let me check the sign-in sheet to see. Looks like last night."

"Can you give him my number the next time he comes in? Tell him it's his little brother. Thank you."

After I hung up the phone, tears welled up. I couldn't believe my brother's life of drugs and homelessness. On top of that, homeless in December—in Wisconsin! As one of the northern Great Lakes states, the temperatures drop below freezing on many days throughout the winter. I hoped he managed to stay at the shelter most nights; I knew I couldn't handle getting a call telling me he'd frozen to death.

Later that night, Lisa and I talked, and I told her, "I've got to get my brother. I can't leave him to die of drugs or freezing to death in the streets. We can bring him here, get him some treatment, and help him get his life together. I am in a good position, and I always promised him I would take care of him when I got older. Now is that time. Hopefully, he'll come."

Lisa understood wholeheartedly, and it was partly why I loved her so much. Having that same talk with my former wife would have guaranteed an argument and a terrible fight. But Lisa understood the life I lived, and she supported me in whatever I had to do to help my family.

Later that night, Anthony called me. "Thank God!" was all I could think. We talked for quite awhile. In spite of our long conversation, the only thing

I clearly recall were the words, "Come get me, little bro."

I solemnly responded, "I will. Just hold on for a day or two. We are going to find a program for you to get into. Just go to the shelter and call me every night. I should know something in a day or two."

I wanted to go get him immediately, but I could do nothing for him at my home. I knew that as a user, he had to have treatment; otherwise, he would simply find drugs in Cleveland and create a problem for Lisa and my daughter.

Lisa called around relentlessly and found a six-month, in-house program for Ant, similar to the one where my mother stayed when we were kids. Déjà vu, except now it would be Ant who I'd wait to see transformed. From the first day I saw him smoke weed, intuition told me this would be his outcome. Of course, I hoped that somehow it *wouldn't* happen, but he had already paved his course. Now, he was like all of my other "Aunts and Uncles" from Stonehedge; he had lost everything. Ant's father, Donald, had always told me that I was my brother's keeper. I sent Ant a bus ticket, and he came to Cleveland on January 1, 2000— a new millennium and a new start.

After seven months of onsite rehab, I asked Ant to come live with us on the 4th of July. Of course, I used the symbolism of that date to reinforce that he emerged as a new and independent man, and that he had more *good* years left on this earth than the number of *bad* years he had already lived. With a fresh start, now it was all about new choices, new opportunities, and a new life.

Ant got a great job at a car dealership doing what he did best—selling. In the first couple of months, he achieved salesman of the month and made a great living; he was living a great life.

Practice, Practice, Practice

With drugs behind him and a laser focus on his passion for music, Dad's singing career blossomed. His first CD titled, *An Affair to Remember,* consisted of ballads from many of the great crooners like Nat King Cole, Johnny Mathis, Frank Sinatra, Billy Eckstein, and Johnny Hartman. The music beautifully symbolized a cohesive journey of love that succinctly paralleled Dad's own life, defined by one love relationship after another. Compiling those works with a voice easily mistaken for Nat King Cole's allowed the world to experience the pure talent of my dad, Sam Gibson, as he finally felt he was claiming his place in life.

The financial boost needed to jumpstart Dad's career came from Pint whose parents had died, leaving her a sizable inheritance. Pint always believed in Dad, so investing a good portion of that inheritance didn't require a lot of thought on her part. With a loan arrangement between the two of them in place, Dad was able to pay for the studio time, musicians, clothes, photographers, and everything else that went into the production of his CD's. He promised to repay every dime when he hit it big. I believe Pint considered her repayment to be the tremendous joy and satisfaction she felt knowing she helped Dad reach that milestone.

About that same time, a tremendous opportunity broke for my dad. He began traveling on a multi-city tour with Mercedes Ellington, Duke Ellington's granddaughter, in a production called *Sophisticated Ellington* that she created to commemorate what would have been Duke's 100th birthday. Paired with a female vocalist, Dad performed all the male vocals for Duke's music in that show.

Mercedes, best known for her dancing and choreography, hit the mark with that production, as it made its way across the country in many great music halls and with some of America's finest symphonies. The musical included a cast of singers and dancers with several scene changes, wardrobe changes, and Mercedes herself as narrator. I made it a point to catch Dad's performances in several different states.

Dad had truly mastered the art of stage performing, captivating the audience with his harmonious voice and the attractive physique he maintained. I enjoyed watching him as the words to each song translated through his posture, the movements of his hands and arms, and through his intense eye contact. Most women thought he sang directly to them, and he could make men feel like the songs belonged to them. With the advantage of great looks, great personality, and a beautiful spirit, Dad had evolved into an incredible entertainer.

Finally, in Dad's second year of traveling with that troupe, he received the opportunity of a lifetime. Their production performed at the coveted venue of Carnegie Hall. As the old axiom goes, "How do you get to Carnegie Hall? Practice. Practice. Practice!" No one deserved the accomplishment of being there more than my dad with all the practice hours put in and the type of commitment to his music that he had displayed for decades without a lot of recognition.

Not only was Carnegie Hall a major moment for dad, but it offered a grand occasion of celebration for all of his family and friends, as well. Many of us experienced Dad's worst of times, many times over. So, to see him ascend to that famous stage, where so many greats had performed, proved magical for us all. Being there was a divine testimony of his strength of character to have overcome such a difficult past. We all wanted to be a part of the occasion.

We represented a proud team of supporters that day in New York City at Carnegie Hall: Aunt Aida, Aunt Freddie, Pint, Nancy, Maeve, Dana, Lisa, Cousin Latrice, and a couple of my fellas, Gary Lewis and Scott Parker. We exalted Dad as our magnificent star, as we watched him rise to meet the vision he had always had for himself. After the show, he looked like a kid on Christmas morning; he was entirely overwhelmed with joy! It was wonderful to behold my father in his glory, living his dreams.

Lotto

Early the next morning, Lisa and I drove seven hours back to Cleveland. I faced an extremely important meeting the following morning, leaving me very little time to re-pack and get to the airport. As soon as we arrived home, I sprinted upstairs; I repacked in literally five minutes, hopped back in the car, and dashed to the airport.

My meeting the next day dealt with one of our products, Relon, which was threatened to be pulled off the market. That required us to prepare a communications strategy for our colleagues, customers, and patients in the North Central Customer Business Unit for Clarke-Smith. In the meantime, we anxiously awaited the press release on the fate of that drug which, until that time, had been heralded as a breakthrough treatment.

Unfortunately, out of the hundreds of thousands of patients who had taken Relon, seven or eight had died. Of course, you never want to experience the weight of anyone dying as a result of your drug, but the sad truth is that death is a reality in our industry when you consider the millions of people ingesting prescribed medications. In actuality, more people die taking over-the-counter pain relievers than almost any prescription drug on the market. Either way, you always hope the benefits of legal drugs far outweigh those dreaded risks.

I arrived in record time at Cleveland Hopkins International Airport. After parking the car and grabbing my computer bag and luggage, I ran, jumped, and dodged my way to the ticket counter. Everything proceeded smoothly from there, and I finally took a moment to catch my breath while the security line inched its way to the conveyor belts and x-ray machines. I had just started mentally preparing for the meeting, when the security agent asked if they could run my bag again.

"Sure," I responded, in a less than agreeable tone. I hoped they sensed my indignation against their trivial routine, as their additional scans would interrupt my already tight trek to the gate.

"What is that?" the security team asked, as my bag went through a second time.

I usually raised eyebrows at security checkpoints because of the loose change and all the cords for my gadgets that I carried with me in my bag. They usually figured it out after the second time. The agent asked if they could run it one more time.

"Sure, but it's just change and wires."

"OK," came his outward response, when under his breath, he must have been thinking, "Like hell it is."

As the bag traveled through the machine a third time, I suddenly remembered something, and my heart sank to my stomach.

"Damn!"

When I got to the hotel in New York City for Dad's show at Carnegie, the valet guy told me if I had any valuables in my car like money, jewelry, computers, or guns they would not be responsible for them being stolen. On that note, I took my 9mm out of the glove compartment and placed it in a zippered compartment in my computer bag.

"Oh, God!" I thought. I never took it out, and that's what they saw.

I asked the security guard, "Can I have my bag? I'll be right back."

"Why?" They asked, with great suspicion at my request.

"I have a gun in the bag," I whispered apologetically.

Boy, you would have thought that I pulled the gun *on* someone. Everybody panicked. They hit some buttons and yelled at people to stay back. Before I knew it, what seemed like an entire police squad ran up on me like I had shot an officer. I remained pretty cool up to that point; then, I realized the magnitude of the matter.

I carefully pulled out my driver's license and gun owner's permit, at their request. The confusion mounted because I carried a Tennessee license, an Indianapolis gun permit, but I was living in Ohio. I had moved three times within two years and never took the time to change those pertinent identification documents. After being escorted to the police station within the airport, they subjected me to a grueling session of accusations.

The first officer said, "Why did you have a gun?"

I said, "Sir, I carry it for protection."

"Why do you need protection?" the second one asked.

"Because I've been shot and robbed before, just to name a of couple reasons."

"Wow, shot. Why were you shot? Where were you shot? Was it in the military?" They fired away question after question.

I explained the incident when I was shot at the night club. Without skipping a beat, they drilled me some more, "Why was your gun loaded? Why was there a round in the chamber?"

I explained "I was an officer in the Army, Airborne Rangers, and have extensive weapons knowledge. Furthermore, if I carry a weapon for protection, what would be the point of having an empty clip or a round not ready for discharge?"

"That's what we want to know, why was it ready for discharge?"

At that point, I realized there was nothing I could say that would be safe from their twisting of words. Finally, they gave me an opportunity to state my case, "Officers, I was on my way to a meeting with the pharmaceutical company that I work for: Clarke-Smith. There's a very important meeting I must attend. I was just promoted to manager, and if I don't show up for this meeting, it's going to really tarnish my career. I apologize for the gun. It ended up in my bag when the valet suggested I get all valuables out of my car when I went to go see my father perform at Carnegie Hall last night; I believe the parking sticker is still in my car as proof. Please, give me a break."

As I concluded my defense, an African-American sergeant came in and heard part of my explanation. He urged the other officers to the back of the room, leaving me stranded at the table where I sat, with a million thoughts—from Relon to jail—all racing around in my head. They came back to the table thirty minutes later, having heard from all of the states for which I had various identifications. All checks came up clean.

"We are going to let to you go, so that you can get to your meeting, but we are going to put a warrant out for your arrest. So, if you get stopped somewhere else, you are going to go to jail. When you come back from your meeting you must go directly to the police station downtown so that they can finish processing the paperwork and render further judgment. If you don't go to the police station, you are going to go to jail if you're caught. Do you understand?"

"Yes sir! Thank you, sir! You have my word I will go straight to the station when I return. You don't know how thankful I am!"

So, I rushed out of that office and to the ticket counter to inquire about another flight. If not, I would have to drive a few more hours and I was already exhausted. Fortunately, they booked me on the next flight.

Once comfortably settled in my seat on the flight, I mulled over all that had transpired. How could I have been so careless? That could have been a major issue, like mandatory jail, according to some states. I wondered if the black Sergeant had a hand in cutting me some slack because the white officers were certainly not showing any indication that I would be getting a break; they were playing the real hard-ass role the entire time. I'll never know for sure, but I still felt thankful that brother stepped in when he did.

At the meeting the next day, due to some logistical error, we did not have a TV in our conference room; therefore, my regional president, John Howard, sent us back to our individual rooms to watch the press conference from there. While watching the TV in my bathroom, a breaking news story came on: "Cleveland Mayor fires the airport security agency for letting two passengers with guns through security in the past 24 hours; stay tuned for more details."

I felt all the stress of the past twenty-four hours—the exhausting drive back from New York, rushing through the airport, dealing with guns and police officers. It all rose up in my stomach. My head hurt. My heart pounded, and I started sweating. Stress churned my lunch a couple of times before everything came running out. Thank goodness, I was already in the bathroom!

How could that chain of events happen now? What a horrible coincidence for all the leadership in my region to be watching the same news as they broke that story. Would they connect that story to the press conference? I could already hear it, "Employee of pharmaceutical company, maker of Relon, gets caught with gun at Cleveland airport—speaking of Relon...." It felt like my entire career at Clarke-Smith dangled by a thread.

I contemplated how to maneuver out of that situation. What would I tell my boss and the Regional President? When I pledged Alpha Phi Alpha fraternity, my frat brothers pegged the name "Lotto" as my "line" name (pledge nickname). That stood for "can't win for losing," based on the things that happened while on line. At that moment, waiting for the details of the news headlines in my hotel room, I felt the symbolism of that name trying to attach itself to me. Voices in my head tried to convince me that name still applied to my life.

Finally, the full story played out on the TV: "In the past twenty-four hours, two people have been caught with guns at the security station, and security failed to apply the appropriate procedures in detecting the weapons. One of the gun carriers...." "Please God, don't do it!" I yelled! "...was a local doctor... The mayor will be replacing the security company with a new company soon. Next in the news....."

Oh, my God; oh, my God. Thank You!! Thank You!! Thank You!! Maybe one day I *will* outlive that name, "Lotto."

When I returned to Cleveland, I went to the police station and cleared up the gun issue. I paid a fine; they kept my gun, and they let me go with that blemish on my record. After that, a security alert must have profiled me for almost two years straight. No one said so specifically, but I'm sure those spot checks linked back to the gun incident. I didn't mind, though. This seemed like a small price to pay in exchange for what could have been a ruined career and some time in jail. With my family's background, that fearful thought hit a little too close to home.

Winning the Right Way

Things were good for us as a family in Cleveland. I performed well on the job. Lisa worked in clinical research that studied drugs while I was selling them. On occasion, she did studies about my company's drugs which was pretty cool. Iman was about a year-old and growing fast. We lived very comfortably. Then, when Pilon bought Clarke-Smith for an astounding $90 billion dollars, I ended up back at the company where it all began. I joked with my old Pilon colleagues saying, "I would have come back for a few million, but you had to go and spend $90 billion."

As my Clarke-Smith colleagues prepared for the transition from one company to the other, the announcement came that I had won our highest sales award as a manager—the "Winners Circle." The award included a trip to Naples, Florida. I chose to take my mother because I wanted her to enjoy the fruits of my labor. She deserved it much more than I did. It was my small way of thanking her for all her struggles and sacrifices. I wanted her to see the people I worked with; I was also hoping she would hear wonderful things about me that would only make her more proud and help her feel good about herself, as well.

The trip was incredible! We stayed at the Ritz Carlton in Naples. Additional perks included a ride in a limo, first class airfare, a stay at a five-star hotel, the finest food, pampering with massages and pedicures, fabulous excursions (including alligator petting!), and entertainment galore. I could not have asked for a better gift for my mother.

Many of my colleagues did tell her wonderful things about me. I did see the pride in her face. One of those colleagues, Clint Lewis, an African-American vice president of sales, spoke highly of me to my mother and treated her very kindly. She was most impressed with Clint and happy for him, too. After all, "he had a good job." Even though I did not work for him at that moment in time, I knew I wanted to. He had an awesome presence, a real facility with words, and a great way with people. I knew I could really grow if I was under his leadership.

On the night of the awards banquet, I savored a special surprise for my mother. I wanted to give it to her at the perfect moment, so I waited until we were dressed and ready to go. I handed her a beautifully wrapped box and said, "Thank you, Mother, for all of your struggles and for all of your love."

As she opened it, the biggest smile spread across her face, and tears flowed down her cheeks. A gorgeous matching set of pearl earrings, bracelet, and necklace waited to adorn her beautiful brown skin. That became her first ever set of pearls. She was fifty-five years-old.

"Oh, Jemal!" I remember her saying, as I gently fastened the necklace on her. It proved one of the best moments of my life. I always dreamed of moments like this, and it felt so good that I could make them real. Throughout the evening, my mother kept feeling her necklace, glancing at her bracelet, and then smiling at me.

Finally, the time came for the winners to be announced. They called my name. As I made my way to the stage, I couldn't help but think, "Wow. I am with one of the top drug companies in the world, and I am one of the best at selling drugs." They showed my picture on the big screen, and I thought, "Yeah, I'm the man!" I walked to the middle of the stage, shook hands with my Vice President, Tim George, as he passed me the crystal eagle. We stood there with clasped hands, smiled for the cameraman, and then I walked off the stage. Leaving the other side of the stage, I saw my picture again and repeated to myself, "Yeah, I *am* the man!"

I had ascended to the top, to a place no drug dealer could ever go. A real pride of being the best at helping people live healthier, happier lives—something no dealer could ever attest to. I felt like the real Nino Brown, Frank Lucas, or Rick

Ross, but a better, much more wholesome version.

As I returned to my table, my mother's eyes were glistening. People kept clapping and shaking my hand as I passed them. That moment felt so magical; it was one of the best moments in my life because I was able to share it with my mother.

The next morning, I flew back to Cleveland, and my mother flew back to Chicago. She sat in the First Class cabin on the plane, rode in a limo to her house, and then placed her pearls in a safe place, so that none of my cousins would steal them.

Can't Live Without Them

Lisa and I have always loved each other; however, at one point in our young relationship, we came to grips with the fact that we needed to work on personal issues in order to solidify ourselves as lifelong partners. After much discussion and consideration, we agreed neither of us was ready for the responsibility at that particular point in time. We decided Lisa would move back to Indianapolis for awhile. It was one of the most difficult decisions I had ever made in my life; yet, at the same time, a mature one. I helped her get her housing situated in Indianapolis, gave her the Grand Cherokee, and caught the bus back to Cleveland. I cried all the way home. It felt as if I had abandoned my beautiful Princess, Iman, and left Lisa to struggle as a single mother.

My guilt over leaving them and my desire for real love battled for space in my heart. Did I even have the ability to believe in true love and hold on to it? My tumultuous upbringing sure hadn't prepared me for it, that is, nothing beyond a few pointers here and there. I had no real examples to follow. So, that inner battle remained a constant force over the next year, particularly after each holiday spent with Lisa and Iman, which was almost every major holiday.

In addition to me visiting them, Iman would come to Cleveland and stay for a week or two at a time with me. I hired a sitter during the day and would arrange less travel with my work schedule, allowing me to take good care of her. I loved being with my daughter, watching her explore the world, and marveling at her discoveries. It fascinated me to watch her. I videotaped almost everything she did. It helped me through the times I spent alone, after she would return to Indianapolis. I would hook the VCR up to a projector and shoot her images on the wall and cover the complete wall, so that it looked like she really stood there. I would just play that video of her all day long; no TV, just Iman—my #1 Princess.

One day, while visiting Indianapolis for Valentine's Day, Lisa and Iman fell asleep in my arms, one on each side. As I stared at the ceiling, a crystal clear revelation came. I realized that there was no other place on earth I would rather be than with my two precious women. On one side of me lay the mother of my daughter, a very kind and loving person who loved me deeply. On the other side, my beautiful daughter who deserved the best opportunity to succeed in life. I knew being a cohesive family would improve Iman's ability to have a good life without any of the anxieties I bore as a child. Her choices in life would be more plentiful and clear if it was not crowded with the kind of pain I had suffered being separated from my parents. So, in that "Ah ha!" moment, I decided to ask Lisa to marry me; I just didn't tell her right then and there.

A few months later, on May 1st, I carried out an elaborate surprise for Lisa in preparation for popping the "big question." I like to think that I'm a pretty romantic guy, but I must admit, I impressed myself with the ideas I came up with for her mystery-filled day.

First, I wrote several letters; each one contained specific instructions for her to follow to a "T." She could not open the next letter until she completed the task listed in the current one. I placed all the letters, along with a dozen roses, at her house after she left for work. Lisa's grandmother helped out by calling Lisa and informing her that she needed to go home due to a medical emergency. When she got there, she smelled air filled with the aroma of lit candles; a dozen roses created a velvety-red backdrop for a bottle of champagne, a fluted glass already filled with the bubbly, and five numbered envelopes with letters enclosed, each neatly arranged in order of the action required.

The first letter, titled "Open Me First," had a brief, intriguing message introducing Lisa to her day full of surprises. It read, "I have learned that life is not promised, but once you find love, it can be…I would like to create a life of love and happiness together, but there are some things that need to be done first. You will need to follow my instructions exactly, or you will miss the true joy of the moment…" It closed with, "By the time you finish this first letter, your chariot will be awaiting you." Lisa peeked outside to find a stretch limo with its motor running. "Take nothing but your purse, the letters, and, of course, the champagne. Once you get into the limo, you can read the second letter." At that point, she knew this day would be *the* day. As she gathered her things, she started making calls and crying to her girlfriends, "I think today is the day! I think Jemal is going to propose!"

Once settled into the immense backseat of the limo, Lisa opened her second letter. "You are one of the most beautiful women I have ever seen…Your hair is so smooth and silky; you belong in the "Dark & Lovely" commercials… But before you can do that you must get it right… Here is some money. Tell your beautician this is a special occasion and she must fit you in immediately. You only have ninety minutes. If you miss the time, you will miss the moment…"

Fortunately, Brenda, her hair dresser and close friend, pushed her other client back and whipped Lisa's hair real "fly" as usual. One and a half hours later, Lisa scurried back to the limo, anxious to get to letter number three. "Your skin is so chocolaty smooth, hands soft and gentle… I want them looking extra special for tonight… Take this money and get your nails done. You have only forty-five minutes…"

As she rode to her nail salon, I later learned she made more calls, cried more tears, and drank more champagne. She began stressing a little while in the nail salon, as time was running out. Manicure and pedicure completed and back in the limo, she slowly opened letter number four, careful not to mess up her freshly painted nails. "By now you are almost ready…Your hair and your hands and feet are looking absolutely beautiful, I'm sure…Now, I want you to find something to adorn your lovely body and some shoes to cradle your soft feet… Here is some money to find something classy but sexy… You have sixty minutes…"

Off she went running through the mall, asking the women in the stores to help her find that very special something—sexy and classy. She briefly shared her fairy-tale adventurous day, causing quite a flurry of excitement, with sales women flipping through racks hunting for the best of the selections. Donning her new shoes and dress, Lisa felt like a million bucks as she slipped back into the limo.

Letter five remained in her hands. "Well, my love, are you ready? The driver knows where to bring you, so just sit back and relax… Another glass of champagne on me, if there is any left." The driver took her to the Sybaris Hotel in Indianapolis. The Sybaris, a very small hotel chain with locations throughout the United States, is known for their luxurious pool suites and romantic getaway packages. I reserved the best suite they had; it had two levels, a plush atmosphere with a beautiful swimming pool encased in the middle of the suite, and a whirlpool off to the side. I also included many other romantic amenities offered by Sybaris.

The limo driver had a remote control for the garage and handed it to Lisa as he assisted her out of the limo. When she opened the garage door, a path of roses and candles wound their way to the inside door. Along that path, lay small gifts and small cards with love sayings. She picked up each card and read it as she made her way along the path, finally reaching the last letter at the door.

"My love you have finally arrived… When we entered this world, we came in it with nothing. All we had was the water that sustained us in the wombs of our mothers and the loving signals sent to us from their thoughts, prayers, and wishes…. When we leave this earth, we will leave with nothing… No earthly treasures or possessions… We will leave only the love we created in the hearts and lives of those we touched. Today you've gathered many earthly possessions. I want you to leave them all at the door. Yes, all of them. When you enter into this next life, I want it to be as when you entered this world—with nothing. On the other side of this door is water that sustained us, but most importantly, a love that will last for generations upon generations…"

Lisa, excited and bewildered, undressed completely and left all the things she bought that day, as well as those she had just picked up along her candle-lit, rose-petaled path. She left it all on the floor next to the door. Then, she entered. There inside the suite I stood in the warm water of the pool, smiling broadly, looking at my wife-to-be as she walked in. She was fine and oh so lovely.

As she entered the water and made her way to me, I could see the tears in her eyes just as she could see the tears in mine. I held her ring on my finger underwater. It was a stunning, thick white gold band with a suspension setting, holding a 1.2 carat diamond of beautiful color and clarity. The suspension setting allowed her to see the entire diamond from top to bottom.

Once she pressed into my arms, I hugged her and kissed her soft lips, now slightly wet from the water.

"I hope you had fun today. I know you may be a bit confused about this ending, but it is actually our beginning. I wanted it to be as earthly, pure, and loving as we can make it. I want us to make a difference in this world with the love we have to give to each other and everyone we touch. Whether we gain worldly possessions or live simply, I want us to always know that it is love that created us, love that will sustain us, and love that we will leave behind. I want to love you for the rest of my life. Will you love me and have me for the rest of yours?"

I put the ring on her finger, as the emotions on her face signified, "Yes, yes, yes!" We then expressed our love for each other throughout the rest of that most beautiful night.

My Greatest Fear

One day in August, 2002, during a typical, hour-long phone visit with Dad, he shared with me his desire to purchase the condo where he lived. He also shared his dilemma of being slightly short of funds for the down payment. The conversation moved to how I thought he mismanaged his money. Dad responded by telling me how he struggled, yet overcame great odds, and how he resented me counseling him on his budget.

As if the topic weren't troubling enough, Dad's reaction seemed off, and his voice sounded scratchy and slurry. I knew something appeared wrong—either he was using again or he'd started drinking, but I couldn't really tell which. Given my suspicions, I definitely didn't want to send him any money because I couldn't be sure it would be used properly. I certainly didn't want to contribute to a new round of whatever he had succumbed to again.

All of it caught me off guard, as I listened to his edginess that day. It especially saddened me because he had been clean for twelve years. Right away, I began contemplating a strategy. How would I intervene? Where in Indianapolis would he go to treatment? What would happen to all of his things? Tons of questions came at me faster than I could bear at that moment. They really required my full concentration.

I heard all I could take for that moment and told Dad I had some work to do. I ended our phone call as affectionately as always with my usual, "I love you, Dad."

He replied in the most sincere manner, "Mal, I love you more that you will ever know."

A couple weeks later, I spent a very productive day in the field with Michelle Taylor, one of my veteran sales representatives out of Youngstown, Ohio. Her territory represented more than a million dollars to me. I coached, and then we strategized and wrapped up what had turned out to be a very nice day—that is, up until the next moment. As I pulled out of the parking lot to begin my two-hour trek to my Cleveland home, I received an Indianapolis call. Normally, I don't take calls from unrecognizable numbers, but that time I did.

"Jemal, how are you doing? It's Henry." Henry, who owned the Bella Vita restaurant in Indianapolis, was one of my dad's best friends. Dad sang at his restaurant every week he was in town. It served as his maintenance job that paid the bills.

"Hey Henry, how are you? What's going on?" I inquired cautiously. An uneasy feeling arose within me, since Henry had never called me before. I thought perhaps the call pertained to my father's condo deal.

"It's Sam; he's dead." Henry certainly didn't beat around the bush. In fact, because he said my dad's name so quickly, it took several minutes to register his words in my brain.

"Sam who?" I asked.

"Sam, Jemal. Sam Gibson." Henry recited slowly.

"Sam Gibson, as in my dad? My Sam Gibson?" I knew my ears deceived me.

"Yes," came an even more solemn response.

"My dad! My dad, Henry? My dad!" I made a statement, asked a question, and made a statement again, all the while yelling and crying out the words, "My dad." I hoped Henry would correct me by saying someone different, but he didn't. He just kept saying, "Yes."

I managed to pull over on the side of the road as I cried hysterically. I asked him over and over again, "Henry, my dad? No, not my dad; not my dad, Sam Gibson."

Henry consoled, "I'm sorry, Jemal. I'm really sorry. He died yesterday, and he's been at the morgue. No one had your number to get in touch with you."

"You mean to tell me that my father died yesterday, and no one called me? His body's been lying in a cold, drab morgue for an entire day? Is that what you're telling me, Henry? Is that what you're telling me?" I could feel the pit of my stomach twist and turn as if someone was choking it. Every time I opened my mouth, it felt like I had to throw up.

"How did he die, Henry?"

"They say it was an overdose."

"No, no, no, no."

I hung up the phone in a total state of shock. All of my life, the nightmare of my father overdosing had haunted me. Yet still, how could this be? How could my father have gone out like that? Why hadn't I intervened a couple of weeks ago when I heard it in his voice? That was my last conversation with him. I played it over and over in my head—especially the part when he said "Mal, I love you more than you will ever know."

I sat paralyzed in my car for countless minutes, unable to move, think, or see clearly. A two-hour drive home still loomed ahead for me. Getting to my dad motivated me to turn the key in the ignition; otherwise, I probably would have sat there hours more in a daze. I knew I had to first get to Cleveland, in order to get to Indianapolis. Intense pain seared my head and chest as I drove home. I imagined a heart attack felt that way.

That man who gave me life—not just physical life, but an insight into my purpose for life—was gone. That man who led me out of the ghetto, like Moses led his people from enslavement, would no longer help me find my way through the situations of my life. That man who taught me the importance of, "I am that I am," like Jesus taught His disciples, could no longer share life's principles with me. That man who enlightened me to things about myself and the world, like Buddha in his time, represented everything to me and so much more.

Somewhere, in the midst of all of that pain and heartache, I felt anger.

I could not believe that not one of Dad's friends in Indianapolis had called me—not anyone! On top of that, my father lay in the morgue for over twenty-four hours, and no one from there called to tell me. Not one person. I started to drive. I don't recall how I made it back to Cleveland. I just remember crying the whole way, barely able to see.

The next few hours became a blur of phone calls; I was calling people, and people were calling me. I functioned in a shocked, zombie-like state while in the car and at home. I do remember crying more and more with every phone call I received, until I got tired of answering the phone altogether. I just wanted to get to my dad. Lisa drove us to Indianapolis that evening. Pint and Maeve were already there, having driven down from Chicago soon after I called them.

Once there and checked into the hotel, we all just sat, and held one another, rocked one another like babies, and cried together most of the night. Everyone remained in shock. My dad meant so much to so many people. He gave of himself in ways that really counted. He struggled financially most of his life, but he so generously offered his knowledge, wisdom, and guidance—all the things that really count in life when someone is in need. He always had time for anyone who came to him with a problem and needed someone to talk to. He shared his street knowledge, his academic learning from his graduate program in psychology, his deep spiritual insight, and his intense desire to communicate.

Those qualities, coupled with great looks and a soothing, melodious singing voice that females found irresistible, made him a loving companion to the many women who adored him and had graced his life. To the many men who crossed his path, he offered brotherly love, a meaningful conversation and good counsel whenever it was requested. He was truly loved by all who came to know him; therefore, his death at such a young age (just one month before his fifty-fifth birthday) made it an even bigger shock.

After crying most of that evening, I took a shower and started to sing all of the songs my dad used to sing: "Misty," "Shadow of Your Smile," "Autumn Leaves," and "My Funny Valentine". One after another, they kept coming out of me. I'm not sure how or why because I didn't even know all the words to many of them, but that night the words came to me as if I had been singing them all of my life. Singing all the songs that he loved to sing connected me to my Sam Gibson—my incredible dad—and comforted me for that moment. Strangely enough, the hotel water stayed hot the whole time, so I just kept singing. I stayed in the shower for at least an hour, not wanting to end that spiritual connection I was experiencing with my dad's voice. When I emerged from the bathroom, Pint and Maeve had planted themselves by the door, and their faces were soaked with tears.

"It sounded just like Sam in there," Pint said.

Maeve chimed in, "It was so beautiful. It was like he was here with us."

The next day, I anxiously drove to the coroner's office. By that time, my brain had processed my dad's death, but my heart held out hope that I would find him there alive. Pint, Maeve, Lisa, Iman, and I were at the door as soon as that office opened that morning. They checked ID's for Pint and me, and instructed us to have a seat in an inside room, while Lisa, Iman, and Maeve stayed outside in the lobby. I figured the workers would come get us once they brought Dad out, but instead, a small TV perched on a shelf in the room flashed on. There on the screen appeared my dad, lying absolutely still on a metal gurney with a sheet to his shoulders and no shirt. Pint broke down and cried while I sat in disbelief. My Dad—my hero, my liberator, my best friend—no longer existed in living flesh. I got up and walked out of that room, without a word to Pint.

Looking back, the appropriate action would have been to hug and comfort her, but numbness clouded my thinking. I knew how Dad was everything to her, too. She had hidden her relationship from her family for twenty-five years. She had heroically saved Dad from drug-related death a number of times, and had afterwards taken him to treatments and let him stay with her while he rebuilt his life. He often bragged about her being his angel on earth.

Not only did she love Dad, but she loved me like a son. I represented the child she never had. In fact, she has adopted our whole Gibson family. Most respectfully, she is Grandma Pint to my daughters, and most graciously she has become a second mother to me. Yes, my dad had many other love interests, but none so true to him and to our family as Pint. So, she sat there, riddled with agony over the loss of the only man she ever loved, and I did nothing to help soothe her pain. No empathy could pour forth from what was my very empty cup at that point in time.

As I walked out of that room, down the hall, and through the building's double doors, my breathing became more and more labored. Once outside, the sun smacked my face, sucking out what little breath remained in me. I wobbled down a wheelchair ramp, using the railing to keep from collapsing. Barely able to see through my tears, I ambled about briefly in a small alley next to the parking lot before giving in to the pressure and falling to the ground screaming, "No! No! No! No! No! No!"

Lisa rushed to me, knelt to the ground, and held me as my arms stretched out toward the sky. I reached for that part of me that was my father, as he left my soul in flight. I couldn't catch him or fly along, so my hands remained empty, and my eyes remained closed. As a child, I had always stated that if my dad ever left this earth, I wanted to leave with him. But he was gone, and I felt it more intensely than I ever could have imagined. While I lay there lamenting loudly, I heard people coming up asking Lisa if we needed a paramedic, or if I was a diabetic or having a seizure or something.

It seemed as though I laid there for at least an hour with a crushing, suffocating sensation upon my chest. I remained in a conscious, yet unconscious, mental state. I knew it looked bad, and it may have even embarrassed Lisa, but she stayed with me, holding me tightly, rocking me like the abandoned baby I was in my mind in those awful moments. A thousand thoughts, a thousand memories, a thousand tears flooded me as I lay in the worst and most incapacitated state I had ever been in.

Pint initially stayed inside, grieving alone. Maeve walked around outside with Iman, entertaining her, carrying her around, and pointing out birds and squirrels to keep her distracted. She kept her away from me and Lisa to avoid having my little girl see her father collapsed in an alley, bereft and so despondent. When I finally came to, we got up from the ground and walked to where the ladies and Iman sat on a curb by the car waiting for us. I had totally forgotten they were even there. Upon reaching them, we all hugged, cried, and thought once more about the man who had changed all of our lives.

From there we drove to Dad's condo. Of course, once I walked in, smelled his scent, felt his presence, and saw his things, I started crying all over again. Each time I cried I felt like it was the first time; it was never-ending. The pressure was so intense, so painful, and so draining. I walked into his closet and hugged his clothes, as if I were hugging his strong body. I lay on his bed and apparently wailed loudly for quite some time, "Not my dad! Not my dad! Not my dad!" over and over until, totally exhausted, I fell asleep. I did not fully remember doing this, but found out later that it caused everyone in the house at the time to grieve for me and the pain I experienced, as well as mourn the loss of my father.

I woke up, still groggy and in disbelief, but faced with the daunting task of finding a funeral home. We located the Yellow Pages and called several funeral homes until we found one willing to pick my dad up right away that day. That relieved me; I didn't want my father left in a strange building in a freezer with a lot of other dead people around him.

Detective Jones had called me several times. I called him back, prepared to hear exactly what happened to my dad. While standing outside, waiting for the detective to show up, one of my dad's next door neighbors came up to me and gave me a hug. He proceeded to tell me that he talked to the police and told them he saw my dad's girlfriend leaving the house looking pretty shaken. He said he saw her leave around 3 P.M. on Wednesday, the day my dad died. Shortly thereafter, he said the paramedics arrived and brought Dad out on a gurney. He said he told the detective exactly what he saw.

When Detective Jones arrived, I asked for his account of how the events unfolded. He told me my dad's girlfriend called the paramedics around 4 P.M. when she arrived at Dad's house and found him dead in his bedroom. Of course, my antenna went up because that contradicted what the neighbor said. At that point, I asked the detective if he had spoken to my dad's neighbor, and he confirmed that he had.

"Well, my dad's neighbor saw the lady leaving out of his apartment at three o'clock, and you are saying that the lady said she came to the apartment at four o'clock and found him dead; that doesn't make sense."

"I'm just telling you what she told me," the detective countered.

He continued reading his notes which indicated that when the paramedics arrived, they found my father dead with a string wrapped around his arm and that there were drugs and drug paraphernalia lying around him. As he continued to talk, tears streamed down my face. I just couldn't believe we were talking about my father. How could he go out like this? Something didn't seem right, but I couldn't stand to hear any more at that point. I told the detective I would be in touch with him later.

As I started going through some of my dad's things in his house, I came across some CD's. They appeared to be practice CD's with over 12 songs in progress on them. I put one into the CD player, and my dad's smooth, mellow voice came softly seeping through the speakers. The beautiful sounds caused everyone in the house to freeze in their tracks. No one there had ever heard any of those songs, and everyone cried as they listened to what would have been the last recorded music from Sam Gibson. All of the songs were ballads, and they all seemed to strike a chord for the moment we were each living through. He sang about loving someone, missing someone, and wondering why someone had gone.

I couldn't help but apply what I heard in the songs to Dad, himself. My greatest fear in life was losing him and it had happened all too soon. I sat there loving him, missing him, and wondering how he could succumb to drugs and leave me like this.

Just One More Time. . .

The funeral home finally called to inform us they had my dad at their location. While still conversing on the phone, I quickly headed to my car. I couldn't wait to have a *real* visit with him, not an impersonal one on closed-circuit TV. I'm sure the coroner's office had its reason for doing it that way, but it certainly felt like a bad way to treat a loved one of the deceased. When I got to the funeral home, they escorted me to the room and there my father lay. I touched his face, his cheeks, his hair. He still seemed so soft and slightly warm which shocked me, considering he had been in a cold morgue. I couldn't stop touching him.

The family members and friends who joined me there respected my privacy with my dad and allowed me as much time alone with him as I needed. I stood there with my head on his chest and tears rolling down my cheeks. I kept thinking, "No, not my dad, not this way." After awhile, I figured I should let others come up, but I couldn't tear myself away. He was my dad, and I, his #1 son; I decided everyone would have to understand me being a little selfish. I hoped they did. So I leaned on him, hugging and kissing him a little longer. It reminded me of my visiting him when I was a child. When the time came to leave him once again, I would hug his neck so tightly, hoping he would not let me go, hoping against hope that he would keep me with him, and I would stay with him forever. As he held me, I would kiss him on his neck as tears rolled down my face. I always hated that moment; that moment always frightened me. Without me saying a word, he would always stroke my head ever so gently and say, "I love you too, son."

I always thought it was strange, yet magical, that Dad would know that I was saying "I love you" in my mind, and that he would be respond with, "I love you too, son," as though he had actually heard me say it aloud. So, there in the funeral home, with my head on his chest, I said in my mind only, "I love you," over and over again, kissing his neck and waiting for him to respond. I wanted God to give my dad one tiny gust of air, a few more seconds of life for him to respond to me just one more time as he always had. But the breath for those words never came.

Finally, I stepped aside and the others all took turns spending some moments with Dad. I had to start thinking about what I would do for his arrangements. He had requested no funeral—just a memorial service celebrating his life. During that service, he said he wanted *Nature Boy* to play repeatedly. He also wanted to be cremated. As a matter of fact, he never wanted anyone to view his body, but I knew I couldn't deprive at least the people who were closest to him the opportunity to say goodbye.

After we finished viewing the body, I set visitation for the next day. I would only invite his siblings, a few extremely close friends, my mother, sister, and Lisa. I decided that I didn't want him to be embalmed. I wanted him to be soft and smooth with a look as if he was just asleep. He still had a hospital sheet over him. I bought a new comforter to place over him, so it looked like he simply lay in bed; this felt appropriate, since it had always been one of his favorite places to be.

Early the next morning, my aunts and uncles arrived from Chicago. As I went to the funeral home alone to drop the comforter off, I stole some more time with him. I sat and talked with him as if we were sitting in the living room of our bachelor pad. He responded in my head, and it seemed real in those moments. I had seen a lot of "afterlife" shows and heard other people say they were able to communicate with their loved ones after death, but I had always remained skeptical—until now. Were his responses just me answering as if I were him? Or, did he really hear me? Who knows?

I went back to Dad's condo to get everyone. As I walked through the door, I sensed such sorrow lingering in the air. I knew the moments to come—seeing him—would prove extremely tough for his sisters and brother. After all, as the baby of the family, it didn't seem right for Dad to be the first of the five siblings to go.

My dad's mother, Evangeline, was a single mother of five and had worked several jobs to maintain the household. That kept her away from home for long hours, forcing my Aunt Freddie, the second oldest, to take on a motherly role toward my dad. Dad, in turn, responded to her as a son, so they formed a tight-knit bond from their early years. The oldest sibling, Auntie Aida, a sophisticated fashion model, operated her own modeling school. Even at a young age, she displayed a business-like, no-nonsense approach to life. She and Dad were very close as well because he so admired her strength and perseverance. Then there was Aunt Arlene. She and Dad were extremely close, not just in age, but also in their shared passion for singing. As kids, they sang duets on their makeshift stage, always entertaining family and friends.

Uncle Charles, my dad's only brother, suffered drug addictions of his own, making for a very strained relationship between the two of them. The story that Dad often referred to, and the one that tainted their relationship, recalled the time he and Uncle Charles sold drugs from Mafia suppliers. At one point, Uncle Charles ran off with the dope, leaving Dad as the target of the Mafia's death threats. They demanded their money or his life.

Fortunately, they liked Dad, and he sang in one of their night clubs, so they granted him extra time to come up with the money. He paid them every dime, too. For years thereafter, he did not see or speak to Uncle Charles. Even when they made up years later, the emotional scars Dad wore made it seem like it had happened the day before. No doubt, he loved his brother; he just found it hard to forgive and ever trust him again.

All of my aunts and uncles possessed a gift for entertainment. They all sang, played the piano, or did something that called for the use of a stage. How unfortunate that all—except Auntie Aida—battled addictions and suffered extreme setbacks at various points in their lives. For Aunt Freddie and Arlene, it was alcohol; Uncle Charles and Dad wrestled with drugs. Although these problems may have thwarted them from reaching their full potential, today they all are happy and addiction-free.

Dad would have loved the sight of all his siblings together. They gathered for a common purpose, based on a deeply shared love for their brother. With each period of success Dad encountered throughout his music career, he had shared with all of them either through money, recognizing them while on stage, or just plain ol' doo-whopping at family get-togethers. They all remembered that and wanted to celebrate him for it.

As we prepared to go to the funeral home, I asked everyone to gather around and listen.

"I want to thank each of you for coming. As you know, it was against Dad's wishes to have a viewing, but I didn't want to deprive you of your opportunity to say goodbye since there will be no formal funeral."

I kept my remarks brief, knowing I would not have been able to hold my composure much longer. They all tearfully thanked me for that opportunity. It turned out to be such an extremely emotional visit, but everyone really appreciated the sense of closure it offered us all.

Later that evening, I threw a "Celebration of Life" ceremony in Indianapolis at the Bella Vita with Dad's band providing the entertainment. Lots of his friends in attendance were granted microphone time to say a few words about what Dad had meant to them. It was beautiful, something he would've loved to have heard. The microphone came to me for the last word.

"I want to thank you all for loving my father. As most of you know, he gave his heart and soul to people and his music. Hopefully his voice and his love will remain forever in your hearts."

That was about all I could muster up. After my final comments, Tony, one of my Dad's best friends, pulled me to the side to speak privately about what had transpired over the past few weeks. As a millionaire who loved my dad, I believe Tony really "pulled" for him to succeed in life, as well. They went to retreats together and Dad always performed at Tony's Christmas parties at his mansion, thereby gaining extra exposure for additional gigs.

"Jemal, your dad had started doing a gig in Kokomo, Indiana," Tony began. "While up there, he met this stripper named Cher, and they started dating. I went up there to see him perform one time, Jemal, and I found him stoned out of his mind. His performance was horrible, and he ended up falling off the stage. I drove him home that night because he was in to no shape to drive."

Tony continued with his explanation, "I told him, 'Sam you need to get your life together and stop doing that sh*t! I'm going to call Jemal.' He begged me not to. He said, 'I will get it together; just don't call my boy.' That was the last time I saw him."

Listening to Tony's story brought me to tears. It reminded me of the old Billie Holiday movie *Lady Sings the Blues*. I couldn't imagine my dad up on stage slurring and ultimately passing out. He had certainly fallen off the deep end. Suddenly, I got angry that Tony never called me, in spite of my dad's request.

While I never said it aloud, I thought to myself "All you said to him was 'get your life together' and that's it? That's the extent of the help and advice you offered my dad? And, you didn't even bother to call me? What in the hell is going on?"

My mind started racing. What *was* going on? My dad's other longtime girlfriend, Nina, knew about this. Tony knew. Henry knew. Everyone knew, yet no one intervened. No one called me. They just let my dad kill himself. While I knew I couldn't project the blame of what happened to my dad onto them, I felt extremely disappointed and defeated.

Tony then said, "Hey, I'd like to have you and your family over to the house tomorrow afternoon before you leave to have a little memorial for your dad. I'll invite a lot of our friends who are not here, get some food, and play his music. By the way, I want to help you with his CD. I heard he had some music that was left at the studio. I've got a great idea for the title and the artwork. It will be great."

I'm sure Tony had great intentions, but somehow I was not feeling it at that moment. Yet, out of respect for him as my dad's good friend, I agreed to attend his memorial the next day.

The next morning, I talked with Detective Jones again, hoping to revisit our previous discussion about what the neighbor saw and the discrepancy in the story Cher gave him. "Sir, I have some concerns about the story from Cher. Can you please talk to her again to see if she re-tells her story the same way?"

The detective answered, "I tried to call her and apparently she has gotten a lawyer, so I won't be able to talk to her anymore without going through the lawyer."

I thought to myself, "Why did she get a lawyer? If she was not there, as she said, what is she concerned about?"

The detective broke my train of thought, "I talked with Tony earlier today, and he told me what had transpired over the past couple of weeks. Additionally, we reviewed records and determined the police were called to your dad's house last week. It appears he was running in the grass park next to his building; he was naked and screaming. This hospital report shows he had major cuts on his feet from glass. It appears he busted out of the shower, believing he was being attacked by bees, and he ran out of the house with no clothes on. So, it seems that it's an open and shut case."

I remembered my dad talking about bees the size of golf balls in Viet Nam, and sometimes he had nightmares about them. I guess the drugs intensified his feelings and awakened the long buried post-traumatic stress disorder he had suffered after Vietnam. Nevertheless, I became deeply saddened just visualizing my dad running naked in a field, scared out of his mind. It cemented for me the depth of his pain and the ugliness of his condition. Upon hearing all that, it didn't make any sense. And, for the case rendered shut, just like that? I told the officer I would call him later, as I needed to think about my next steps.

After the detective left, I immediately called my Uncle Larry who had been a Chicago police officer for thirty-plus years. "Uncle Larry, what charges can be brought against someone who's present when someone else has an overdose?"

I thought surely they could be charged with something.

Uncle Larry informatively responded, "Nothing could really happen to someone in that position."

That still just didn't sound right to me. Of course, as a non-legal professional, I couldn't debate the information fed to me, but for someone involved in an overdose to not be charged with something for leaving without getting help for the victim hardly seemed fair. Nonetheless, I trusted Uncle Larry's confirmation. Therefore, the girlfriend's presence didn't matter unless it was proven that she administered the drugs. How could I prove that?

Later that afternoon, we arrived at Tony's huge house on many acres, where lots of people had already congregated. Dad and I loved going to Tony's house in the summer where we'd play volleyball on his sand court and then jump in his pool to cool off. I often used his house as a part of my visualization for the type of house I wanted to own one day.

As soon as I walked to the back of the house, Tony came up and gave me a big hug. Without a doubt, Tony had loved and respected my dad. I knew his sentiments were pure. He introduced me to several people I didn't know. One of them was Ray, the guy who tried to get the real estate deal through for my dad. Ray was at Dad's house when he and I had one of our final conversations. My gut told me Ray probably used drugs, too. Dad appeared stoned that time when we spoke. Being there with him, I imagine Ray must have been stoned, too. Pure speculation on my part, but I trusted my instincts.

Then Tony pointed out Cher, my dad's girlfriend, the stripper. She walked over and held her hand out. "I'm so sorry to hear about what happened to your dad. I really loved him."

At that moment, something felt absolutely wrong! I sensed her lying; her sorry sentences registered with me as disingenuous, to say the least. Furthermore, what right did she have being there?

"Get out of my face," I said to her, ignoring her still-extended hand.

I thanked Tony for putting the memorial together, gathered my family, and left. I never spoke to anyone at that party again. I never called that detective again, either. In fact, I stopped trying to figure out what happened altogether. I chalked it all up to my dad using drugs. Had he not been using, he would not be dead. I do not believe that "ignorance is bliss," but sometimes it might be 'better' than knowing a painful truth.

The challenge of accepting his death was wearing heavily on me already; I certainly didn't want my emotions tied to the "how's" and "why's" of his passing. The real truth that remains is that he's not gone from me. He is, and always will be, as close to me as my next breath.

Butterfly

The day came for Dad to be cremated. A co-worker of mine, who owned a crematory in Indianapolis, graciously offered their services. I went to the crematory by myself and asked the personnel if I could sit in the room and watch. Before they put my dad in, I had to have a few last moments. I rubbed his hair, stroked his cheeks, and kissed him like I did as a little boy. I laid a picture of us on his chest and closed the box. They came in a few moments later and started the heating process for the chamber.

The room started to get hot, and they asked me, "Are you sure you want to stay in here?"

I quietly replied, "Yes."

Once the chamber reached the cremation temperature, they opened the crematory door, and my dad's cardboard casket slowly disappeared. I sat on the floor with my arms folded around my legs and my lips pressed against my arms. The tears flowed freely down my cheeks, onto my arms and onto my pants, as I watched the man who meant everything in the world to me go to ashes. I sat there for an hour daydreaming about the times we spent together eating White Castle® cheeseburgers and Hostess Ding Dongs®; I saw us doing push-ups, contemplating life's principles, learning words on 3x5 index cards, and going on double-dates. I started to think about how I would soon join him, and a part of me felt it really would be sooner rather than later.

I searched for some sort of consolation to help ease the excruciating pain of my grief-stricken core. I found such solace in knowing the needles from years ago that had broken off in dad's biceps would finally be gone. Realizing that the crematory fire would melt away the injection tracks on his arms, hands, and feet, comforted me as well. I allowed my soul to catch a glimpse of a silver lining in the revelation that my dad was returning to his purest state of being; any drugs in his tissues were burned off in the process and purged from his body forever. Yes, Dad would finally be free of all his inner struggles, cleansed of the addictions that devastated and ultimately ended his life. That did console me. It was a small peace.

When I left the crematory, Dad remained in the chamber. I sat in the car and watched the smoke from the machine hover above the building for a moment and then drift calmly away into the sky. I remembered how Dad always dreamed of flying, and I thought, "Dad, now you get your chance to fly."

Suddenly, one of the most beautiful butterflies I had ever seen landed on my driver's side window. It stayed very still, as though it dared me to study its brilliance and flair—and study it, I did. Its wings sported black and blue markings of incredibly intricate patterns, while the edges were tapped with tiny splashes of white. Orange spots stylishly encircled the dazzling blue background. I allowed my mind with its imaginary force to consider, "This must be Dad coming to say goodbye."

There I sat—me and my Dad/butterfly—for what seemed like a very long time. As it finally took off, fluttering into the sky, my trance broke, and I decided to head back to the hotel to join the rest of my family. Just as I prepared to put the car in reverse, the butterfly came back, this time balancing on the antenna. I quickly put the car back in park and once again watched that butterfly for as long as it stayed. Once again, it took to the air, and I started to drive away again; I had almost made it out of the parking lot, when it came back again—the same exact one!

That third butterfly landing convinced me that it was, indeed, my dad! At that sign, I wept hard. "Be free, Dad; the world is yours to see. Nothing can hold you down now. I'll see you soon, real soon." He flew off once again and never came back.

The next morning, I picked up Dad's cremains before we all drove to Chicago for his second and final memorial service. I spared no expense on that service. Dad's friends, family, and acquaintances gathered at Chicago's DuSable Museum of African-American History, America's largest and oldest independent institution of its kind[14]. Dad graduated from DuSable High School, so the museum, under the same name, seemed appropriate. The museum has dedicated itself to preserving the history and culture of people of African descent and is filled with incredible sculptures and artwork; this made the decision to celebrate my dad at this location even easier. We catered delicious food in abundance. Pint and Maeve lovingly put together four large collages of pictures. They covered Dad throughout his life and included an entire panel of just Dad and me, a pictorial history of his singing engagements, and a representation of all the friends and family he had so affectionately shared his life with.

We played Dad's music for the couple of hundred attendees. We sold his CD's and t-shirts, and people shared stories and loving memories of time spent with him. That event exceeded everyone's expectation of a memorial. It moved my mother to say she wanted her memorial service to be just like it. I certainly didn't want to hear anything about her death at that moment; nonetheless, I duly noted her request.

Within a week and a half, having pulled together two memorials in two different cities had left me physically drained. All the planning, reminiscing, and crying left me emotionally depleted. On top of all that, Lisa and I were scheduled to be married in just three short weeks, with Dad slated as the best man. He had been my "best man" for my entire life, so I didn't know how I would deal with such a gaping vacancy that would feel so apparent on that special day of mine. Unfortunately, all of the unexpected circumstances, responsibilities, and emotional turmoil left me in no mood to even get married. I didn't want what should be one of the happiest and celebratory days of my life to be filled with condolences and hugs, due to the loss of my father.

I asked Lisa if she still wanted to go forward with the wedding. Once she told me, "Yes," I told her that I needed to go to the mountains for two weeks, which meant I'd be back just a few days before the wedding. I explained to her that if she could have the entire wedding worked out by then, it would be fine, and if she didn't, then we would simply postpone our nuptials.

I investigated some travel getaways and found a mountain range called "Worlds End," a part of the Endless Mountain region of the Alleghenies in Pennsylvania. I found the location's name very fitting because I certainly felt that my world had ended. I packed my Jeep with just a few food rations, pictures of my family, and my 9mm handgun. The beautiful drive relaxed me. My Jeep Wrangler could only muster up about sixty miles per hour through those winding Pennsylvania mountains because of the thirty-inch mudder tires, so the trip remained slow and easy.

The long trip gave me some time to contemplate life after death. Did spirits meet and know each other once they left earth? Was Dad hanging out with Kyk? Kyk, one of my favorite cousins, had died just four months prior to Dad. We weren't real cousins; he was one of Enner's six children. We met in Peoria and had known each other since we were six and seven-years-old. When I lived with Enner, during Mom's relapse treatment, Kyk and I shared everything. That included a bedroom, sometimes the same bed, our clothes, and sometimes even each other's underwear. We had a break-dancing crew, and we used to compete against others in the park or around the block on Douglas and Christiana Streets.

Unfortunately, Kyk died of AIDS, another dreaded illness wreaking havoc on the black community. While blacks only make up 12% of the population, we make up about 50% of those living with AIDS in the US.[15] My cousin, Michael, died of AIDS a few years prior, due to intravenous drug use. One might say that drugs and AIDS were both devastating my family. Nevertheless, most of Kyk's family, including his brothers and sisters, found out he had AIDS only a few months before he died; others didn't know the cause until after his death. For years, we were always told he suffered from tuberculosis or meningitis; there were all different reasons given why he remained so sickly and often stayed in the hospital. Kyk never wanted anyone to know his real ailment, so he made Enner and Wright promise not to reveal the truth.

It devastated me when I found out. Fortunately, I was able to spend some quality time with him during his hospice care before he died. I bought a couple of books to keep in his room for people to read to him each time they visited. He had lost his sight and could barely speak, so reading seemed to be a good use of time for his visitors, especially since most people didn't know what to say or do. I enjoyed reading to him, and he seemed to enjoy it as well. Words can soothe us.

One day, instead of reading, I reflected on all the time we spent together swimming, bike riding, break-dancing, and looking for pop bottles as kids. We used to call ourselves PBH's (pop bottle hustlers) because sometimes collecting them brought us our only little bit of spending money for candy. Pop bottles cashed in at five or ten cents, depending on the ones you found. We spent hours walking down alleys, looking in weeds, in brown paper bags, or around garbage cans. It may sound gross, but it was a lot of fun, and represented part of how we survived without being totally deprived as kids in our impoverished neighborhood. Memories flooded my mind, and I began to cry. The nurse came in to check on Kyk and saw me in the worst state, overcome with tears, slobber, and snot. She comforted me, said a prayer, and then left.

Most times, I did my best not to break down in front of Kyk, but that time, I couldn't help it. I leaned up toward his bed, held his hand and said, "I'm sorry."

He whispered back, "It will be OK."

Kyk died a few days later. I took it extremely hard, but for the most part, internalized it. I tried to be strong for Enner, Wright, and all the rest of Kyk's family. Dwight—my other play cousin and another young man raised by Enner—and I hugged Enner after the funeral and assured her that although we could never replace Kyk, she had two more sons to love, and that we loved her dearly. From that day on, Enner stopped calling me her nephew and began calling me "son."

The afternoon of Kyk's funeral, my face began tingling. Soon, I started drooling and slurring my speech. Thank goodness, I had the sense to go to the emergency room instead of ignoring it. A doctor later diagnosed me with Bell's Palsy, a virus that attacks the immune system when its resistance is low due to stress or other illnesses. It causes inflammation in the nerve that controls facial muscles. The doctor's exams and lab work didn't detect any other related issues, so he narrowed down the cause to stress. The emotional strain I endured during Kyk's illness leading up to his death took a greater toll on me than I ever realized.

As I drove through the mountains, I felt kind of jealous of Kyk because I was thinking that he got to spend time with my dad, and that they could zip all over the universe just having a ball together. I finally reached Worlds End, and I immediately could see why they called it that. The mountains created a spectacular view. Their ranges went on as far as the eye could see. With nothing beyond the mountains, one could truly be or feel at the end of the world.

I requested a rustic cabin with literally no amenities. For days, I cried, read, prayed, and slept. Finally one day, I put my gun in my pocket, my rucksack over my shoulders, and decided to go for a walk. My mind told me this would be the day, the day I would reunite with my father.

As I walked, I chanced upon a small creek with a few benches backed up to it. In front of the benches stood a podium, giving it the impression of a small outdoor chapel. I decided to take a seat on the bench in that outdoor chapel and listen. Except for nature's sounds, silence dwelled there. I listened to the silence. I focused on the silence beyond the water running from the stream and the muffled sounds of birds chirping. Both the beauty and serenity hypnotized me for hours as I sat there. Little by little, I felt the tension in my face loosen; my teeth unclenched; my brow unfolded, and I smiled—something I hadn't done for quite some time.

Just as I started to completely relax, I heard my father's voice clearly say, "Mal, now is not your time. You have more life to live, more to give, more to do. The world is yours, and you must find a way to live without my physical presence, but know I am always with you."

I cried, but finally the tears were more joyous than painful. I felt my dad had released me from that horrible decision I had planned to carry out. In my plans, I thought about my mother and my sister. I had rationalized that my mother had lived a full life and my sister still had my brother and mother to look after her. I also thought about my soon-to-be bride. I knew she would miss me and be extremely sad, but probably not as sad as me without my dad. Iman was the only person who truly made me struggle with my plan of ending my life. Thinking of her made me think about the love I had for my dad and how wonderful it felt to have him in my life. I thought about how he shaped and molded me to become the man that I am and that I would, in turn, deprive my own child of experiencing that same love if I took myself away from her.

Yet, I still rationalized some more that although it wasn't right to do that to Iman, at only three-years-old, she would soon forget about me. On the other hand, I had over thirty years of fond memories of my dad that I would never forget. I figured I had possibly fifty or sixty more years of life to suffer without him, and I simply couldn't envision living through that.

The pain of longing for more of my dad's love overwhelmed me. I had missed so much with him during my childhood; therefore, I had always yearned for more from him—more time, more love, more encouragement, more support... more everything. Finally, through our time spent together as adult men, the void had started to be filled in with all the fun we had and all the sharing we did. We became two best friends—an inseparable father and son team. Suddenly, the team ceased to exist. How could I continue? I again heard Dad's voice saying, "Mal, it's not your time."

I sat there for a couple more hours, praying and meditating on peace, strength, and how to live without my dad. I pondered how to find the same joy in my daughter that Dad had found in me. I knew I wanted to create a relationship with her that made her feel like I supported and completed her life, the same way my dad completed and made mine whole. I owed her that, and I wanted to experience that as a father, too, just as my dad had experienced it with me.

Finally, it started getting late. I took a few pictures of the surrounding area and even wrote a sign that said, "I'm going home," and taped it to the Worlds End sign. I then took a picture of that sign. I wanted a reminder of how close I came to the end of *my* world. The next day, I left.

When I returned home, Lisa had everything worked out for the wedding, and it turned out beautifully. Since Dad was supposed to be the best man, we put a flower on a pedestal in his place because no one could ever fill his shoes or the gap that his absence created.

A lot of my family and many friends showed up, and I appreciated them all. Instead of a day filled with condolences, everyone there really helped to brighten my moments and the entire day. Lisa and I danced our first dance as a married couple to the song Dad and I recorded just a few months earlier, "The Very Thought of You," by Nat King Cole. As we danced, I remembered Dad and me together in the studio. Needless to say, that first time recording a song found me quite nervous. Dad stood behind me, and every time my part came up, he had to tap me on the shoulder; then, I would jump in. I didn't quite have his impeccable musical timing. I could hold a note but didn't really think I had a career in music. We laughed and sang in the studio until the wee hours that morning. Singing together like that felt like a dream come true for both of us.

Since Dad really struggled financially throughout his artistic career, he didn't want me to ever do the same; therefore, he always jokingly told me that I could sing, but only *after* I made my millions. I knew he had always wanted to do a father and son duet, but he waited for my voice to mature. Now, I was dancing to our song at my wedding with my new bride in my arms. It was the first time anyone had heard Dad and me together, and though he wasn't physically there to see everyone's reaction, his voice singing that song made him present for all to hear. I really couldn't tell if everyone's tears were tears of joy or tears of sadness; I suspected they presented a nostalgic mix of both. At that point, I suppose it didn't really matter. We were all listening and remembering, and then, just at the right moment, I felt Dad tap me on the shoulder as my part in the song came up. I closed my eyes, tenderly held my wife, and sang our song.

Wolf

I don't know what happened, but my brother's life clearly spiraled downward. After observing strange behavior and a few things missing from my house, I searched his room and found a spoon under the bed that he was using to cook his drugs. I changed all the locks to the house, wrote him a letter stating the he needed help and that he couldn't stay with me anymore because he was endangering my family. I taped the spoon to the letter and left it at the back door entrance where he usually came in. Putting my brother out really tore me apart. During the first few days following that letter, we had some tough conversations and made some hateful statements that I know we both regretted.

A week later, my phone rang, and out of the clear blue I became the recipient of Ant's distress call. No niceties such as, "Hi. How are you?" Instead just, "I need you to come get me."

My instincts told me what I needed to know, but I asked anyway, "From where, Ant?"

"Jail."

"Why are you in jail?"

"Grand theft auto."

"What? What do you mean? You stole a car, Ant?" I expected drug charges, never that.

"No, little bruh, let me tell you what happened." He explained how he let someone borrow his employee-authorized vehicle from the Cleveland auto dealership where he worked, and the person never returned the car. I wanted to ask him so many questions, but our phone call on a prison public phone might have been recorded.

"Ant, I don't have the money to come get you; I just gave you $800 a couple of weeks ago. So, you are going to have to wait."

"Well, can you click over and call my girl, Cynthia?"

"What's the number, bruh?" I clicked over and called her.

"Baby it's me, Anthony. Awe baby I miss you."

"I miss you too, baby," she replied in a half-whiney voice, displaying a lot of sympathy for him.

The way they carried on, you would have thought he had been in jail for a couple of years. I sighed heavily at the whole ordeal and put the phone down until that fast busy signal came on. I was so disappointed and, quite frankly, speechless. I didn't even tell Lisa. I didn't even want to think about it.

The following day, Anthony called me and asked me to make another call for him. To Cynthia again, I thought as I pressed the numbers on the keypad, but this time a guy answered the phone.

"What!" The salutation sounded very gruff and agitated before even knowing what the caller wanted.

"Wolf, what's up man? It's Anthony," replied Ant.

"What you want?" he snapped back.

"Hey man, they got me locked up, and they need the car back. They think it's stolen."

"What the f**k you talkin' 'bout?" Wolf shouted. "Where you callin' me from?"

Ant softly replied, "Jail."

"Jail! Don't be callin' me from no f**kin' jail, talkin' 'bout a f**kin' car! I don't know what the hell you talkin' bout!" Click!

Wolf hung up, leaving Ant and me on the line.

"Ant, who the hell was that?"

"Wolf. I'll explain it later. Call Cynthia for me."

I dialed the number he gave me and the same crap went on, 'Hey baby. Hey baby. I miss you. I miss you too. Blah, blah, blah.' I angrily put the phone down and left it there until the busy signal. It appeared my brother had one of his "usuals" going on, and I was about to get caught up in it.

Ant asked me to go to his court hearing, since they said it looked favorable when family members supported you there. So, I went.

"All rise," the bailiff commanded. The judge walked in and shortly thereafter, my brother and several other guys filed in and stood facing the judge. Once the judge sat down, the bailiff issued another command, "Take your seats."

As I looked at my brother, it took everything in me not to cry. I hadn't seen him in a couple of weeks, and he had been in jail for about one of those weeks. He looked horrible and old! His unshaven face and the hair that grew long only on the sides of his head added almost twenty years to his actual age of thirty-seven. He had lost a lot of weight and had dark blotches all over his face.

I can't remember all the details of his case, but the judge let him out on one condition—that he return the car in a certain period of time. I waited in the lobby of the courthouse for him. Once in the car, we rode in silence. I stared at him. I couldn't help but stare; he looked really bad.

Finally I broke the silence, "What's the deal with the car?"

Ant shared the full story, which only took several seconds, "I let Wolf use the car in exchange for some drugs. I got caught up getting his money back, so Wolf never gave me the car back."

I went back to staring at him. My brother used to be a handsome man, dark-complexioned, with a nicely trimmed beard. He reminded me somewhat of the late R&B singer, Gerald LeVert. Upon leaving jail, though, Ant looked more like "Gator," the drug addict character from the Spike Lee movie, "Jungle Fever." When we got to my house, Ant walked into the kitchen where Lisa stood at the counter. As she turned toward him, I could see the shock on her face; she was not prepared for what she observed. Tears welled up in her eyes. That assured me it wasn't just my critical assessment of him; he really did look bad.

Ant headed right to the fridge, grabbed a Corona beer, opened it, and drank it straight down with the refrigerator still open. That served as confirmation to me that he was continuing a hundred miles per hour down the wrong path, perhaps not even cognizant that there *was* another path for him to take. I don't know which felt worse to me, knowing he was unaware of a better way, or knowing that there was nothing I could do to make him choose that better way.

"Jemal, I need you to take me to see Wolf. I gotta get the car." That request instantly broke my train of thought, and I sensed trouble brewing. After hearing Wolf on the phone, I knew I never wanted to meet that man in person. Ever! But I also heard the judge say that the only way Ant would stay out of jail would be to return that car.

He had to go, so I had to take him. My Ranger instincts kicked in, and off I went planning for any possible scenario. I figured I would drive the Jeep Wrangler with the top off, so that I could have a good visual of our surroundings. I would take a couple of my guns and pray that I didn't have to use any of them.

I quickly changed my clothes, packed my guns, and off we went. As we drove, I started to think, "What in the hell am I doing? I'm a manager at a major Fortune 100 company, responsible for tens of millions of dollars. Why am I driving with my brother, a criminal, to see another criminal, with the possibility that something criminal could happen? I could go to jail for carrying these weapons, or worse still, get injured or lose my life! I'm prepared to kill someone, and for what? What am I thinking? I am about to throw my life down the drain." Then, I started to rationalize in the other direction.

"This is my only brother. What if something happened to him? I would never forgive myself, knowing I didn't do everything possible to help him out."

I *am* my brother's keeper. I kept remembering what Ant's father, Donald, always told me, "You better take care of your brother."

Then, my mind raced back to, "This is crazy. Please, God, don't let anything happen. I've got a wife who loves me, a beautiful daughter who needs me, and so much to give in life. Please, God, don't let anything happen to me or my brother." At that point, I clearly sensed I had made a poor decision in getting involved in the whole situation. I knew that only God, fate, or whatever you want to call it, could get me out of it; I knew I, alone, could not.

We arrived at Wolf's house. Ant hopped out of the Jeep while I positioned myself in a strategic place in the Jeep where I could see the house but could take cover, if needed. Before my brother could get close to the steps, the front door of the house burst open, and out came one of the scariest looking dudes I had ever seen in my life. Damn! I instantly deduced why they called him Wolf. He actually looked like one. He had a prominent Eddie Munster "widow's peak" and everything, with the rest of his hair styled in a small afro. He lunged off the porch straight at Ant. I thought, "Oh crap, it's about to go down." He landed right in my brother's face.

He seemed to tower over my brother, muscles bulging through his shirt, his neck bigger than my thigh, and a vein bulging down the center of his head. When he started talking, it sounded like he howled. After hearing that, I definitely knew why they called him Wolf. He started cursing at my Ant. "Motherf**ker, why you call my house with that "motherf**king bullsh*t. I oughta beat your a**."

Ant tried to get a single word in, but Wolf kept going on. Then a girl came out and walked past them to a car parked across the street, but she didn't get in. I thought she must be "packing" and possibly trying to position herself with a good shot at me.

"Please God, don't let this sh*t go down. Don't let us leave this world like this."

I grabbed my 9 mm, and I pushed the safety lever off. I looked back over at my brother and Wolf. Ant finally got in a few words. I heard him say, "I never told them who had it, but I've got to turn it in or I'm going to jail for grand theft auto. All you gotta do is leave the car somewhere and I'll call it in. Once they get it, I'm good. And, I won't say nothin'." You could still see the vein bulging out of Wolf's head. Every exhaling breath he took sounded like a growl. Ant said Wolf had just gotten out of jail for serving a life sentence for murder and drugs. I am not sure if that was true but there was no doubt in my mind that this animal didn't care about anyone's life.

My brother was slick. I knew if he got a word in, he could turn that whole thing around. It's no wonder he'd won so many sales awards, regardless of where he worked or what he sold. When he talked, people liked him. I looked back over at the girl, who still manned her station. I realized I hadn't put myself in the best position. I hadn't expected someone to come out and cover me. I looked back over at my brother, and he started backing away from Wolf who glared but didn't howl anymore. I expelled a huge sigh of relief, thinking he must have it worked out. Ant got to the Jeep, hopped in, and we sped off!

"Thank you, God! Thank you, God!"

I just kept repeating it silently to myself. My brother leaned back in his seat, and it appeared he must have been saying the same thing. He still looked very scared, and both of us kept looking behind us. I was happy nothing happened to my brother and ecstatic that I didn't throw my life away over something that didn't even involve me. That situation justified my belief that although I could leave the ghetto, the ghetto just wouldn't quite leave me. Someone or something would always pull me back in.

Learning Curve Goes Vertical

I had been performing well as the Cleveland District Sales Manager for Pilon. At that time, the way to become a Regional Sales Manager was either as a Director of Area Operations or a Director of Management Development. The Director of Area Operations worked closely with the Vice President, going to meetings with or for them and drafting their communication and presentations. It was like being a glorified assistant. There were limitations with that opportunity in that you did not get to learn real leadership skills to help you become a better leader.

On the flip side, the Director of Management Development position gave you tremendous opportunity to develop as a leader. You were certified to teach all of the leadership models and tools to include Situational Leadership, DiSC, Emotional Intelligence, Civil Treatment, and many more. The only problem with this position was that you had to network a little harder with the vice presidents because you were not directly 'in the circle' for a regional slot. Nevertheless, both roads could lead to a Regional Sales Manager job, one of the most coveted jobs in the industry.

Regional Sales Managers generally ran a $1 billion operation with approximately 150 employees. They also had medical, marketing, human resource, and legal teams supporting their operation. Most of the Regional Managers retired in this position, and it took a long time to get there. With salary, bonus, and stock options, you could easily make about $300,000 or more a year. Most retired as multi-millionaires. Needless to say, with my competitive nature of always striving to be the best, I wanted the job. But, I was ten to twenty years younger than most managers in that job, and there were very few African-Americans accepted in that role. So, I did a week-long internship in both positions.

My first week was spent at Pilon's New York headquarters in Manhattan, New York. During the week, I shadowed Joann Yeksigian, Director of Operations. She was extremely smart and appeared to be a good fit for Vice President, Tim George, because he appeared to be a very cerebral guy. When they started talking about business models from graduate school and how they thought it applied to a situation we were going through, I felt a little out of my league. But that's what I admired about Tim. Even though he appreciated the value of thinking from a more structured thinker with an MBA, he also valued the experimental, "out of the box thinker" who might be unfamiliar with graduate school systems and models, but who generally knew how to apply ideas in pragmatic, functionally effective ways.

The week came quickly to an end. I am not sure what valuable task Joann accomplished that week, as everything she did was for Tim or someone else. I am sure the exposure in certain meetings made a positive impact on her, but I struggled to find how she was being developed as a better Regional Manager.

The next week, I went to Management Development. That was at Arrowwood, Pilon's state-of-the-art training facility in White Plains, New York. Each room contained thousands of dollars worth of high-tech equipment including projectors, flat screen monitors, and a sound system rack with computer integration. It was truly a trainer's paradise. The cafeteria was like a dream. Just about anything you ever wanted to eat or drink was provided. Throughout the halls were food stations with candy bars, ice cream, chips, assorted drinks, and protein bars, and everything was free. It was a snacker's paradise, and I was a master snacker! Fortunately, during the week I was there, a training session for new District Managers was held.

Art Thurnauer was the Team Leader for the group. I sat in on his class, adding tips and advice along the way. He asked me to do a presentation on

"How to Conduct Effective POA Meetings." POA (Plan of Action) meetings were our quarterly meetings where we discussed state of the business, strategy, and product updates. We also practiced selling skills and recognized top performers. They gave me the standard deck they used for training groups. After reviewing the deck, I knew there was a lot more value I could add to help DM's have more productive and inspirational meetings.

I was known to be pretty hard, yet fun and fair. After being trained as a US Army Ranger, I certainly didn't like things that were soft, unchallenging or a "cake walk," but I realized in corporate America I would be crucified if I applied the same training intensity or philosophy, so I mixed purposeful intensity and fun together. I resembled the college professor you loved because they really challenged you without being a pain in the butt. That's what I strived for.

So, I added some of those intense, purposeful activities and ways to have fun, and I rewarded people for their participation. Additionally, I always found a way to add the principles of visualizing and believing by using love, controlling thoughts, and other positive boosters. Quite honestly, that was the most important part of the workshop to me. There was definitely content that needed to be disseminated and learned, but the value of understanding how to be successful, how to think, and how to believe could apply to anything during any session. So, as people were thinking about how they could apply the lesson to their work, many contemplated how they could apply it to their personal lives, as well. That kind of integrated thinking proved valuable in all areas of life, so I always made sure I gave them examples of each.

I often used something I learned as a visualization exercise at the Leadership Institute held by Bob Proctor and John Aserath in 1997. One of the speakers had us do a simple exercise that taught the value of visualizing. For over a decade, I used that exercise with most groups I trained or led. It then became common at Pilon because others started to replicate the exercise with their teams or groups. Needless to say, just that one simple exercise not only changed my life but also impacted those with whom I shared it. I sought out other exercises like that one.

Whether it was an exercise in movement or in thought, I wanted to connect some very important life principles into my workshops.

With that training group, I did the visualizing exercise at the end of my presentation. People were amazed at how it worked. Then I told them how important it was to visualize the POA and see it going exactly as planned; I stressed seeing it in color, seeing people laughing, learning, practicing, and understanding, as well as seeing the full atmosphere essential to the success of any meeting. I also told them how important it was to visualize situations in their personal lives. Seeing it, of course, is only the first step; then, you must have true belief in the vision. I am a believer that the subconscious does not know the difference between what is real and what isn't. So, whatever conscious thought we begin to program ourselves with is what our subconscious will start to act out or bring into realization.

At the end of the presentation, I received a standing ovation. I loved that type of instant gratification and immediate impact. It had been a long time since I had that feeling, not since my job as a new hire Training Manager, in fact. Even so, an ovation was unusual for that type of training. Art sat in the room observing and was very impressed. They had an opening in the department and that presentation served as my interview. I was hired a couple of weeks later. My learning curve went vertical in that assignment in terms of developing people to be better coaches and leaders by utilizing the models we subscribed to at Pilon.

I enjoyed training more on conceptual issues like leadership versus technical issues like product knowledge. It was not a stretch to add life principles to leadership trainings because leaders always looked for ways to connect with their people in order to get better performance and happier employees. Additionally, most leaders, at some point in their careers, are faced with challenges of leading an individual or a group. So, they were hungry for tools to help them deal with the myriad of challenges they faced each day.

In my training sessions, we often talked about seeing someone's "light bulb" turn on. The bulb always seemed to be much brighter with true leaders because their struggles usually affected them greatly, both personally and professionally.

Seeing others find solutions, strategies, and concepts on how to better lead people brought a tremendous amount of joy to me. That was one of those jobs where I never felt like it was a job. I loved it.

My colleagues and I would often work the week-long classes together. I tried not to compare myself to them because a successful class was a success for the team. However, in observing the feedback on all the workshops, there were higher scores for the sessions I led than for the sessions that my peers led. It was good for me to see that the value I delivered was indeed differentiated from everyone else's. It confirmed the effect I wanted my personal development and teaching to have on others.

At the start of my assignment, Pilon had just purchased Panacea, another company. That constituted a major purchase at approximately $70 billion. My department needed to train all of the acquired managers and regional managers on all of the leadership models and core coaching tools. That was my "baptism by fire" as they say. We brought on thousands of colleagues, so I had to get certified in all of our leadership workshops in a short time period. We trained groups by the hundreds all over the country. I remained on cloud nine, as people came up to me after every session I conducted and talked about how I had great articulation, excellent platform skills, and the ability to motivate others.

I soaked up every comment like it was a bonus check. Those were the type of checks my mind could re-cash over and over again for the rest of my life. They were the fuel that inspired me to continue to give my all. For instance, I can't tell you what I did with my cashed bonus check in 2003, but I can tell you almost every authentic compliment I've received. They say that most Americans care more about job satisfaction than money. I could truly attest to that during this time in my life.

Time flew by, and before I knew it, seven months had passed. I had trained hundreds and hundreds of colleagues. Colin Powell's concept of Performance Impact and Exposure (PIE) was starting to play itself out with me. My performance was terrific. The impact of my performance worked its way around, and they asked me to be on certain projects. I chose other projects I thought were great opportunities for me to learn and add value, as well.

I made an impact with a group of Pilon vice presidents who others thought of as the new school leaders; those on the cutting edge included Clint Lewis, Tom Griffin, and Bruce Birtwell. They challenged the old paradigm of experience over talent. Many of them were beneficiaries of the talent argument. As long as you demonstrated the aptitude to learn and had the talent to perform, it didn't matter how long you'd been on the job, how many years of experience you had, or how old you were. They were "out of the box" thinkers, and they created a team of leaders who had an "out of the box" approach to the business.

Fortunately, I had the opportunity to work with each of those vice presidents on key projects. I knew with each of those projects I would be evaluated, and that the evaluations would determine whether or not I would earn a spot on their team. Thankfully, their observations of my high quality work brought me positive exposure I otherwise would never have been afforded.

Help is on the Way

A few Regional Sales Manager positions became available at Pilon, but I didn't take true interest in any of them for several reasons. First, I felt I had a lot more to learn before advancing to that level; secondly, I believed many of my peers expected to be shoe-ins for some of those openings because of their length of time with the company, and I didn't want to hinder their chances. Lastly, I had wisely learned to select a job according to the boss versus picking a job based on the position only. Regardless of the industry, taking a position where you inherit a horrible boss could severely hinder your career, since that person could make or break the job for you.

One day, during a meeting with a colleague, I learned about an opening in Chicago. I tuned out the information fairly quickly, as Chicago had never been on my radar screen. I guess you could say I'd always been nervous about going back to my hometown. Since most of my family still lived in the "hood," I would no doubt be sucked back into the environment one way or another, if for no other reason than just visiting family. Plus, I kept having a bad dream that I would get robbed or killed while visiting or chilling on the old block, so I quickly dismissed any opportunities leading me home.

However, as my colleague spoke more about it, I learned the position reported to Clint Lewis. That turned my ear and got me totally tuned into the conversation. Clint Lewis, an African-American Vice President of Sales and an awesome leader, held the respect of many. As I have mentioned previously, when

I first met him and heard about his reputation, I knew that I would do anything to be on his team. It gave me a lot to think about. I knew some of my other colleagues would post for the position, and it would be a long-shot for me. Despite that, in my head, I started listing the pros and cons of moving back to Chicago.

My mother had been ill and seemed to be getting worse. I heard it in her voice every time we talked. I knew she stayed either intoxicated or high because she would slur through most of our conversation. I tried to get her to tell her job that she was having a problem and needed help. She agreed, but my cousin Valencia, talked her out of it. I got so angry at both of them, but what could I do from a thousand miles away? I began thinking that if I moved home, I could help my mother turn her health and addiction around. Looking back, I am fascinated about how matter-of-fact these things were to me. I wonder how many of my colleagues had to break from their work mentally to consider how they were going to get their parents off drugs.

Another pro to applying for the position came down to logistics. Most of the other positions after Regional Sales Manager were in New York. Therefore, if I didn't choose to go home to Chicago now, I would probably never get the opportunity to do so later. Of course, that move would allow me to spend time around all my family, not just my mother. I did at times feel a little guilty having missed so many events with them throughout the years. Those pros were pretty strong ones.

To be objective in my decision-making, I had to equally consider the cons of moving to Chicago, as well. Two big ones were definitely the cold weather and my old neighborhood. I didn't want to become a victim of the influences of my old "hood" any more than I wanted to deal with those sub-zero winters. Taking everything into account, I decided the pros outweighed the cons. I could manage the cold by limiting my time in it, and I would figure out ways to be careful when visiting my family. I put my name in the hat for the job and secured an interview.

I spent days preparing for the interview and thinking about all of my leadership experiences and successes. My "brag book" had grown as thick as a

Bible, and I only had ninety minutes to sell myself. So, I worked on focusing on just the key elements from those successes, those that were suited toward the interview. I had also prepared a very special sentimental surprise for the interview.

The day finally arrived. Several other candidates were scheduled on that day, as well. Unfortunately, my turn would be last. I remembered an interview I had years prior where I had been scheduled as the final appointment of a long day. I recalled that the interviewer kept drifting off to sleep during my interview. So, I made it a point to figure out ways to keep those interviewers awake and engaged, just in case the same thing happened. The interviewers were Clint Lewis and Paul Cartabiano, the out-going Regional Sales Manager. He'd been promoted to another position but was asked to help with the selection of his replacement.

My turn finally came. A couple of days prior, I had sent an email telling them that it would be difficult to cram over one hundred thousand hours of work and leadership experience into one hour or so, but that I would do my best. I received a positive response which led me to use that as the ice breaker. No sooner had I finished my icebreaker, than Clint jumped right in and said, "Let's talk about your leadership experience. Why do you think you are a great leader?"

Fortunately, as a Director of Management Development, I had developed my leadership philosophy by teaching a class called "Teachable Point of View." We referenced a book called *The Leadership Engine* by Noel Tiche to help frame the workshop, so I prepared myself for a question like that. My leadership philosophy was as easy as E.I.E.I.O. Yes, that simple. It may sound like the chorus to a children's song, but it stood for Emotionally Intelligent, Execution, Integrity, and Optimism. I expected those four principles from others, and others could count on me to deliver them as well.

After I explained each of them, Clint said, "Now, give me a couple of examples of how you exude or exemplify each of these qualities."

That's how the interview started, and it continued in that vein non-stop for almost two hours. I felt really good about how things were flowing. As we prepared to close, they asked if I had any final comments. I closed the interview with the story of how I got to FAMU:

"I left Chicago, basically on a one-way trip with $40 in my pocket and with many hopes and dreams in mind. During that twenty-plus hour trip, I reflected on all that transpired with my life and, more importantly, all that was to come. Now, you can help me fulfill a dream. By my family's standards and those of most Americans, I have made it, earning approximately $170k a year. Most of my family lived on welfare, bringing in maybe $5,000 a year. So, I guess in their eyes, I have definitely made it. I believe in visualization, so I have already visualized myself going back home. I have bought my one-way bus ticket. That one-way journey to Chicago will give me the opportunity to reflect on all that has transpired with my life and, most importantly, all that I would be able to do for my family now that the 'village son' is returning home."

I slid them an actual bus ticket I had purchased before the interview. "Trust that your business will be in good hands, and now, I trust you to help to fulfill a dream. Will you hire me?"

That close proved powerful. It was one of those situations where you had to have been there and seen the looks on their faces, in order to feel the impact of the moment. A couple of days later, they called and offered me the job. The moment became one of the happiest of my career, mainly because of the financial potential and security acquired. Everyone who retired from that position retired as a millionaire. Therefore, at age thirty-three, I had basically secured my dream of becoming a millionaire.

I sat on top of the world! I would finally be able to fulfill my promises to take care of my mother and siblings. I would be able to help other family members and be a positive role model to my nephews and cousins. I had made it. I would have a $1.75 billion quota for drug sales, certainly the envy of all the drug dealers in my family. Many of them could have accomplished something similar, if they had been afforded a little more guidance and made better decisions.

The "Other" West Side

During the time I had worked in New York City, we lived in a small, historic town called Brookfield, in the northern portion of Connecticut. We chose Connecticut for its lower taxes and Brookfield for its charm. Unfortunately, what we gained in charm, we sacrificed in diversity. Of course, in selecting a home in a predominantly white, affluent community with a black population of only .76%, we weren't so naïve as to think there wouldn't be any repercussions or a consequence or two to have to deal with. I suppose what we didn't consider was the *depth* to which we would have to deal with it.

One day, my Little Princess, Iman, came home from daycare saying she didn't want to be black anymore; she wanted to be brown instead. When questioning her desire, we discovered that apparently a little four-year-old white girl in Iman's class told her that black was ugly and that she was ugly because she was black. I must say I wasn't prepared for the powerful sting Iman's innocent request caused when I realized my child had been told that kind of foolishness and had taken it as fact. Just as disheartening to me was the notion that the white girl had that kind of ugly thinking embedded in her mind at such an early age. Racism had to have been taught in her home.

Needless to say, Lisa and I agreed our next neighborhood had to be more diversified. We hoped that would decrease the probability of dealing with those types of racial issues with our children, since I found it difficult to try to explain racism and discrimination to a four-year-old.

Finally, we moved to Chicago. While searching for the perfect place to live, we took up temporary residency downtown. It fulfilled a major childhood dream of mine of living in downtown Chicago near the Magnificent Mile (our version of Manhattan's 5th Avenue)! Growing up in the projects positioned us just a mile west of downtown. Therefore, as a young boy, even though I lived in such a poor neighborhood, I enjoyed the most spectacular picture-perfect view of the city's buildings from my bedroom window. While looking out at night at all the lights and shapes of the Sears Tower, Standard Oil Building, and all the other wonderful architecture that makes up one of America's most impressive cityscapes, I imagined being there experiencing the energy of downtown living.

As our interim home, we rented an apartment on the twenty-second floor of Millennium Park Plaza, one block east of Michigan Avenue. Having a doorman to greet me, the opportunity to walk home with shopping bags full of clothes, shoes, and many accessories proved a far cry from pee-stained hallways and rats and roaches running around my feet all those years back. From my window, I *could* have looked back to my old neighborhood, but instead, Lisa and I spent hours staring out the window at the skyscrapers, Michigan Avenue, the beachfront, and Lake Michigan. It had become a part of the view I gazed at as a child while I had fantasized about living there. We would walk to Grant Park where Chicago hosts numerous free summer festivals, such as *the Taste of Chicago, Blues Fest, Jazz Fest* and many more. We shopped, took walks, and went to all those festivals, just like I dreamed I would. As I did so, I smiled and thought, "Chicago, I'm home!"

After looking at quite a few homes and neighborhoods around Chicago and its surrounding metropolitan area called "Chicagoland," we decided to build a home in a small subdivision called Ballantrae in Flossmoor. Flossmoor, located some thirty miles south of downtown, is part of the metropolitan area, and is therefore considered just a suburb (or Village), not its own town. With its 27% African-American population (instead of .76% like Brookfield), we were pleased that the diversity level would give our children a better representation of the "real world" in which we lived.

To put into perspective just how large the Chicagoland area is, it extends 9500 square miles, housing over ten million people and encompassing ten area codes! Some of the streets are amazingly long, taking you practically from one end of the city to the other, and many streets run clear out into the suburbs, as well. Several of them that come to mind are Pulaski, Kedzie, Western, and Cicero Avenues. Cicero Avenue is a main throughway from one end of Chicago to the other, and Western Avenue has been dubbed the longest continuous street in America.

Now, in light of all that vastness, imagine this irony: Pulaski Avenue runs right into the affluent community where Lisa and I built our 6200 square foot home; it's the same Pulaski Avenue that runs through my childhood neighborhood! The same Pulaski Avenue where I was robbed on the #20 Madison bus as a teenager! We fell in love with the area first before realizing the street connection. We were literally on the same street that led to my family's neighborhood, except we were some thirty miles south. I could take Pulaski Avenue from my house almost directly to my mother's house. It is about one hour's worth of traffic lights and slower going than on the expressways, but it can be done.

Ballantrae is an affluent, all African-American community. Most of the homes there were newly built. Most are 4000-plus square feet and occupied by middle to upper middle class families with the majority of the heads of households just in their thirties and forties. Rarely in this country do you find a community that boasts such a profile, other than perhaps in Atlanta or Washington, D.C. Sure, you can find similarly affluent, predominantly black communities in Chicago, but many of them are full of older homes with residents in a much older age bracket.

Our new neighborhood epitomized southern hospitality, as well. Residents spoke to each other, little kids rode their bicycles up and down the street, people waved when you drove by, and we knew all of our neighbors. It reminded me of what I had learned about Rosewood, Florida in the 1920s— a peaceful, lovely symbol of black prosperity within a tight-knit community.

In that case, unfortunately, all that's left now is a ghost town (even ninety years later) after the neighborhood's massacre by spiteful whites resulted in burned down homes and murdered residents. It is a tragic piece of history few people seem to be familiar with these days.[16]

Ballantrae fit our lifestyle perfectly. So, when our final construction bill went over our set budget, topping out close to a million dollars, we were okay with that because we planned to stay there a very long time. After all, we had designed it as our dream home with a pool, movie theatre, and lots of marble and granite. You name it, we included it all.

Greater than all the beauty that living there could deliver came an intriguing reality that I'll always remember. At one end of Pulaski Avenue, which we call the West Side or the *Wild, Wild West*, I grew up knowing K Town, L Town, drugs, gangs, prostitution, poverty, crime, death, and destruction. Even after escaping those gripping jaws of oppression, I'm haunted still by my past at that other troubled end of Pulaski Avenue.

It seemed as though my old and new neighborhoods represented "bookends" to my life's journey (not just at that point—I would later learn—but beyond as well). There I sat in my spacious, upscale home, surrounded by the finest furnishings and collectibles I had ever owned, yet thirty miles, thirty-plus years, and millions of dollars couldn't separate me from the crowded quarters, shared beds, roaches, rodents, and burglar bars. One stretch of asphalt—Pulaski Avenue—reminded me that I was still connected.

Control the Controllables

As a new Regional Sales Manager (RSM) with a sales quota of $1.75 billion, my job grew very intense. I felt that being one of the youngest RSM's in the entire company, coupled with the fact that I'm African-American required extra hard work on my part to quiet any would-be critics. I had over eight states in the Midwest, each with different market dynamics, so once again my learning curve went vertical. If I failed, I would be failing Clint Lewis and failing other African-Americans who desired this opportunity in the future.

I worked extremely hard, sometimes seventy hours a week, just to stay up to speed. I needed to be sure I was delivering value instead of just consuming it. Fortunately, my previous experience in Management Development in New York allowed me to deal with the people and coaching issues with relative ease. Many of my counterparts who took the Director of Operations position (shadowing their VP) struggled because they did not have the people development exposure or experience. I relied on that strength to help build a cohesive and motivated team fairly quickly.

Despite my hectic work schedule, I got my mother settled into an in-patient alcoholic and drug center called Keys to Recovery at Holy Family Medical Center. I loved being in Chicago where I could help her because she needed help for other medical conditions as well; she was dealing with lupus, diabetes, and high blood pressure. There were so many health issues she had to deal with due to her years of drinking and using drugs that she could only be stabilized in the hospital.

I visited her almost every night, and I also went to most of the family support meetings the program offered. The physical stress of long work hours, the mental stress of excelling in my new position, along with the emotional stress of being by my mother's side seemed insurmountable at times. Nevertheless, I wouldn't have traded being there for anything in the world. My mother needed me, and I needed to be there for her.

One night, driving back from the hospital to our apartment, I mentally prepared for a series of major business analysis meetings coming up over the next several days. Those meetings required all of the regional sales managers to go to the various markets they're responsible for, where the respective district managers would update them on their market opportunities and challenges. Each market had at least four or five district managers, so this would entail a whole lot of updating and analyzing. Once again, I knew that my peers and district managers alike would be testing me on my knowledge and, more importantly, on what value I could bring to the table.

My ringing cell phone broke my deep train of thought. It pleased me to see my brother's number displayed, since I hadn't talked to him in several days. His tone of voice didn't seem to be as jovial as usual, but due to the late hour, I presumed he had experienced a long, tough day at work like me.

"How's Mommy doing?" he started off the conversation.

"She's doing fine. I'm really pleased that her counselors were happy with her progress. What's up with you?" I asked.

"I went to the doctor earlier today," he reported. "I've been having some pain in my chest and my shoulder. The doctor told me that it must be indigestion. He told me to take an over-the-counter medicine called Tagamet, but I don't think it's working because I am still having problems…"

I interrupted him, "Ant, you should try Prilosec. I think it's better than Tagamet, and it works faster. If you have any more problems in the morning you should go to the doctor."

Ant switched subjects, "How's the job, li'l bro?"

"It's going fine. It's just really intense, but I enjoy what I'm doing."

"I am really proud of you," Ant said in his still-tired voice. "You know, I've been bragging on you at work." I knew that to be true because every time I met one of my brother's friends or co-workers, they told me how much he talked about me. "You shouldn't worry about anything at that job because you're just as talented and smart as any one of them."

I took comfort in my brother's words, as I always did. "Thanks bruh, I really appreciate you and love you, but I'm really tired right now, so I'm about to shut it down. I'll call you tomorrow."

"I love you too, li'l bro." And with that, I clicked my brother off and pulled up to my building.

The next day, the meeting with the Chicago North district managers convened at the Wingate by Wyndham Hotel, off Interstate 290 close to Schaumburg, a northwestern suburb of Chicago. That group represented one of our most important teams, responsible for hundreds of millions of dollars in annual drug sales. I definitely had to be on top of my game. Constant ideas flooded my mind on how I would engage this team and help them find ways to deliver more. We refilled our coffee cups in preparation for the start of the meeting. As we stood around talking, I happened to look down at my phone in my briefcase on a chair and noticed some missed calls. Just as I discovered my sister had called five times, the phone vibrated and I answered it. On the other end, Eboni cried hysterically.

"Anthony's dead! Anthony's dead!" Her voice shrieked.

I only remember responding with, "What?"

She cried, "Anthony's dead!"

I grabbed my briefcase and laptop and walked abruptly toward the door, saying to those standing near me, "I've got to go; I'll give you a call." I told my sister I would call her right back.

Before I got to the elevator, a floodgate of tears opened. Ebi's words repeated again and again in my head. Such horrific words: "Anthony's dead!"

"No, he's not. I just talked to him last night. I've got to wake up from this dream, this nightmare. That's it. That's it; it's a nightmare," I told myself. Fragmented thoughts of "How?" "Why?" and "Did he suffer?" tormented me as I traveled down the elevator. I passed one of my other coworkers, Tom Hensley, in the lobby downstairs. I whisked right by him as fast as I could, not able to talk to anyone at that moment. I'm not sure if he saw me, but at that point it didn't matter; nothing mattered except Anthony Holloway.

Once through the double doors and into the parking lot, I called my sister back. "Ebi, what happened; what's going on?"

"I don't know. I have been calling the hospital, but they won't give out any information to me because so many people have been calling claiming to be family members. I talked with his friend, JB, at work and he said Ant passed out while at work. They called the paramedics, and that's it."

I sat in my car in the Wyndham parking lot, rocking back and forth bawling, "God, why? Why my brother? Why my brother?" I'd just lost my father a little over a year prior, and now my brother followed. Reality started sinking in.

"Ebi, what's the number to the hospital?" I called them, and unfortunately, they wouldn't release information to me either, even though I identified myself as his brother. They said they would only release information if his mother called. And then more reality set in. My mother had to be told her oldest son was dead. *I* would have to go to rehab to tell her that her son is dead.

Of course, at that point, with Mom doing so well in rehab, I feared the news would potentially cause a relapse for her and quite possibly be one she might not ever recover from. Ant's death would be a huge blow for my mother, as most likely she would try and take the blame for it happening. She always felt guilty that she had not been a better mother. She would tell me that if she had lived her life differently, things would've turned out so much better for all of us.

I drove to Tee's to pick up Ebi. I thought about how Tee would be taking the news, especially with not being granted any information by the hospital. For many years, Tee raised Ant as her own son, so no doubt she had a right to that information, but hospital rules are hospital rules. I remember over the years on Tee's birthday or on Mother's Day, some of Ant's cards to her would say, "Mother," while others would say "Grandmother." I can only imagine what deeply seeded confusion that relationship brought about for him, especially given the fact that Tee was neither mother nor grandmother to him, but his aunt. Confusion or not, in her eyes, he was her son who could do no wrong, a sentiment shared by most mothers toward their sons.

When I walked through Tee's door and saw her standing there, I completely broke down. She had a few tears in her eyes, but she was much more composed than I thought she would be. She told me, "This is God's will, and you have to be okay with this. You have to be strong. I know you lost your father, and now your brother, too, but you have to let go and let God." Given Tee's religious lifestyle, I expected that from her, although maybe not quite so soon after hearing this awful news.

Eboni came down the stairs, and we hugged and cried for a long time. She and Ant enjoyed a close relationship, one that grew even closer after I left for college. They resembled each other in many ways, but mainly in that both were quick-tempered and extremely emotional, but with soft and compassionate hearts. As Ebi and I stood there in Tee's townhouse and embraced for what seemed like eternity, we both understood that we grieved not just for Ant, but for our mother as well. In minutes, we would have to tell her.

After we tried to pull ourselves together, we drove to the hospital and asked the counselor if we could see her. The counselor came out and said, "It's too early for visiting hours, so you will have to come back."

I told the counselor, "My mother's son, our brother, passed away this morning." I emphasized to her our need to see our mother immediately. She obliged. I added, "Please do not tell my mother anything. Allow us to do so."

They put us in a conference room, and they brought our mother in. There, my sister and I stood with tears running down our faces.

"What's wrong with Tee?" my mother asked right away, as my sister cried a little bit louder.

"Ma," I said as I approached her, "it's not Tee; it's Anthony. He died this morning."

"Anthony?" my mother asked softly, "How?"

I said, "We don't know, Ma. Too many people have called the hospital, and they won't give us any information. They will only tell you. I'm so sorry, Ma; I'm so sorry." We all hugged. My sister and I cried profusely while my mother barely shed a tear. She appeared to be in shock and, more than likely, in denial.

The counselor came back in and indicated that my mother could not leave the facility. It shocked and angered me that, at a moment like this, they wouldn't be a little more empathetic toward a patient's personal emergency. I remember saying pretty sternly, "Ma'am, we are leaving in five minutes *with* my mother. We are going to Cleveland to get my brother. As soon as everything is done, I will bring my mother back."

My mother had to sign a few release papers, and we left the hospital. While driving back to Tee's house, my mother called the hospital in Cleveland. It appeared by her responses they asked a battery of questions. After being satisfied, they finally released the information about my brother. They said that he died of a heart attack, and they pronounced him dead on arrival at the hospital.

Next, we called the Ford dealership in Cleveland, where my brother worked, and spoke to JB. "Hey JB. It's Jemal, Anthony's brother." I immediately asked, "What happened to my brother?"

JB answered, "Anthony got his check and went to get it cashed. When he came back, he went to sit at his cubicle. I started to see him shake, and his head rolled back. So, me and a couple other guys pulled him off of the chair and sat him down on the showroom floor. He started to vomit, and we didn't know what to do. We called the paramedics and when the paramedics arrived they started CPR."

As JB talked, I cried. I tried to summarize for my mother and sister what he said. "JB, did anyone do CPR while you guys waited for the paramedics?"

"No," he said.

I couldn't believe that no one in that establishment did CPR! Suddenly, it hit me that just the previous night, my brother had told me that he had chest and shoulder pain, and the doctor had diagnosed him with indigestion. Those are common signs for a heart attack, and the doctor missed them! I missed them! Instead when talking to him, I kept thinking about things I could not control—my meeting the next day, my mother in rehab—and in the process missed the signs that my brother shared with me.

At that point, I could barely even see the road through my tears. I pulled the car over and began harboring a serious guilt trip, blaming myself for Ant's death. I could have saved my brother's life if I had not been so caught up in my mother's health and my job's demands; I was selfishly thinking of my own life. I missed all the signs of my brother's heart attack. It felt as if a dagger pierced my heart as I began choking on my own tears. How could I have missed it? How could I have missed it?

It took me a little while to gain my composure, but the guilt remained. When we arrived at Tee's house, Lisa was there with our belongings. My mother and sister quickly gathered their things, and we started the drive to Cleveland. I cried, rocked back and forth and sobbed almost the entire way. In my mind, I kept apologizing to Ant for leaving him there. I remember the day Lisa, Iman, and I left Cleveland to move to New York for my new position with Pilon. Shortly after pulling out, I stopped the U-haul in the middle of the street. With extremely mixed emotions, I walked to my brother's car behind us, leaned in the window, and kissed him on his head, letting a few tears run onto his bald head. I said, "Please take care of yourself, bruh. Please. I love you."

He responded, "I will li'l bruh. I love you, too."

I got back in the U-haul and my gut kept telling me that he wouldn't really be OK; something inside said that he needed me. It wasn't a case of me being a worry-wart either; it went deeper than that. I felt like I abandoned him there, much in the same manner as with my dad when I left him in Indianapolis. I left them both for a promotion, an opportunity to grow, to make more money, and do more for my family. Again, one of my greatest fears had come upon me. I'd left my brother, just like my father, and both of them had died. How could I be my brother's keeper if I keep leaving my brothers?

The tears wouldn't stop coming. In my sadness, the only relief I found was knowing that my brother did not die of a drug overdose or by the hand of violence in the streets. A violent consequence always seemed a likely possibility, for obvious reasons, with drug struggles for over half his life. However, I still couldn't get over the fact that I felt I had let his life slip through my fingers.

Once we got to Cleveland, we went straight to the city morgue. Fortunately, the coroner was there, and we had a chance to talk to her. She said from her initial assessment, it looked like Anthony had had a series of small heart attacks that may have been transpiring over the past couple of days, and that he must have had one major blockage that actually caused the fatal heart attack.

I shared with the coroner that my brother had gone to see a physician the day before his death, and that they had diagnosed him with indigestion when he complained of chest and shoulder pains. It appeared that the doctor he went to see misdiagnosed him, and that he could have potentially still been alive if he had gotten a more thorough workup. The coroner said there were still a few more tests and analyses to be run before she could give her final report, so we were not allowed to see him. I gave her my telephone number and asked her to give me a call when she finished.

I wanted to get my brother out of the morgue as soon as possible. Just the thought of having him lying in a morgue with a bunch of strangers sickened me. Before we left, we went to claim Anthony's belongings, a very tough thing to do. I grabbed his clothes and they still smelled like him. I pulled them close to my chest, smelling them, and wondering what would have happened if I had been more alert. I kept damning myself for not being my brother's keeper.

After we left the morgue, we drove to the Ford dealership to meet with JB. He had taken my brother's keys and a few personal items so they would not be misplaced or stolen. That day marked one month to the day that Anthony had celebrated his 39th birthday. I sat in his cubicle and ran my hands across his desk, touching everything that he'd once touched. I spotted a Polaroid picture taken on his birthday of him receiving balloons, flowers, and a singing telegram from Cynthia. He told me then that he had just celebrated one of the best birthdays of his life. Now, it would go on record as the last birthday of his life.

While I sat there, many of the sales staff and managers spoke with my mother. I heard them telling her how wonderful Anthony was as an employee, as a co-worker, and as a person. As I watched my mother, she still seemed to be in shock since she was maintaining quite a stoic demeanor. Finally, after packing up the personal belongings from his desk, we bid our goodbyes, assuring them we would notify them soon of Anthony's service arrangements. We then headed to Ant's apartment.

As we approached Ant's apartment unit, his door stood slightly open. We walked in and saw that some items had been taken. There appeared to have once been a TV and VCR in one of the spaces, but they were no longer there. I immediately knew that someone had broken in. How low down could a person be to break into someone's home after he's died? That's just down-right dirty and immoral. We called the police, and while we waited for them to arrive, we tried not to touch anything, but I couldn't help myself. Just as I had done with my father, I walked into my brother's closet and grabbed his clothes as if I were embracing him, and I buried my face deep within them, hugged them tightly, and cried.

I recalled the good times we spent in Peoria during my mother's sober and clean stage, the times when he protected me from the violent streets, the times when I attended his Narcotics Anonymous meetings, and the times when we would hug and I would kiss him on the back of his head by his ear. Now, I just hugged the empty clothes he once filled and smelled the scent of cigarettes, cologne, and my brother's essence.

The police came and confirmed the burglary. After they dusted for prints and asked some questions, they left. We gathered some of my brother's things and left the apartment, as well. It had gotten late, so we finally went to the Marriott downtown and checked in. One of our close family friends, Sharvishia (Fee), worked there and got us a free suite for as long as we needed it. What a blessing, as we already had to think about so many other things.

I called around to a few funeral homes, and we finally found one that would get Anthony the next morning. That next day, we woke up bright and early. The funeral home called to tell us they had my brother, so we could come down to see him. I knew that would be an extremely difficult moment, just as it was with my father. My mother and sister had never lost anyone that close to them before, so I tried to brace myself and make myself strong for them.

Once we arrived at the funeral home, they took us to a room in the back where Ant lay on a gurney. For the first time, I saw my mother break down. "My baby!" she cried out, "Oh, my baby!" She hugged and kissed him and wouldn't let go of him.

Anthony was her firstborn. I wasn't born until four years later. Iman and Zhara are six years apart. I realize that I could never love one child more than the other; however, my firstborn, Iman, created so many more lasting impressions of fatherhood because she ushered in that new experience for me. My mother, more than likely, relived all her lasting impressions of Ant as she hugged him on that gurney. I knew I couldn't console her at that moment.

I grabbed my brother's soft hand. He looked as handsome as he always had with his beard still neatly trimmed and sketched out. He had one of those beards you could do almost anything with; one week he'd sport a goatee, the next week it would be thin lines. Before you knew it, he'd show up with a full beard. Because of his dark, chocolate skin and his beautiful smile, his beard truly accentuated his handsome face. But, all that must go to our memory banks now; we would no longer see the beard change. No longer would we see that engaging smile. He lay there lifeless.

My brother, one of two men I loved more than any other men in the world, was gone. My two most powerful catalysts—my father and my brother—

were both gone. Dad and Ant both had a push/pull effect on me, sometimes pushing me forward to achieve, and other times pulling me back into their own difficulties and the kind of life I desperately tried to escape. Both of them, however, provided great insights that guided me. My dad imprinted me with his example of being a voracious reader and lifelong learner, who constantly yearned for more knowledge. My brother showed me the sheer importance and consequences of the choices we make in life. They represented my biggest cheerleaders and most cherished teachers.

As I grabbed by brother's hand, I lost what little stamina I had. I collapsed on his chest, sobbed hysterically, and wished I had never left Cleveland. How could I have left him? Now my sister started jumping up and down, crying. She had totally lost her composure. The funny thing about death is that we all know it will happen, and we all know people who've lost a family member or someone extremely close, but we never know what we each may truly feel or how we will handle it, until we are actually standing in that room viewing our loved one's body.

We had a short funeral service (more like a viewing) in Cleveland. Many of his friends came to pay their respects. Some I'd met while attending Narcotics Anonymous meetings there with my brother from time to time. Some I met while going to the sober club with him. Lots of others I didn't know. A couple hundred people all together showed up. They all mentioned how much he loved me, how much he bragged about me, and how proud he was of me. It was all too overwhelming, and I melted again. I remember seeing Cynthia, but for some reason I don't remember much about our interaction.

Finally, with that service over, I had my brother shipped back to Chicago, where the funeral there was simply beautiful. We held it on the West Side at Corbin's Funeral Home. Lots of people from all the various cities he had lived in showed up. Almost all of his other brothers and sisters from his dad's side of the family attended. Hundreds came to pay their respects. Afterwards, we hosted a beautiful "Celebration of Life" ceremony for Ant at the Wingate by Wyndham

Hotel, close to Schaumburg. It was the very hotel I attended for my analysis meetings the day I found out about his death. I spared no expense. I knew that if given the opportunity, I would've paid for his wedding. So instead, I laid his memorial out! We had an ice sculpture with his picture inside the ice, balloons, picture boards propped up around the room, and plenty of food. To cap it off, we showed video with footage and pictures of him as a baby, all the way up until the day before he died.

While the video played, Ant's dad, Donald, came to me with tears streaming down his cheeks, and he whispered in my ear, "You really loved your brother; this is incredible." Those words meant more to me than any other words spoken to me during that entire experience. Donald had always told me to take care of my brother, and his words gave me some peace and consolation that I had really tried to do that to the best of my ability.

Ant's autopsy came a couple weeks later. *Heart attack—cocaine induced.* That statement rocked me hard! I felt almost more devastated than when I first learned of his death. My brother really did succumb to the streets, just like my dad. How did that happen? Why did it happen? I still held onto the thought that I could have potentially saved him because he had reported having symptoms of a heart attack.

In the long run, I knew the cause didn't really matter. Therefore, I needed to shake off that sense of failure. Okay, so I had missed the signs of the heart attack; I had missed the signs of drug use. Dwelling on that didn't bring my brother back. On top of that, I then felt embarrassed that my boss and mentor, Clint, stood in front of a couple thousand people at a meeting at Pilon and told them my brother died of a heart attack. Ironically, at that meeting we launched a new drug used to treat cardiovascular disease.

How would I then tell them the truth about how he died? I wouldn't. None of them knew how my dad died, either. It was fine that way. I vowed to not focus on how or why they exited this world, but celebrate the fact that they lived and loved as best they knew how. Who would understand the dichotomy of drugs in my world anyway?

Like Brother, Like Sister

In 2005, Lisa and I hosted our first Thanksgiving dinner in our new house. We were really excited, as lots of members from both our families attended. Thanksgiving had always been my mother's favorite holiday. She actually loved anytime we all came together as a family, but as holidays go, Turkey Day ranked on top. Having me back, living in Chicago, made that holiday an extra special time for her. Although I was back, Ant was gone; it felt bittersweet for all of us, though no one said it out loud. As our first real family gathering since Ant's sudden death, I anticipated the day being a challenge for me. However, with seventy-five plus people converging upon us, I found little time to think or do anything about it, let alone to be sad.

Additionally, just a few days prior, we had had our second daughter, Zhara. How blessed could I have been? She was beautiful, with big, brown eyes, lots of hair, and beautiful brown skin. Most of my older relatives said she looked like my mother when she was a baby. That certainly made my mother happy. Once again, there were lots of reasons to be joyful that day.

Even aside from our special reason that year, I love Thanksgiving almost as much as my mother because I truly believe in the principle of giving and receiving. It amazes me how great we can be at giving but at the same time be poor at receiving. And when we don't receive, we are denying others the ability to give, thus blocking them from the joyous feeling of giving. It is the same joyous feeling we get when we give. So, I love using this time to teach my family to give and receive graciously, allowing the reciprocal nature of the principle to manifest.

In addition to that, I love all the aromas that permeate the entire house: greens, dressing, roast, macaroni and cheese, green beans, turkey, baked chicken, fried chicken, fried corn, sweet potato pie, peach cobbler, chocolate cake, and of course my favorite—'chitlins' (chitterlings). Even chitlins' controversial aroma seems acceptable on Thanksgiving Day!

Lisa loved to cook. She cooked everything except the chitlins; that remained my job, and I always hooked them up! Each year, they were devoured first. Well, I suppose that could be partially because there were so few of them. You see, I would get the pre-cleaned chitlins, and to be on the safe side, I would still clean them as if they were the regular ones. Therefore, by the time that whole process was completed, they had shrunk considerably. Nonetheless, they were still a hit.

That year Ebi brought a new boyfriend, Pablo, to the holiday celebration. He looked like he had been to war, sporting a nasty scar from the back of his head almost to the front. Initially, I thought *car accident* as the culprit, but my instincts told me *gunshot wound*. My suspicions were later confirmed. He stood at only 5' 5" and appeared to be a body builder, with shoulders spanning what seemed to be the width of the doorway. Immediately, I thought either *prison-build* or *use of steroids*. I instantly became skeptical of Pablo; his presence just rubbed me the wrong way.

Actually, many of my sister's boyfriends kind of rubbed me the wrong way, so I made it a habit to have a man-to-man talk with them about her, as soon as I met them. I would generally tell them how much I loved her and that she was like my own daughter. I made sure they knew unequivocally that I would do anything to protect her. So, I pulled Pablo aside and asked my sister to come along. I gave him "the talk." In concluding, I reiterated, "She is like my own daughter, and I love her dearly. If you have any children, I'm sure you understand. I hope you treat her like you treat your kids."

To that, Pablo smirked and replied, "Yeah, I'll treat'er like I treat my kids. They don't like me 'cause I tear dat ass up, ain't dat right, Eboni?"

At that point, my sister shut down in a way I had never seen before. She could be quite sassy and usually dominated her men, but this time, she reacted very submissively and with a demeanor of fear. Right away, that bothered me, so I repeated myself, "I love her like I love my daughters and I will do anything for her."

I sensed there would be issues. Later that evening, I pulled my sister aside. "Ebi, something doesn't seem right. And you've got scratches on your neck. Are you okay?"

She quickly consoled me. "Yeah, everything's okay. CJ did that."

"Well, we haven't talked in a while. You've been more distant, and I feel really uncomfortable about this cat." My gut feeling led me to ask, "Is he hitting you?"

"No," came her nervous reply. It was not reassuring to me at all. She said it again, as though reading my mind, "No."

At that point, I conceded with, "If you ever need anything, just call me, 'kay? Just call me."

I didn't hear from my sister for a couple of weeks. That alone concerned me, so I called and text messaged her a couple of times. No reply. My mother and sister usually spent every day together, so I decided to call my mother to check on her. I figured if trouble brewed with Ebi, my mother would mention it. Well, my mother seemed fine and she mentioned nothing out of the ordinary with Ebi.

Several mornings later, while I was preparing for work, Ebi called. Crying softly, yet hysterically, she managed to utter, "I need your help!"

"What's wrong, Sis?" I anxiously asked.

"It's Pablo. He's been beating me, and I really think he's going to kill me."

"Ok, I'll be there as fast as I can—probably an hour, though!" I slammed my cell phone shut and began muttering, "I knew it! I knew it!" Rage rose in me instantly. Why do men do this to women? Why do men feel they can do this to women *I* love? They really don't know who they're messing with. Apparently, the corporate facade had them fooled. They failed to realize I grew up in the same environment as them. In addition, I am an Army-issued, trained killer, and now they want to try me.

Just as I began plotting how to kill Pablo, rational thoughts interrupted, "Jemal, what the hell are you thinking about? You have a wife and daughters. You are an executive with a Fortune 100 company. You make a handsome, six-figure income. Why are you about to throw all that away? Okay, you shoot him. You kill him. You go to jail. Then what? Or say you *don't* shoot him; he shoots you. *You* get killed! What happens to Lisa and the girls?"

"I don't give a damn," my other self scolded. "I told that punk that Ebi's like my daughter. I am my sister's keeper. So, I guess I've got to show him I mean what I say." As I furthered the plan of attack in my head, I decided not to drive my company car because I could not afford to get caught with a gun in the car. That would be cause for immediate dismissal. Amazing how I rationalized how to keep my job in the midst of potentially losing my life or throwing it away with a jail sentence. I continued to rationalize, thinking I should put on a suit to lure him into a false sense of superiority.

Just then, Lisa came into the closet where I was rapidly dressing. Looking puzzled at my haste, she inquired "What are you doing?"

I hurriedly told her the situation, anticipating the resistance that quickly came. As I reached for my gun, she started to cry. *That*, I didn't anticipate.

Through those tears of fear, she shouted, "What are you going to do? Throw your life away for some stupid crap your sister has gotten herself into? You have a family and children. What about us, huh? What about your mother? You're going to throw your life away just like that? What about the rest of your family, Jemal?"

I stood there for a moment and respectfully looked into her eyes. Lisa spoke from a place of logic. No doubt what she said made perfect logical sense. I thought about my beautiful daughters and my beautiful wife. I thought about the wonderful storybook life we lived with a million-dollar home in the suburbs, great job, and great friends. Yes, by all standards, I had made it. By all of *society's* standards, I had made it. So, why would I throw it all away for my sister?

For that reason alone—she's *my* sister. And that presented a whole different set of standards. She's *my* "shugah bum." She's the one I taught how to talk and how to walk. She's the one whose tears I wiped away as we struggled and lived with family after family, sometimes together, sometimes apart. She's my sister, and I'm her keeper. There was no other answer.

I couldn't explain it to my wife, so I didn't. Society and what "they" would think of my actions at that moment had no effect over *my* thought process. Logic certainly had nothing to do with my decision. I kissed my wife, dashed downstairs and kissed my children, thinking that could be the last time I saw them. I left.

While driving to the West Side, the raging battle continued in my head. "Gib, what are you doing? Are you really going to throw your life away? What if he kills you?"

The other side chided, "What if he kills your sister and you did nothing to stop it? What about her kids? How would you feel?"

The mental debate carried on the entire time I drove. Once on the Eisenhower Expressway, I called Ebi to find out exactly where we would meet. Being too scared to go home and too scared to go to Tee's, she told me to meet her at the Dollar Store on Laramie Avenue near Jackson Boulevard. When I pulled into the parking lot, I spotted her in her car crying. We got out of our cars and I gave her a big hug, kissed her on the forehead, and said, "I'm here, Sis."

It took a few moments for her to control the flood of tears that sprung forth on impact when we hugged. After that, we got in my car and I drove off. I didn't know yet where to go, but figured it would be best to at least keep moving. "What's going on?" I asked.

Ebi finally broke down the entire story, as tears trickled down her cheeks. "Pablo is a Chief for the 4 Corner Hustlers (4CH) on the West Side. He ran the block where we once lived on Lotus from Central all the way back to Lake. He ran all the drugs, the soldiers (gang members), and everything happening on that street. He's been beating me for a while."

One part of me got angrier and more furious than ever before; the other part of me got justifiably scared. Now, it's me against a Chief and his entire gang on the block! How did I end up here? I previously told my sister back when I had a beef with her babies' father, Montell, that she had to protect *me*, too. Keep me out of the drama! At age twenty-seven, I figured she needed to stop making stupid decisions about men. I needed to really think through everything.

Ebi continued her account: "I found out he was cheating on me with another girl. The girl called me and told me that he picked her up in my car and he even took her to my apartment. So, after I talked with her, I told him he needed to get his stuff from my house. Listen to this."

She then played a voicemail message that Pablo left earlier that morning. "Eboni, you better call me. I need my money! Every deal I miss, that's how many times I'm gonna beat yo' ass. You better call or I'm gonna f**k that ass up, b***h!"

I couldn't believe what I heard. That dude was crazy. But, my sister was crazy, too. "Ebi are you holding his dope money?"

She reluctantly answered, "Yes, I've got about $1800 at the house."

"Dammit, Dammit, Dammit! Ebi, why are you holding his money? How could you get involved with a gangbanging drug dealer and get caught up in his shit? I can't believe you!!"

"I know, Jemal. I'm sorry, I don't know why I did it, but I'm here now."

She certainly had that right—*we* were here now. I kept driving.

Soon, we made it to Madison Street and Western Avenue. Like every other time I'd driven down Madison Street, I started reliving the horrible experience of being robbed at gun point and having most of my clothes taken off my back while on the #20 Madison bus at age sixteen. But right then, I needed to focus on Pablo, so I quickly pushed that memory away. Instantly, the thought came to call my cousin, Charmaine. As a police officer, she could certainly shed some light on the matter. I told her the whole story and then asked her opinion.

"I know she is your sister," Charmaine began, "and I know that you love her, but you won't be there to protect her every day. What will happen tomorrow, or the next day? You are going to have to go to the police."

"You know, Charmaine, you are so right. Thank you, and I love you."

"I love you, too," came a relieved sounding voice over my cell phone's receiver.

We hung up. I don't know if Charmaine knows it, but she probably saved my life with her advice that day. At that precise moment, the game plan started falling into place. "Ebi, here is what we're going to do. We are going to go to your house, get his clothes and his money and drop them off where he can get to them. Do you know of a place?"

"His cousin's," she said.

"Okay, cool. You are going to call your apartment's office and tell them that someone is trying to harm you and that they have a key to the building entry door and to your door. You need to get the locks changed for both immediately, and we will pay for it. You said he paid part of your rent, so I will give you his portion of the rent money to give back to him. You will leave him a message and tell him that you have left the drug and rent money at his cousin's and tell him you have filed a restraining order. After that, call the phone company and change your telephone number. Lastly, we will go to the police and file the report. What do you think?"

She smiled and nodded, affirming her agreement, and we began executing the plan in the order I laid out. We arrived at the Kedzie Avenue police station. As we headed across the parking lot, I felt the weight of my gun in my overcoat. Thank goodness I caught that in time! I recalled that airport security incident I experienced several years back when I had forgotten to take my gun out of my computer bag. I certainly didn't need to deal with anything like that again. Besides, Chicago enforced mandatory jail sentences for carrying a handgun back then, so I'd probably be walking right into a jail sentence, if caught. I sprinted back to the car, got in, and placed the gun under the seat. I met Ebi inside the police station where we filed the abuse report. Almost instantly, they issued a warrant for Pablo's arrest.

Ebi's entire countenance improved. In the midst of her relaxed expression, I could tell she remained nervous, but at least she cracked a smile every now and then. I loved to see her smile. She had the deepest dimples. They served as beautiful accents on her light-skinned cheeks. I always considered my sister very attractive.

I started to feel a little better myself, knowing we had involved the police. In spite of a very bad situation and a couple of less-than-civilized intentions on my part, in the end, I made some good decisions that probably saved my life and Ebi's—at least for the time being, I thought. It made me think of Mo'Nique, the comedian, and a comment she made while doing a show at a women's prison, "We are all just one bad decision from prison."

The thought of being able to see my beautiful babies and my wife that night brought a spontaneous grin to my face. Thank you, God. The situation became another reminder that although I'd made it out of the ghetto, my heartstrings stayed strongly attached to the people in the ghetto. A sad reality, but it remained *my* reality. And because of that, I realized *I* would never be truly free—mentally or physically—unless I totally freed *them*. At least, I must free my mother and my sister.

Next, Ebi had to pick up her sons, Markell and Chris Junior, known as CJ. As I dropped her off back at the Dollar Store parking lot, I instructed her to get the boys and then come stay at my house for a couple of days. "Pablo probably doesn't remember how to get to my house, so you'll be safe there."

As soon as I said that, my familiar gut feeling told me I'd better go with her to get the boys and have her follow me. We first picked up Markell at St. Catherine Siena-St. Lucy School in Oak Park, where he was a student. He came out with his mom, sporting a big smile on his face. Ebi must have already told him I came with her. He ran right to my car and hopped in. I was happy to see him, too. My mind flashed through everything that had transpired that day. Man, how our kids are totally unaware of the things we go through as adults.

"What's up, Uncle Mal?" Markell squirmed his little nine-year-old body into the seatbelt in the front seat, as I helped him fasten the buckle.

"Hey, what's up Buddy?" The kids teased me because I called them both "Buddy" all the time. We followed Ebi to the nearby daycare, *A Small World*, to get CJ. The director of that Oak Park facility happened to be our cousin, Teresa. Ebi parked in front of the daycare center, and I parked right behind her. She hurried inside while Markell and I stayed in the car talking.

All of sudden, Markell pointed out the window and said, "There's Pablo!"

I glanced out the window just as Pablo slammed the passenger door closed on a white Buick that pulled up next to Ebi's car. Pablo ran into the building, while the Buick sped off down the street. As soon as it left my sight, I reached down under my seat and slid my 9mm into my coat pocket, trying not to let Markell see it. I ordered him to stay in the car and be still, and I told him not to worry. I felt bad that he saw my gun anyway, but action took precedence over apologizing. I hopped out and ran into the daycare.

My abrupt entrance added to the nervousness already apparent on the faces of some daycare workers and parents standing in the front hallway. A few mothers grabbed their children and rushed out the door. The daycare's hallway had a couple of twists and turns, and I just followed the eyes on those nervous faces to determine which direction to go. I finally got to a second hallway and someone pointed to the men's bathroom.

I busted through the door (only later realizing how stupid and risky that was). Pablo stood facing Ebi and holding her shirt by the collar. Tears streamed down her face as she tried to hold her composure for CJ's sake. My nephew stood behind her, with his slight four-year-old body pressed up against the wall. He looked scared, too, and I could see the tears welling up in his eyes. He, too, kept his composure—ironically, for the sake of his mother.

I glared at Pablo so hard, my face felt hot. "Let my sister go!"

He ignored me and kept his stare fixed on Ebi's eyes, his face just inches from hers. "Come on, Eboni," he said with such vengeance.

My sister looked at me with lips trembling, as she kept resisting Pablo's pull. I felt more anger rush through all my veins until my whole body boiled. Once again I shouted, "Let my sister go!"

A moment of silence fell, then, "Click." I released the safety lever on the 9mm. Pablo looked at me, looked down at my coat pocket, and looked back at my eyes. I knew he heard it. I knew he saw the look of death in my eyes. I knew at that point he understood I meant business. He abruptly released my sister and backed out of the bathroom.

As he exited, he snarled at me, "You're gonna need a lot more than that." "The only thing we'll need is an ambulance, home boy," I snapped back at him. He and I kept eye contact, like two Pit Bulls, until he backed entirely out the front door of the daycare center.

The white Buick was waiting outside for him. He ran and hopped in. At that same moment, the police arrived responding to the call my cousin Teresa made as soon as Pablo cornered Ebi and dragged her to the bathroom.

The police, hopping out of their car and walking swiftly past the Buick, had no idea that the suspect sat in that very car they passed. Realizing his lucky break, the driver of the Buick quickly maneuvered to the left and sped away once more. I bolted out the door, pointed to the Buick, and informed the police that the guy just got away. One police officer jumped back into his squad car to chase after the white Buick. The other officer proceeded inside the center to get the complete report from witnesses inside.

While I stood listening to Teresa tell her side of the story, the battle began in my head again.

"You idiot! Do you realize you could have caused a shoot-out in a daycare center with lots of kids and babies around? With your nephew in the bathroom, you could have harmed him or scarred him for life, depending on what he saw. Thank God, nothing happened!"

My other self kicked in, "Way to go, Mal! You just saved your sister's life from some asshole. That's what big brothers are for!"

As the debate in my mind raged on, I walked outside to the car, got in, and told Markell to relax. I took the gun out of my pocket, put the lock on it, and slid it back under the seat. I thanked Markell for being such a trooper and told him to stay in the car a little while longer while I went back inside to get his mom and brother.

After the police officer gathered all the facts he needed, he told me and Ebi to go file another report at the police station. This time, we had to file it with the police station in Oak Park, the jurisdiction for the daycare. After that, Ebi and the boys followed me home. Next, we had to tell my mother what happened. We purposefully excluded her until we were totally finished with the whole ordeal, so we wouldn't worry her.

Once Lisa and I got everyone settled at the house, I called my mother. Before I could even say anything she said, "I just got home and Pablo was sitting in the dark on the porch across the walkway, where I couldn't see him. When I put my key in the door, he lunged at me said, 'Tell Ebi she better give me my money or she's going to get hurt.' Then he walked away. I was so nervous and had no idea what he was even talking about."

I could feel that anger rising again. So, the cops never caught them, and then for him to be messing with my mother? Oh, he really didn't know when to quit. He *was* a crazy fool for real. Before my mind could wander again down the *what-I-am-going-to-do-to-Pablo* road, I heard Charmaine's voice of reason, "You can't protect her every day."

I proceeded to tell my mother what happened. She expressed both anger and relief. She knew I probably saved my sister's life, but she also knew I could have caused a lot more damage and lost my own life in the process. I gave the phone to Ebi, so she could tell her version. I overheard my mother scolding her for dragging me into her mess.

Pablo hung around my sister's job a couple of times as a scare tactic, but eventually left her alone. A few weeks later, we learned he got shot again—five times and he still lived. Unfortunately, some fools never die.

Not Now

My mother never quite bounced back to her old self after my brother died. I believe what they say is true—when a parent loses a child, it upsets the natural order of things. No mother wants to see her child go before her. However, with the drug-filled lifestyle my brother led, one might have guessed that day would come sooner than any one of us would want to imagine.

My mother was an introvert. I am not sure if that was her natural characteristic, or if experiences during her young life on drugs caused her to retreat into a shell. Either way, before Ant's death, she pretty much stuck to herself, but did socialize with family and did some things out in the community; after Ant's death, she spent most of her time in her room and hardly anywhere else. She would go to work, come home, and go to her 10 x 10 square foot bedroom at Tee's. She would stay there unless she had an Alcoholics Anonymous or Narcotic Anonymous meeting, a function with the West Side Club, shopping with my sister, or visiting at my house.

Fortunately, my mother had been clean and sober since my brother passed. Her Sober Day began March 1, 2004, the day I took her to the hospital/rehab. My brother died eleven days later, and she seemed to still be in a trance when she got out.

In July of 2007, the company where my mother worked for almost nineteen years laid her off. They were bought out several times, and the name had changed, but my mother's job did not. However, each time they were bought out, Human

Resources reset her timesheet as if she was a new employee. Therefore, she left that company after all those years with no retirement account, no savings plan, and no 401k. Nothing! That made me so angry when I found out. How could a company get away with that? And, her boss, who she had known for most of those years didn't even call her to say, "Thank you." Pathetic! I realized how fortunate I was to work for Pilon; they would never treat their people that way.

Since I had a decent amount of money saved up, I knew I needed to help my mother. I didn't want the stress and financial pressure to cause her to have a relapse back into drugs or drinking. I asked her to tally up all of her bills, which she did. They added up to $10,000, plus a car note and auto insurance. So, I wrote her a check for $14,000. I told her to pay off all of her bills, stash $2,000 away in a savings, and give $2,000 to Eboni. I also told her I would pay her car note. She only had to pay for her auto insurance and household goods each time she received her unemployment check. I left her with some items to pay, so that she could feel like she contributed toward her own well-being, and for her self-esteem.

When I gave my mother the check, the glow in her eyes was worth a million dollars to me. Without saying it, I felt her love and her pride in how successful I had become. She cried and hugged me. I felt overwhelmed with emotion, too. It truly made me grateful that I had reached a level in my career that afforded me the opportunity to care for her, as I had always promised. All those years of struggle and sacrifice paid off not just for me, but for her also. The funny thing is that $14,000 no longer represented a lot of money to me, but it did to her.

I wanted to buy her a house, but she would never leave Tee, especially since Tee had become so ill. But, at least she didn't have to worry about a thing. It was almost like she retired. I told her now she could devote her time to worthwhile causes, or do some things that she had always wanted to do. I encouraged her to make the best of the time and be productive.

I really tried to reinforce that because a lot of times when people retire from working all their lives, they slip into a myriad of health problems because their brains and bodies are no longer as active. Often times, people experience an increase in blood pressure or a worsening of diabetes due to lack of physical activity. In addition, depression or mild dementia can result from lack of mental stimulation, engagement, or active thinking. So, my mother increased her support of the West Side Club, went to more meetings, and did more things with her friends.

One time, I paid for her, my Aunt Hannah, and my Aunt Bob to go on a cruise for Aunt Hannah's birthday. I've tried to do special things for all of those who were special to me as a child or as a man. I love Aunt Hannah and the way she inspires everyone she comes in contact with, so it felt good to do that for her, especially since she had never been on a cruise. Plus, Aunt Hannah suffered through her own battle with drugs. Back in the '70s, she and her husband were big time dealers in the projects, selling marijuana. One day, while they were being robbed, she was shot in the stomach. She stayed in the hospital for a month after that and almost died. She later continued using drugs, but has made a wonderful recovery today.

On the cruise, they all had a great time. But after the cruise, I learned from my sister that my mother began spending even more time in her room than before. If she didn't have a meeting or function to go to, she would stay in her bedroom all day.

Early one morning, my sister called me, speaking fast and hysterically. I had gotten a call like that from her before—when my brother died. My heart sank to my stomach as I asked her, "What's wrong?"

"They are taking Mommy away."

"What do you mean, 'away'?" I asked.

She said, "In an ambulance. She can't talk, can't move. They think she's had a stroke."

"Where are they taking her?"

"Loretta Hospital," she said.

I thought to myself, "Oh God, a community hospital. Why not Northwestern Hospital, Rush Presbyterian, even Cook County for the immediate trauma intervention?" But, it was too late; they were on their way.

I was fortunate to be in town. Pilon had asked me to move to Atlanta or take a severance. My boss, Michelle Keefe, and mentor, Clint Lewis, really believed in me. I chose to stay with the company and move to Atlanta because of my tenure and potential. I thought it to be the best move, but now with my mother having potentially had a stroke, I couldn't help but second guess a decision, once again. Loved ones I had moved away from always died shortly thereafter. I tried not to look at it that way, but the outcomes were beginning to speak for themselves.

Certainly, there were some valuable lessons to be learned, like making the most of moments while we are with the people we love. Frankly, I'd learned all the lessons I could stand in one lifetime, but I knew more had to come. "Just not now," I hoped in my mind, "not with my mother." Luckily, we had not moved to Atlanta yet, even though I was traveling back and forth to the office there. I was in Chicago that morning, so I could get to the hospital to see about her.

I was about forty-five minutes away from Loretta Hospital, but it may as well have been four hours for the anxiety I felt while driving. I hadn't quite recuperated from the emotional draining from losing my dad, then my brother, and now my mother was seriously ill? It proved just too much for me. I prayed asking God, "Please, not now." I felt I shouldn't be asking selfishly for things or specific outcomes, but I found myself doing it anyway. "Please God— not now." When I got to the hospital, some of her friends were in the waiting room. They all looked incredibly sad. My heart sank even further. Lisa, one of my mom's closest friends from the West Side Club, got up and gave me a hug.

"Where is she?" I asked.

Several answered in unison, "She's in the back."

So, I hurried up to the desk. "My mom is here. Her name is Evelyn Farmer."

"Go on back," the lady said. As I walked through the doors, I could feel the tears welling up. A stroke is a terrible event. If it doesn't kill you, it can leave you paralyzed, demented, and unable to take care of yourself. The nursing home had plenty of stroke patients, sometimes entire wards of them. When asked, most people say they'd rather have a heart attack than a stroke because they could potentially recover from a heart attack, but a stroke can leave a person and their family devastated physically, emotionally, and financially.

I finally found my way to her room. My mother laid there with my sister next to her. Her eyes were open, and she talked. "Thank God—she's alive!" I thought. "Thank you, God!" The next thought that came to my mind, "Is she paralyzed?" She held my sister's hand, but I couldn't really tell who did the holding. As I walked in, she started to cry. I bent over the bed, and she wrapped her arms around me. Thank God, no paralysis! This must have been a mild stroke.

Just as I thought it, my sister said it, "The doctors believe it was a mild stroke."

"What happened?" I inquired.

My mother explained, "As I was lying in bed, I found myself unable to move or call out for anyone."

"For some reason, I got the urge to go check on Mommy," Ebi jumped in with her version, "When I walked in, I saw that something was wrong, and I called the paramedics."

As they continued talking, my mind wandered to getting my mother out of Loretta. I talk about heart attacks, strokes, and other serious health challenges for a living. I talk about the ramifications of them and the relief of them. I missed the opportunity to put my knowledge to work with my brother; I would not miss it with my mother. Aggressive therapy is key, especially with a stroke because the probability of having a second stroke within the first year is extremely high.

I interact with some of the best cardiologists and neurologists in the country. From all of their lectures, I knew the first few hours were critical. I knew the workups that needed to be done, and I also knew that Loretta Hospital didn't have the equipment or the expertise with which to do it. Therefore, I asked the nurse to call around to a few other hospitals to see if we could get her transferred. Unfortunately, unless you're brought in by an ambulance to one of the other major hospitals, you had to wait as a new admission. Both Northwestern Hospital and

Rush Presbyterian Hospitals were talking three-day waits.

So, we were stuck with an inadequate hospital with an inadequate staff, at least for me and the high standard of care I desired for my mother, but I had to focus on the good news. Having her alive and with just transient paralysis indicated a good possibility for full recovery. Not many people are that lucky. My cousin, Chucky, at age forty, had a stroke the year prior, and he stayed in the hospital for months. He lost use of one side of his body and had a speech impediment. Fortunately, with therapy he recovered, but his job put him on permanent disability.

My mother fully recovered, and I got her in to see one of the best neurologists in Chicago. He did a complete workup and said my mom would be fine. He put her on 80mg of Lipitor and a few other meds. Aggressive therapy— that's what I'm talking about.

Loretta Hospital is located in the "hood." It is my opinion that some "hood" hospitals are contributors to the healthcare disparities between blacks and whites. Tee had been going there for years. I asked to speak to her doctor to discuss her progress. Tee, a diabetic, had high blood pressure and high cholesterol; she had survived breast cancer, a heart attack, and bypass surgery, and had weathered a few other health challenges. Her health was a total wreck; however, the family joke was that she would outlive us all.

I tried to stay involved with Tee's healthcare, so I asked her doctor about some of the basics like what were her HbA1c, LDL, and HDL levels. He had no idea. None of it appeared on her chart, and the chart went back a couple of years. He told me her total cholesterol, her glucose levels, and rattled off a few other numbers, but those were all in-office measures. They were either too cheap or didn't care to do a full blood panel to check the real indicators as they related to her health. That type of mediocre or substandard workup should not be the standard of care for a patient with that kind of health profile.

I told the doctor how disappointed I was with their care and demanded a full blood workup on Tee. Thank goodness I work in the drug industry, or I would have had no clue. It saddens me as I think about the millions of people who don't have the medical knowledge needed to ask the right questions or to challenge the care being delivered. I am not saying that all doctors are bad, but I am saying they are not all great. Sometimes, you could have a good doctor with managed care restraints, budget restraints, and/or policy restraints.

Perhaps a bigger problem is that so many people look at doctors as gods who have all the answers. They don't. They are scientists who do not always have all the answers and often speculate, strongly relying on how well patients report their own information and answer the questions posed. Those patients who are not well-educated or cannot communicate effectively are at a distinct disadvantage for receiving the best healthcare.

Wish it Was Anthony

I attended the American College of Cardiology meeting in New Orleans in March, 2007. It felt great to be back in New Orleans, especially after the hurricane. I had traveled there twice since the tragedy, and each time the sites were still heart-wrenching. New Orleans is one of the most unique cities in the country. The people, the music, and the history all hold the key to the incredible depth and originality of its diverse cultural landscape. Like most Americans, as I watched the devastating effects of the flood that killed thousands and left hundreds of thousands homeless, I wondered what role I could play to help rebuild New Orleans.

I requested special permission from my company to take my management team to New Orleans for our quarterly meeting, and my boss approved. We went almost one year to the day of the hurricane. The first day, we did community service. It surprised me to see how extremely organized the efforts were for volunteering.

Our project helped rebuild a house on Musician's Row. This project really hit home for a couple of different reasons. First, I felt pure joy helping my fellow Americans, and then to be on Musician's Row was just simply a treat. I thought of my dad and how proud he would have been for me helping his fellow musicians. In 1981, one of his early gigs, when he was starting out as a singer, brought him to New Orleans. Maeve had helped Dad get the booking in a Holiday Inn lounge for a month. It turned out to be a big gig for him at the time, and it was his first road trip with his "Sensitive And Mellow" band.

Dad enjoyed the audiences and getting to know his way around the city. He spoke of sitting in the French Quarter in open air cafés, where he would eat oysters on the half-shell with hot sauce, talk with other musicians, and watch the myriad of interesting people stroll by. Dad would have loved the work we did.

The rebuilding strategy for the city was to make sure musicians had homes. After all, New Orleans has always been known for its great jazz, and the musicians are a key element to the tourism there. So, my team and I took great pride in building a home that day.

After that, we took a tour of the Ninth Ward and other devastated areas. It felt like being in an episode of *The Twilight Zone*. As we walked down streets of neighborhoods with homes that appeared to be intact, a deep quiet fell; there were no sounds of birds or dogs, no movement of any kind—nothing. It was eerie to think how quickly all life disappeared from miles of neighborhoods. I finally walked over and looked into a house and saw that it had been completely gutted on the inside. No walls, stairs, wood, nothing.

In home after home, there remained nothing but empty shells with merely an outer brick layer. On every door, a marking contained a circle with an "X" in the middle. And, in each section of the "X" were numbers and letters. Each of these meant something specific to officials who inspected the homes either immediately after the hurricane or later, as specific data became available. The most heart-wrenching was the number written there. Our tour guide explained to us that the number meant the number of people found dead in the home. Many homes had zeroes, but quite often you would see a one or a two; in rare cases, there was a number three or four. But, when we saw a number six, that's when the tears really fell among all of us.

Another house I looked in had not yet been gutted. I saw baby toys, dolls, and trucks. It looked like toys for different age groups of boys and girls, so I assumed there had to have been a couple of children living there. It had a #5 on the door. It immediately made me think of my own daughters, Iman and Zhara.

I wondered what a final moment would have looked like if we occupied that home and were unable to evacuate. I imagined the horror of watching my babies reaching for me with a confused look of why I didn't help them that time as I had done so many times before when they scraped a knee or fell off a bike. But this time, I would only watch them drown. Their innocent precious lives tragically stripped away as the water filled their lungs, until I met the same tragic fate. Just envisioning that for one minute was too much for me! By then, the tears were flowing, and I realized the magnitude of the devastation. While I only fearfully envisioned it, so many people had experienced this fate.

As we passed by hundreds of homes, I just couldn't believe the tragedy. We saw boats and cars on the roofs of houses and homes with water marks eight feet high. Imagine standing in the middle of your block, and your entire neighborhood is underwater.

That trip created a defining moment for my team. We represented Pilon with our community service, but we also represented ourselves and our families. It changed the hearts of many of the members of my team. Some went back to New Orleans with their families while others took their church back and did community service. I was really blessed to have exposed them to that experience; because of that exposure, more work, more love, and more compassion went into New Orleans.

Being back in New Orleans in 2007, I could see that a lot of progress had been made since my previous visit. The Annual American College of Cardiology meeting was always a great meeting to attend. There were thousands of doctors from all over the world, sharing and learning all of the advances being made as it related to cardiovascular disease. Of course, there were also hundreds of vendors and their employees exhibiting all of their products and services in the convention hall.

Pilon always had one of the largest booths with thirty or forty colleagues working every corner and section of the booth. The pace went either extremely fast or extremely slow. Most of the time, I participated in meetings with world-renowned doctors, leaders in the cardiovascular arena like Dr. Steve Nissin of the Cleveland Clinic—one of our nation's top hospital and research institutions. Newsmakers like top epidemiologist, Dr. Charles Hennekens and cardiologist Dr. Michael Koren; others contributed as well.

On the second day, I walked a few short blocks from the W Hotel to the convention center. As I walked, I saw a man about fifty feet ahead of me beginning to stagger. There were at least twenty other people walking between him and me, so I was sure other people saw him as well. He continued staggering until he fell into the street with traffic coming at him. I dropped my briefcase and sprinted toward him.

It surprised me that people just stood and looked at this elderly man lying partially in the street. Fortunately, the car driving in that lane stopped in time, which created a safety block for that man from other cars. I picked the man up and dragged him over to the sidewalk. He appeared to be barely conscious. He had a name tag on, so I started calling his name, "Dr. Jones, Dr. Jones."

For a moment, he looked at me and then his eyes rolled to the back of his head. Once I saw that, I checked his breathing and realized he had stopped breathing. I immediately administered CPR. Since he looked frail, I decided not to press hard on his chest, to avoid cracking his ribs. One, two, three, four—I counted as I pumped on his chest. Just as I got ready to do mouth to mouth resuscitation, I remembered that a Japanese study I had recently read stated you should only do chest compressions for potential heart attack victims because they may still have enough oxygen in their blood system to sustain them. The technique would be different for drowning victims as air would be needed, hence mouth to mouth would be the way to give it.

So, I continued with the chest compressions for what seemed like ten minutes, but in reality was only two. All of a sudden, Dr. Jones wet his pants. I thought, "Oh crap, I'm losing him!" So, I pumped a little faster. Sweat dripped off my face onto Dr. Jones. The adrenaline, the anxiety, and the hot New Orleans sun caused me to sweat profusely. I prayed that I wouldn't pass out.

Finally, a doctor stepped up and said, "How can I help?" Suddenly, it dawned on me; most of the people who saw him fall were doctors. As I looked around, I noticed that many of the tags had MD after the name. As a Pharmaceutical Representative, I scraped up my knees and tore up my suit to save that stranger, while doctors stood around watching. For heaven's sake, we were at the American College of Cardiology, a cardiologist was having a heart attack in the midst of cardiologists, and a non-cardiologist was the only one who sprung into action to desperately save the man's life!

I told the inquiring doctor to check Dr. Jones' pulse and his breathing when I broke from compressions. Together, we worked as a team for another sixty seconds which now seemed like sixty minutes. At one point, while waiting on him to check for heartbeat, I glanced up and noticed my boss, Michelle Keefe, out of the corner of my eye. Her eyes widened in confusion, but I could sense her encouragement as I continued.

The doctor helping finally said, "I've got a pulse!"

Shortly thereafter, Dr. Jones started to breathe.

"Thank God! Thank God!" was all I could say.

Dr. Jones opened his eyes and still dazed, tried to sit up. At that point, I knew things would be okay.

"Dr. Jones, you are okay, you are okay, but I need you to relax, just relax," I said. I could hear the ambulance sirens, which appeared not to be far away.

"Thank God," was really all I could say. The paramedics finally got there and took over.

When I stood up, I did not realize a big crowd had gathered. Then, everyone started clapping and cheering. I felt a little embarrassed. You usually expect applause when you win something or sing something or make a great speech, but not for saving someone. But, I guess I wouldn't know that, since I had never saved anyone before, at least not in such a direct, physical sense.

Then the doctor who helped me gave me a hug and asked for my card. I didn't have any on me, but Michelle gave him one of hers and wrote my name on it.

"That was an incredible thing you just did, absolutely incredible," the doctor repeated, as he accepted the business card.

Other people started coming over and giving me hugs or shaking my hands. At that moment, I did not want to take credit for saving his life. I just felt grateful that I could allow him to once again see his wife, or his children, or his grandchildren. I kept thinking that day was not his day to go and how blessed he was to have another one.

I told Michelle I would get to the meeting with Dr. Koren a little late, as I needed to go back to the hotel and freshen up. When I got to my room, I looked in the mirror and thanked God for working through me. Then, I began to cry. Not for Dr. Jones, but for my brother, Anthony. I wished I could have been there for him when he had *his* heart attack. I wished that someone like me could have been there to save my brother.

With tears still flowing, I tried to pull myself together to get back to the meeting. As I looked at myself in the mirror while putting on my tie, I knew I needed to let go of the guilt and negative thoughts I had about Ant and focus more on the positive and controllable issues, like Dr. Jones.

I wondered how Dr. Jones was doing. Before I went back to my meeting, I took a cab to the hospital where he was taken. Because of laws and guidelines that protect patient health information, they refused to tell me his status. His name tag identified the hotel he stayed at, so I decided to go there and leave a message. I left a brief description of the incident and who I was; however, I never heard from him. Some of the key people at the convention said that he remained in stable condition, but that's all I ever found out.

Pilon wrote an article about that incident and distributed it to our divisions worldwide. I felt overwhelmed and humbled by all the comments I received from all over the world; I got messages from Ireland, Germany, South Africa, and many other countries, so many responses, in fact, they actually crashed my email box! I knew in my heart that it was a time for Pilon to be proud and a time for me to be grateful to have been in the right place at the right time, prepared to take the right action.

Let's Fight This Thing. . .

A few months later, my mother began having pain in her side so badly that she decided to go to the hospital. I believe the pain had been there for quite a while, and she just bore it until she couldn't anymore. The initial diagnosis, without any lab work, indicated ovarian cancer. When my sister called to tell me, I was dumbfounded. She said mommy had to go in for follow-up visits. When I talked to my mother, she seemed to act as if nothing had happened. She appeared very calm and impassive. She simply said, "I'm OK."

They scheduled my mother's appointment a week or so later, and I assumed they would do a biopsy and other blood work. Naturally, that night I Googled everything I could about ovarian cancer. While the news seemed daunting, there appeared to be a glimmer of hope and a decent survival rate if it was caught soon enough. My company had a couple of cancer drugs on the market, but not for treating ovarian cancer. I figured with chemo and radiation, there might be a chance. Being the optimist that I am, I remained hopeful. Besides, we had already been down that road supporting Tee as she suffered through breast cancer twice and was currently battling it again because it had come out of remission. Since my mother didn't work anymore, she had been taking Tee to radiation treatments, so it was kind of ironic that my mother would now be needing help getting to treatments for herself.

A few days later, the pain for my mom became excruciating, and she couldn't breathe properly. My sister took her to Cook County, and they admitted her. I had

Ebi get the doctor's information, and I called the next day. The doctor confirmed that my mother had cancer, and it appeared to be pretty severe, but they would have to do a biopsy to be certain. Of course, I didn't get any sleep that night.

I flew up to Chicago the next day. I did not get in until after visiting hours, but the resident doctor I had been talking with met me outside and took me in the back way. As we walked toward her room, he told me that my mother's cancer was very serious and that she might only have a few months to live. It took everything within me not to buckle to my knees and hit the floor. I could not believe what I heard. "This must be a bad dream; this can't be true. I am not going to lose my mother. Not right now. There is so much I still have to do for her, so much more of my promise to fulfill, so much of her life to live."

I felt the tears well up in my eyes, but I knew I had to be strong for my mother. The doctor walked me to the room, and as I walked through the door, the tears fell anyway. My sister was there, as she had been staying overnight. My mother lay in the bed, still looking beautiful to me. She wore her hair a little longer than usual. She usually kept it short like a high top fade with waves and dyed with a slight blonde tint. Her cheeks were big and soft as pillows. She had light brown eyes that matched her smooth, caramel brown complexion. As a kid, I used to put my eye up to hers to see if I could see her eyes any better. Of course, I couldn't, but it was my way of telling her how beautiful they were. My daughter, Iman, has the same eye color. I now do the "look in the eyes" thing with her.

So, there she laid, my "Mommy," with only a few months to live. I walked over to her and reached across the hospital bed and hugged her, kissed her cheek, and laid my cheek on hers. I knew she could feel the tears running down my face onto hers. I knew from that moment that she knew her condition was serious.

After hugging my mother for a few minutes, I finally gave Eboni a hug. I knew she must have been emotionally drained and physically tired. She had been at the hospital for a couple of days, and I'm sure she needed some rest. Because they spent so much time together, she and my mother became best friends. My sister did not have very many friends. She had some mood swings where she didn't want to be around people, and I guess people didn't want to be around her. Also, my sister lived with my mother most of her adult life. When my mother moved back in with Tee, my sister went right with her. Even when Eboni did have her own place, it was just two blocks from my mother and Tee's, and she still stayed with them most of the time.

I could relate to how my sister felt since I, too, had lost my best friend, my dad. I realize, though, that every relationship is different and every loss is different. Just because I lose my father and you lose your father, it doesn't mean that we understand how each of us feels. The only thing we have in common *is* losing a father. Since relationships and life experiences are totally subjective, how we feel about a loved one and how we process our experiences and express our emotions is absolutely an individual thing. I learned that great lesson from my father's death. Since then, I've learned to empathize better and be compassionate without projecting my feelings or experiences onto someone else. At the same time, I try my best to respect whatever they feel and whatever process they are going through.

It occurred to me that I shouldered a two-fold burden. I was a son, feeling helpless in his quest to keep his mother alive and pain-free forever, and I was a big brother, empathizing and trying to stand strong for the baby sister who was walking out her last days with her best friend and mother. We share the same mother, but as I said before, we cannot share the same pain. Ebi's facial expression that night looked as if my mother had already died, and I had to respect that. I hugged Ebi and tried to temper my emotions to be strong for her. It didn't quite work.

This had to be a painful sight for my mother, looking at her only two children who were still quite young, and knowing she would not be with us much longer. Painful on another level, too, for as Ebi grieved for her mother and best friend, I also grieved for Ebi's personal anguish over our mother.

I told my sister to go home and get some sleep and that I would stay that night. I asked her where the pull-out couch was, but there wasn't one. She had been sleeping upright in a chair for the past two nights. What a trooper. I heard a cough and turned around and saw another patient in the bed next to my mom's.

I hadn't even realized she shared a room. I had walked right by the lady. My mother said she'd been coughing all day. "Interesting," I thought, as I made a mental note to talk with the doctor about that. My sister gathered her things and left.

I sat next to my mother and held her hand. I asked, "Ma, how long have you been living in pain?"

"A few months," she said.

"Why didn't you go to the doctor sooner?" I softly scolded her.

She just shrugged her shoulders, as if to say, "I don't know." Her actions convinced me that the loss of my brother and then the loss of her job had both catapulted her into a downward spiral of sadness and depression. Sitting in a dark room for many hours a day proved depressing all by itself. Nevertheless, we were at the point that we were at, and there was no need rehashing how we got there.

We talked a little more and, finally, she fell asleep. I slept on and off, waking every time a staff member came into the room. As a teaching hospital, there were nurses, residents, medical students, and fellows from different specialties popping in and out regularly. I suppose my mother came to them as an ideal teaching opportunity with the host of other challenges she presented: lupus, diabetes, high blood pressure. Knowing this did not leave me with a comforting feeling, and this was another reason I wanted her transferred.

The next day came, and I looked forward to speaking with the doctors. I wanted a good and thorough explanation of the diagnosis and, more importantly, a prognosis. Certainly, I did not want her to stay at Cook County. They were a great trauma hospital, but not the place I wanted my mother to be for cancer treatment. The doctors came around at mid-day. Typical me, I pounced right on them with a bunch of questions, and they quickly realized that I wasn't the average "Joe Loved One" they normally counseled.

During conversations that are medical-related, I am usually asked, "Are you a doctor?" One of the greatest gifts from working in the drug industry is either knowing what's going on or knowing the right questions to ask to get a better idea of what's going on. To learn something I didn't know, I would either call a doctor I've worked with before or one of our internal doctors who work on our research teams.

Instead of answering my questions right away, the attending doctor asked me to step out into the hall. I did so, as the resident doctors trailed behind. My sister timed that perfectly, as she arrived at that point and joined in on the conversation. I could still see the pain on her face, but she at least had a little more pep in her step. Getting a good night's rest in her own bed had worked wonders.

The doctor asked me "Do you know what's going on?"

"I've had some informal discussions, but please enlighten me," I quickly turned the floor back over to them.

The one doctor began, "We believe your mother has stage IV cancer and maybe has just a few months to live. The MRI showed masses in the ovaries, pancreas, large intestine, peritoneum (stomach lining), and the lungs. Her condition is very fragile due to all of her other medical conditions. We are going to do a biopsy in the next couple of days, so we can determine the origin."

Hanging on the doctor's every word, and then hearing those words reverberate in my head, brought forth my tears. I respectfully asked, "Are there any experimental drugs or studies we can get her enrolled in?"

A different doctor answered, "In order to do that, we must know the origin of the cancer. Because lung cancer treatments don't work for pancreatic cancers, and pancreatic cancer treatments don't work for breast cancers, and so forth. So, before we can do anything, we have to get a biopsy."

On that note, we all went in to see my mother. She sat up in the bed and said, "Well?" The doctors told her everything they had just told us in the hall. My mother remained very stoic. Tears rolled down her face, but it was a quiet, calm cry. My sister and I hugged her, and that's when the tears really started to flow from all of us. I could see the doctors slowly retreat to give us some privacy.

"My babies. Who's going to take care of my babies?" That's all my mother kept saying, over and over. "Who's going to take care of my babies?"

The next day, I had an important meeting at work. Nothing more could be done regarding my mother until the biopsy. I knew the next couple of months would challenge me. My boss, Michelle Keefe, certainly one of the best bosses I've ever had, advised me to take a concomitant leave of absence. That would give me flexibility to continue working during the week, but take off on days that I needed to support my mom. She had just done it for her husband, Ralph, who had an aneurism. It allowed her to take care of him and their daughter, Taylor, but get key things done at work, too. I submitted for the leave and it was approved instantly.

Just like with most other companies, you have people who are always trying to find something to hold against you, to drag you down with, or more insidiously, to make you less of a competitive threat to them. So, I knew if I missed a lot of key things at work, someone would begin questioning my commitment or ability. "Is he engaged?" "Where is he?" "We haven't seen him in a while." Those were the kinds of questions that floated around about me—behind my back, of course—after my brother died.

Yes, I came to work a little dazed and challenged at times during that period, but I put my nose to the grindstone, as they say, and worked harder. Working harder for me meant being out in the field with my team and my customers and not in the office being "seen" by my peers. It disappointed me to think that people used my most vulnerable moments to take a dig, but because I had experienced it already, I anticipated it with my mother's illness.

I determined within myself not to let work distract me from that precious, yet painful, gift of quality time spent with my mother before she made her transition. I flew home to Atlanta later that night. An awful feeling came over me. I started to regret leaving Chicago to go to Atlanta. I felt it that night, as well as when the company had transferred me. Pilon had just downsized and lost a third of the Regional Managers. Of those who were asked to stay on, six of us were the "overages" in our office, meaning we had a choice to move to another city that had openings or we could take the severance package.

That severance package was sweet; it was approximately two years worth of salary and bonus, medical benefits for one year, placement support, and some other enticements. I was the only one who made that difficult decision to move. The other five people took their $300,000 to $400,000 and left the company.

With my mother dying in a hospital where I didn't want her to be and me working a thousand miles away, the guilt settled in. It would have been much easier to be in Chicago. I could have moved my mother in with me and made sure she had good nutrition and great care. But, I chose Pilon and selling drugs over my mother. It had been the same with my dad and with my brother. I was caught up in the prescription drug world of Pilon. Kind of funny that those selling or using illegal drugs often make the same choice—drugs over family. There I was faced with the same old dilemma. Only I wasn't an addict with an uncontrollable habit; I engaged in logical and straightforward thinking, and yet I had still chosen the drugs.

I knew participating in self-guilt like that constituted "stinkin' thinkin'" which never helps anything. Besides, chances are I may not have been able to change any of my family's outcomes had I even been there the whole time when their lives were going awry. I must never forget that selling drugs has allowed me to do some wonderful things for a lot of my family members. Also, it's difficult in Corporate America to find fine bosses you can believe in who have your back. I found that in Clint and Michelle, and I did not want to jeopardize that for another boss. I decided at that point to just make the best of the situation and really balance my time wisely between my mother and my company.

Early the next morning, my sister called me with a problem. "They said Mommy has developed pneumonia."

We found out the lady they had my mother rooming with had pneumonia. I couldn't believe what I heard! How stupid could that hospital be? Why would they put a cancer patient, whose immune system was compromised, in the same room with a patient who has pneumonia? That example validated why I didn't want her at Cook County.

Most people think doctors are incapable of making mistakes and that they all know better than anyone else. Well, somebody had to graduate at the bottom of the class, and that's the person you probably don't want treating you or your loved ones. Unfortunately, that's probably the person who works in an inner city hospital. Additionally, sometimes a hospital's policies and systems can be so dysfunctional due to incompetence or cutbacks, and it allows things like that to happen. People get wrong medicine, wrong surgeries, wrong rooms— wrong everything.

I paged the doctors immediately. When one of them called back, I couldn't help but chew her out. I knew that wouldn't solve anything, but it satisfied me in that moment because I felt like I was fighting for my mother's life. The doctor was so apologetic, but I didn't want to hear an apology because apologies couldn't cure the pneumonia. Finally, I asked, "What's her condition?"

They told me they had started her on an antibiotic and that it should kick in fairly quickly. I hung up and called my sister immediately. She said Mommy looked really bad; she wasn't really talking, just sleeping a lot. I could tell Ebi was really concerned.

That incident sent me back to Chicago that day. I figured I would drive. I needed the time to think, anyway. The trip took twelve hours, so that would be plenty of time for me to be alone in thought. I packed, got in the car, and took off by ten o'clock that same morning. I enjoyed the beautiful drive, especially through the mountains of Georgia, Tennessee, and Kentucky. I cried most of the trip. I didn't think I had that many tears or that much pain to spare, but I cried a river once again. I reflected on all my special moments with my mother. I remembered Ma singing lyrics to Anita Baker's song "Angel" to me, "You're my angel, oh angel." I felt so loved during those moments. A lifetime of moments flowed in and out of my mind as I drove.

Every hour or so, I called my sister to get an update. Each time Ebi reported, "Somewhat non-responsive." So, I drove a little faster.

About three hours outside of Chicago, Eboni called, hysterical, "Jemal, they said the antibiotic isn't working and that they may have to put mommy on life support, and if they do that, they are asking me to sign a *Do Not Resuscitate* form."

"Let me speak to the doctor," I said.

The doctor got on the phone and repeated what my sister said.

I "read" into him, "You will *not* put my mother on a machine! The antibiotic hasn't even had a chance to start working yet. It's a seven-day course, and you just started it today!"

"But, Mr. Gibson, her condition is deteriorating. I don't believe she is going to make it."

"If we put her on a machine, most people *don't* make it off the machine," I firmly stated, trying to be respectful and not yell. "That said, you will *only* put her on it if her oxygen levels absolutely require it. And if you put her on it, we will *not* sign a *Do Not Resuscitate* form. We will wait seven days for the antibiotic to start working! Do you understand?"

"Ok, Mr. Gibson. We will keep a close watch," the doctor obliged.

"Please give the phone to my sister," I said. I told Eboni what I told him.

My Aunt Bob happened to be there, too. I told her the same thing I told my sister and said I would be there in about three hours. I hung up the phone and started praying and crying. "God, please keep my mother. Please allow me to make it to see her before she passes on." I headed down the highway at about ninety miles per hour, hoping I wouldn't get stopped by the police.

My sister sent a text, "Where r u? She's getting worse." Just ninety minutes and I would be there. Suddenly, I felt the car start dragging and leaning to one side. "No, no, no! This can't be a flat. Please, no!" Sure enough, I had a flat tire. My mother lay dying in a crappy hospital, I still had a little over an hour to go, and I got a flat. Lotto!

I pulled the car over and pounded the steering wheel several times, as though that would make a difference. Why is this happening to me? After engaging in my one-minute pity party, I had to get moving quickly. I jumped out and started fixing the flat. Just then, while the sweat was dripping profusely down my face from the pace of things and the adrenalin, a police car pulled up. "Great,"

I thought, "another deterrent." As the officer walked up, I kept working. I didn't say anything because I really didn't know what to say.

He finally asked, "What are you doing?"

Really? Did he really ask me what I'm doing? What a stupid question, and I sure didn't have time for stupidity. I realized, though, that I didn't have time for my ego to get in the way of the real business at hand which was getting to the hospital.

"Fixing a flat," I nonchalantly answered.

"You from Georgia?"

"Yes." He could obviously read license plates.

"Can I see your license?"

"Sure." I thought about explaining my situation to him, but I didn't feel I would be able to keep myself composed. Plus, I was sure he'd heard enough sob stories in his time. So, I gave him my license and hurriedly went back to the tire-fixing. By the time the officer came back with my license, I had the tire and all the tools back in my trunk.

"Have a nice day," he said, as he handed me my license.

"Thanks," I said as I put the license back in my wallet.

I hopped back in the car and prepared to take off. I had lost thirty precious minutes, and I had a donut on, so I could only drive about sixty miles per hour. Just then, another text came from Eboni asking again, "Where r u?"

I replied telling her I had a flat and would be there in an hour. I then pulled onto the road and continued what had become a much more arduous journey than I had anticipated. Thinking once again, I felt I should not have left Chicago and my mother for a job. I should have stayed to make sure everything was taken care of. Why do I keep choosing work over family? Why do drugs continue to curse me? Even the good drugs...

I finally arrived. I paged the resident doctor, and he arrived shortly to take me up the back way because it was after hours. As soon as I walked into the room, I saw more equipment and IV's going. I leaned over my mother's bed, "Ma, it's me." She opened her eyes and looked at me, managed a little smile and closed her eyes softly. "I'm here, Ma. We'll take care of you," I whispered.

"She hasn't responded to anything in awhile," Eboni said. I knew Ebi probably needed a hug. So, we hugged for a good five minutes. Then, I finally hugged my Aunt Bob.

My mother slowly recovered over the next couple of days. I knew she would. It really troubled me that the doctors were trying to write her off so quickly. They should know how important it is to wait sometimes. Maybe they didn't care because she didn't have insurance, and it would cost them more money to wait. I didn't know, but I had faith, especially in the drugs they were giving her. I suppose like anything, it's been my constant faith and belief in the prescription drug industry that has allowed me to perform so well in it.

In that moment, I thought about the twisted duality between legal and illegal drugs. While my mother's illegal drug use did nothing but shorten her life, the legal drugs had been working to extend her life. In order for me to provide the assistance for my family's hospital stays or even funerals as a result their illegal drugs, I had to allow the demands of my legal drug job take me away from them. I was so grateful for Pilon.

They did several biopsies, but they all came back inconclusive. The majority of the issue stemmed from the negligence of the hospital to do things right. The Resident failed to get the right sample the first time. The attending physician got it from the wrong spot the second time. Totally ridiculous! They finally got some of the fluid from the peritoneum. By that time, my mother was so sore and weak from all the procedures that they couldn't do it again.

They diagnosed her with adenocarcinoma. That is a cancer with an unknown origin; however, they speculated that it was either pancreatic or ovarian because of the size of the masses in those organs. The doctors asked for a family discussion. That meant time to do some planning. We sat in my mother's room, and they explained all the options: hospice, treatment, do not resuscitate, power of attorney, and so forth. While I did not want to influence my mother, I hoped she would say, "Let's fight this thing." Sure enough, that's what she said.

I asked what our treatment options were. Fortunately, the ovarian and pancreatic cancers are treated with the same chemotherapy so we put a plan in place to do a couple of treatments, and the doctors would evaluate her progress. My mother also opted to resuscitate and she gave me the power of attorney. I understood the significance of that decision at that exact moment.

I looked at her and said, "Ma, trust that I will fight for you to stay alive, but I won't allow you to suffer either. Should we get to a point of no options, I will do what is best." The mere fact that those words were coming out of my mouth was earth-shattering to me. I stood there talking about the imminent death of my mother. It all became so overwhelming.

I found that any moment during those weeks could turn into an uncontrollable crying moment that would hit me without warning. I started thinking about death a lot more. I thought about my death and the death of other loved ones. I talked about it a lot, to the point where it started bothering Lisa. But, I was learning the very valuable lesson that tomorrow is borrowed time, and today is the only guarantee we have. We can choose to love and choose to live each moment or we can save it, hoping or planning to have it to fill the next day. But, for some, that next day may never come and we may have lost the moment in which to love someone or be loved by him or her.

In the midst of all the pain, I had spurts where I loved on my daughters like there would be no tomorrow. I talked with friends I hadn't talked to in months or years. I knew this principle, but it was now real, as real as it could be.

They let my mom out of the hospital. She started her chemo, and things started to seem a little promising. I kept flying back and forth from Atlanta to Chicago, helping my sister out. My aunts were coming over on certain days to help out when neither Eboni nor I could be there. My mother, though weak, started to respond to the chemo. They revaluated after two treatments and thought she was strong enough to receive the other four treatments, so they continued on.

We needed to hear that great news because my mother's birthday was fast approaching. I wanted it to be a special birthday for her. I thought over and over about what I could do to top her sixtieth birthday party that had been held at our house in Chicago the previous year. I had invited all of our family, her friends from her old job, and friends from her AA/NA group. There were over a hundred people there enjoying that beautiful event. I created a video of her life that I projected on the biggest wall of the house. She showed her friends all around the house or the "mansion" as she called it. At 6200 square feet, it hardly measured up to what we call a mansion, but she proudly called it one anyway. If that's what she wanted to call it, so it would be.

Her celebration culminated with a "Ceremony of 60 Roses." I had purchased sixty roses and placed them on a table. We gathered the entire party around and sat my mother in the middle. I asked everyone to think about a moment they shared with my mother that touched them, changed them, or moved them in any way. Each person would grab a rose, stand with my mother, share the moment with the group and my mother, and then give her the rose. I nervously planned it, knowing that it could either be a bust where no one would get up and say anything or that it could be a moment that my mother would never forget. Most people never have the opportunity to hear at one time what people feel about them, except at a funeral and, of course, they aren't hearing it then, or at least most of us don't believe they are.

I wanted my mother to know how much love people had for her. I wanted her to hear examples of all the love, joy, and support that she had given to others. Once I finished explaining how the process would flow, people were up grabbing roses—Aunt Hannah, Aunt Bob, Nita, Illandus, and so on. It turned out beautifully. My mother cried the entire time, and so did most of the people in the room at some point or another. I finally closed it out, "Mommy, on behalf of my big brother, Anthony, and my little sister, Eboni, we want to thank you for all the love that you've given us. Thank you for all the moments that you struggled but persevered to keep the family together. We are so thankful to have a loving mother like you. Happy Birthday."

That original moment could not be recreated. While I knew it would be hard to top that, her upcoming birthday had to be very special, nonetheless.

One day, while talking with Ebi about our mother's birthday, she said, "Well, I have a surprise. I want to get married on Mommy's birthday."

Definitely surprised, I said, "First of all, congratulations! I am really happy for you, if that's what you want to do. Secondly, have you really thought about it, because it could be a sad day for you, and you wouldn't want to spoil your anniversary with your husband by crying all day and night missing Mommy. On another note, do you really want to get married, or are you just doing it so that Mommy can see you married?"

"Both," she responded honestly. She decided to get married the weekend before our mother's birthday, on May 24th. Then, the plan would be to celebrate my mother's birthday and Eboni's wedding reception on the same day. The next day would be my birthday, and the greatest gift for me would be to spend it with my mother.

The next few weeks were pretty good. I continued back and forth between Atlanta and Chicago, as usual. My mother continued getting stronger. Yet, one day when I happened to be in Atlanta, Eboni called me, crying. I thought, "Please don't let it be now. Please don't let it be now."

Eboni spoke in between sobs, "We had to rush Mommy to the hospital."

"What happened?" I asked.

"She almost burned herself up! She was smoking a cigarette and fell asleep. The oxygen from her machine caused the whole bed to go up in flames."

"How's Mommy?" I asked, scared out of my mind. Who ever expected something like that in the midst of everything else going on?

"She's got burns on her legs and just a little bit in her face, but she'll be OK."

"Smoking? Why is Mommy smoking? We are trying everything we can to keep her alive, and she's continuing to kill herself! How is she getting cigarettes? She can't even leave the house, so who's bringing her cigarettes?"

"Tony," Ebi said. Tony, a cousin of ours, had his own challenges with drugs and alcohol. He was very helpful most of the time and had an extremely kind heart. Unfortunately, Tony died while celebrating his 50th birthday after partying all night. I was never told the cause, but I could only assume it had something to do with drugs and alcohol.

So, I flew up to Chicago the next day. I didn't really want to blame Tony. I needed to talk with my mother, though. There she was hanging on by a thread, and not only did she make it worse by smoking, but then burning herself in the process! The cancer was already compromising her immune system, which meant any little infection could kill her.

When I arrived at the house in Chicago, I noticed cigarette butts in the ashtray and under the bed. In a small paper bag, I found a couple of packs of cigarettes. Suddenly, I found myself daydreaming about back in the day, sneaking into my mother's room with my brother showing me her drugs hidden in her dresser drawer. I clinched the bag of cigarettes in my hand and started to cry to her, "Why Ma, why?" In response, she shrugged her shoulders.

Addictions are a powerful force, and my mother had several of them throughout her life. She had gone from one type of addiction to another, and each one landed devastating blows on her life. Heavy drinking and smoking is a typical pattern for many who have pancreatic cancer. I hated to associate my mother's cancer to addictions, so I tried not to think about it.

My mother's party and Eboni's wedding reception were very nice. Most of our family came to celebrate both, but it was special for my mother because most people assumed it would be her last. I held on with faith and hope that it wouldn't be; I didn't want to turn the moment into a sad one and neither did my mother. Therefore, both of our speeches at the event touched on celebrating the moment and loving family more. After my mother's speech, she went outside and smoked a cigarette.

The next day, on my birthday, Enner coincidentally got re-married. I took my mother to Enner's wedding, where everyone excitedly greeted her. I could tell she really enjoyed seeing that part of our extended family. We took lots of pictures, and most importantly, I got to dance with my mother. At any party we went to, we would often Step (Chicago's urban version of Swing Dancing). That time, the dance felt very special. My mother tired very easily and could barely stand, but I knew she wanted to dance with me as much as I wanted to dance with her. I sensed that we both thought that would perhaps be our last dance.

After the wedding, I took my mother home and carried her up the stairs. She slept for the rest of the night. A few days later, she welcomed her sixty-first birthday. I really didn't know what to get her since I didn't know how long she had to enjoy it. She had never gone to a play before, so Lisa and I decided to take her and Ebi to see the Broadway play, *Wicked*. She liked it, but slept through most of it. We then took her to Red Lobster, her favorite restaurant, and she barely ate, but we knew, more importantly, that we had shared and created moments we would remember.

Things continued to yo-yo over the next several weeks until my mother was hospitalized again. Now, a breathing machine and feeding tubes helped to sustain her. She slept most of the day, and when the medication wore off, she got really agitated. That generally happened at night, so I stayed at the hospital every night, and my sister came in during the day.

One day I went home to Atlanta to see my girls, and once again, the day I got home, my mother had a major issue. Her heart stopped beating, so she had "coded" for the first time. I certainly could not risk driving, so I took the next flight back to Chicago. Fortunately, she recovered, but the doctors had a conversation with my sister while I was on my flight. They told her our mother would not make it, and we needed to decide whether to keep her on life support. My sister told them they needed to wait for me. Once I landed, I called my sister and she told me what they said. I told her to tell them that our mother wished to be resuscitated.

Eboni said that Mommy had been non-responsive for hours and somewhat catatonic. When I walked in, I yelled out, "Ma!" and she opened her eyes, looked at me, and then drifted back to sleep. I knew in my heart it wasn't her time. She eventually recovered and became fully alert. She could not talk because of the tube down her throat. We waited for her to get strong enough to receive a tracheotomy. Once she received a trach, she would be able to go home.

We ultimately had to have the conversation again with my mother about what we should do if she coded again. Even though she couldn't talk, she gave her Evelyn stare like, "You better revive me!" and she also took the time to write it out. That relieved me because I certainly didn't want to have to make the decision to not resuscitate or remove her from the oxygen.

We relished the next few days of watching my mother get stronger. She wrote a lot, and we would laugh at the things she was saying. She ate food through the tube but soon got tired of that. She would always ask for a hamburger or ice cream. She seemed like such a little kid, like one of my daughters, the way she would look when we said "No" to those foods. And like a father, I wanted so badly to get her whatever she wanted. I couldn't wait for her to get out of the hospital.

It was July 4th, 2008 and I could see the fireworks from her hospital room. Chicago, being so wonderfully flat, made it possible to see the spectacular Navy Pier fireworks display from miles away, as long as one of the skyscrapers didn't block the view. One could also see fireworks hosted by any number of far away suburbs, way off in the distance. I loved fireworks.

That night's display had an extra special flair because I watched them with my mother. It reminded me of my childhood, living in the projects and looking out over the city. I remembered the world being a big unknown place to me. Going through cancer with my mother was part of that unknown world that I didn't care to know. As I sat there, I hoped that it wouldn't be our last Independence Day together.

Fortunately, she got stronger over the next couple of days. As soon as she could breathe a little better, the trach would be removed. One morning, I went to Tee's to take a shower and take a nap. Eboni called me on the cell crying, "Mommy coded again."

I jumped up and went to the hospital. It always seemed that when I left her side, she would have a near-death experience. It made me wonder if she just didn't want to die in front of me. But, that was my ego talking. She didn't want to die, period, because she recovered every time.

Over the next couple of days, my mother coded three more times. The doctors were bewildered by her will to live. Unfortunately, coding took a toll on her; she got weaker and less responsive each time. That last code was all I could bear. After they cleaned her, I sat and held her hand. As the tears rolled down my face, the reality of one of my greatest fears had come upon me. I would have to make the decision.

I finally hoped that my mom would just pass away in her sleep, peacefully and pain-free. Quietly, deep down within, I prayed to God to please take her. She had coded five times. She began to look lifeless, her eyes slightly open, breathing on the cue of the machine and moaning every now and then. I would stay with my mother until late in the evening. I decided to leave her alone that night. A part of me wanted her to rest and a part of me wanted her to transition naturally. So, I went and slept in the car, in the parking lot, until morning.

When I went back into the hospital, my mother still lay non-responsive but alive. I asked the doctors to back off the pain medication and sedatives to see if she would respond. They backed them out until almost no pain medications or sedatives were on board, and she still lay there unresponsive. Eboni and I discussed it, and we agreed that Mommy had gone through too much, and it was time.

I can't describe in words the depth of the pain in my heart having that conversation, but we had to have it. Afterwards, we called all of her siblings and close friends. I told them we were going to take her off of the machine that day and they might want to be there, in case she didn't make it. So, everyone arrived in the early afternoon. Everyone took turns saying something special to my mother.

I couldn't believe we were there. I couldn't believe that moment was upon us. The doctors were supposed to turn the oxygen off at four o'clock that afternoon. They were a little late getting started. We stood around my mother's bed in a circle and the nurse turned off machine. I held my mother's hand, whispering to her,

"Come on, Ma; you can make it. Breathe, you can make it."

My mother gasped a few times, never waking, never talking, just gasping in what appeared to be a completely sedated state. Then, a tear rolled down her left cheek, and she took her last breath. I sank my head in the pillow next to her and cried out until I couldn't breathe. "I'm sorry, Ma! I'm sorry!"

She left us, and I felt that I had given up, that I'd played God and made the decision that it was my mother's time. The pain in my cry was deep and thunderous. That was *my* mommy, and now she was gone. And, now I was there alone. I was orphaned. All those who would love me unconditionally were gone. Those who would inspire me to do and be my best were gone. I was alone. No one moved; no one touched me. They respectfully gave me my moment.

On the other side of me was my sister who was crying uncontrollably, too. While I had lost my mother, she had lost her best friend. I knew what that felt like having lost my dad, so I walked to the other side of the bed and Ebi and I hugged and cried a little while longer. Everyone gave us our moment. Then others came closer to her side. We were encircled by Aunt Bob and Uncle Larry, Aunt Hannah, Aunt Betty, my wife Lisa, my mother's friend Lisa, and my best friend, Mike Brock. It was beautiful to see that love surrounded the beautiful woman who had given me life.

My mother's home going service could not have been more perfect. We held the "Celebration of Lynn" at the Marriott Hotel on Ashland Avenue near Roosevelt Road. A couple hundred people showed up to celebrate her life. I presented it just like my dad's and my brother's; it was just like she wanted with ice sculptures, balloons, food, music, family and friends, all telling stories about her.

The next day, my sister and I went to where the cremation would take place. We had our chance to say our last goodbyes, hugging and kissing her as we would a sleeping, newborn baby. My sister and I stood holding each other as they slid my mother into the cremation chamber. One might think it morbid to want to watch, but there were so many stories about people not being cremated and families being given fake ashes of their loved ones. I didn't want that to happen, so I wanted to watch. I was my mother's keeper. Just like I watched and waited with my dad, I wanted to do the same with my mother.

After a few minutes, I had to step outside. We didn't leave immediately. Eboni and I walked to the corner of the crematory and just stood there looking up at the sky. I turned around and looked at the smoke from the chimney as it floated and faded into the sky. "There she goes," I thought to myself. "Now, she's back with Dad, and they will be looking after me together."

Suddenly, out of nowhere, came a butterfly. It landed on my shirt and didn't move. Even when I turned and moved about slightly, it stayed right on my shirt. I could have passed out! It was just like with Dad outside the crematory in Indianapolis six years before. She flew from my shirt to my hand and just sat there.

"Hi, Ma," I said under my breath. I didn't want my sister to know what I was thinking. But, she was just as shocked because butterflies were very special to my mother. In fact, my mother had a butterfly tattooed on her chest. During Anthony's birthday, she would let a butterfly balloon go in the air. So, my sister instantly connected the butterfly with my mother, too. While the butterfly sat on my hand, I shared with my sister what had happened when my dad died, and we both sat there in complete shock. Finally, after a few minutes or so, she flew away. "Be well and be free, Ma," I whispered.

Tired

Two months later, Tee died. She had just had a check-up before my mother died. The doctor said she was fine, considering the cancer; the radiation seemed to have worked, and she was given a "good" bill of health. I guess that didn't mean anything. Tee said she was tired. She had lost her husband, Harry, my brother Anthony, all of her siblings except two, and finally my mother, her only daughter. She simply gave up trying to live.

Unfortunately, Tee's death caused a rift in the family because my mother's siblings didn't want my mother to be recognized as Tee's daughter or any of us to be recognized as her grandchildren. We weren't trying to fool anyone or disrespect my real grandmother, Dorothy, but everyone who knew Tee thought my mother *was* Tee's daughter and that we were her grandchildren, so I didn't see any reason why we could not be a part of her eulogy; it was her life.

Tee loved everyone equally but, for the most part, she treated us like we were hers. We spent many birthdays, Thanksgivings, Christmases, and lots of other special moments with Tee; we were always at her house. My mother was raised by Tee for most of her childhood years and had lived with Tee for the last ten-plus years of their lives. My mother had always called Tee, "Mother." It dumbfounded me that people didn't want to recognize someone in death as she was in life. Even though Tee had specified how she wanted things done, people still did it their way and acted foolishly in the process. After Tee's funeral, I just took a much needed break from the family for a while.

Tee had been a major force in my life, directly and indirectly. She always shared her wisdom with me and wanted me to call her more often. She truly saved my mother and my brother on several occasions from their own self-destruction while on drugs. Her love for them and her faith in God allowed me to have them in my life a little while longer. I understood that, and I loved her for it. I only told two people at work that Tee had died. I grew tired of grieving, and I felt people might be getting tired of grieving for me.

What Path Will You Take?

We were in the midst of layoffs at Pilon again; this was our third layoff in four years. Years ago our company bragged about never having layoffs in the company's one hundred and fifty years. Now, within a few short years, we had almost caught up with other companies in our industry. Naturally, every downsizing announcement came with a tremendous amount of anxiety. With it being late in 2008, and with our country suffering what some called a recession and others called a depression, most people in corporate America couldn't think of a worse time to be let go from their jobs.

I had just moved to Atlanta, bought a house, and hung some pictures on the wall. A month later, I got the announcement. The Florida region had some very talented leaders who had great performances over their entire careers. There were four of us Regional Managers, and the company planned to only keep two, so I knew it would be close. That time, however, I mentally prepared myself to leave. The severance package would be several hundred thousand dollars, and I knew I could make it on that for a couple years, even in a bad economy. And, I was honestly ready to try something different. Most importantly, I wanted to have some time off to grieve for my mom and for Tee, who had just passed away. Quite frankly, I had not taken the time to finish grieving for my father and brother, either, so I really hoped I would get the package.

Many people had the same ideas as I had. Those who were close to retirement and had lost most of their 401k's thought of it as a great windfall. Unfortunately,

I couldn't just volunteer for it; I had to wait for it to be offered. On the flip side, to be told your talent, skills, and capabilities weren't needed or valued by the company could be a major blow to the ego. I struggled with it for a moment or two.

Fortunately, at the time, I was reading *A New Earth*, by Eckhart Tolle. The teaching about ego and how to manage it proved extremely helpful for me. One Sunday after re-reading a chapter and meditating, I took a completely new perspective. I realized that Pilon did not define me, and that only *I* could define myself. I would not be defined by status, finances, other's perceptions of my successes, or the challenges I faced. All that mattered was the love I had for life and a genuine belief that, as John Wooten says, "Things turn out best for those who make the best of the way things turn out."

While I found inner peace regarding my fate with the company, I knew it would be difficult communicating with those who would stay and those who had to leave. I understood that many were not in the space I chose for myself. For them, Pilon was their life. Many had spent twenty or thirty years with the company. They were between a rock and a hard place, too young to retire, yet at an age where companies would avoid hiring them. I decided I would work through that challenge, as well, if I had to.

In the meantime, I had launched an African-American Network called PFAAN (Pilon Field African-American Network). Those types of networks were common in other areas of the company, but we never had one in the field, so it seemed the right time to create one. Our engagement and inclusive scores from a Gallup survey showed African-Americans felt less included and less engaged than our white counterparts. Less engagement usually led to poor performance, which usually led to termination.

Currently there are four hundred colleagues involved in PFAAN. I lost some political capital in getting the organization off the ground, but that's okay. The reward is already paying off, as the objective of the network is already being achieved. The engagement from those involved in PFAAN is getting better, with hopes that the organization will continue to improve as time goes on.

Our next downsizing meeting was scheduled to be in Dallas in January, 2009. I looked forward to traveling there because my "twin," Tricie, lives in Dallas, and I had hoped to see her. We are not real twins, but cousins, both Gemini's born on the same day, albeit two years apart. My Aunt Freddie and several other cousins lived in Dallas, as well. Dana, the only male cousin in my generation, besides his brother who I'd never met, lived there, too. Dana got out of jail in March, 2007. He had actually spent most of his adult life in jail. In his early teens, he got involved with the Black Gangsta Disciples, one of the notorious gangs in Chicago. Most of my cousins belonged to that gang.

Anyway, Dana got into a fight, killed someone, and went to jail for manslaughter. When he got out, he got hooked on drugs and went back to jail for armed robbery. He got out again, and then went back in shortly after for another armed robbery. I think since the age of eighteen, he has only spent a total of four years free. He was now forty-two. What's fascinating is that Dana's brother who was adopted as an infant by two lady friends of my grandmother, Evangeline Koonce, had a totally different outcome. I was told that those ladies raised him in a very loving and supportive environment and that today he is a rocket scientist for NASA!

One might argue there is the probability that both those boys' lives could have turned out the exact same way, even if they had both been raised in the same household—one a great success and the other one with a life riddled with crime. However, one cannot deny that parental guidance and support and social environment play a major role in a child's development and success. Unfortunately, after connecting with our distant NASA cousin one time, we've not been able to reconnect. Intuition tells me he may prefer it that way.

When Dana got out of jail that last time, he moved to Dallas to be in a better environment, away from the people, places, and things that he knew and that could trigger the same old behaviors. Tricie graciously took him into her house. It had been a long time since any of us had seen him, so we had a big family event planned for him. My Aunt Arlene (Dana's mom) came down along with other family and friends to welcome him home and celebrate what we hoped would be his "new" life. I enjoyed seeing him. He had stayed in good shape, his heart seemed to be pure and full of good intentions that he would not go back again, and I believed him.

Thus far, he had remained good and clean. He drank occasionally, but he said he could handle it. I didn't think his occasional drinking was a good idea, though, as it only worked to weaken him, so that when a trigger appeared, he wouldn't be strong enough to resist it or control his choices. Then before you know it, down the slippery slope he would go.

Dana and I had spoken around Christmas and made plans to spend a day together when I got to Dallas for my meeting. I would come down a day early, and he would take a day off from work. I really looked forward to hanging out with him, since I hadn't seen him in two years. The last time we were together he had just been released from prison. I had taken him to a strip club, and we hung out the whole night. It had felt good to be around him, as we were close when we were young. Since I had lost my brother and my father, I felt their presence in him.

There were rumors running through Pilon that we would find out at that Dallas meeting whether we were placed or not. The tension levels were pretty high in the office and so was the backstabbing. I had never been more disappointed in some of my peers than during that time. The office turned into an "every man/woman for themselves" environment, with people spreading vicious rumors about each other. People questioned work ethic, strategic skills, and coaching skills. You name it, they were spreading it.

I landed in Dallas, checked into the hotel, and called Dana. "Hey what's up, Cuz? I'm in town. What's the haps?" I asked.

"Aw man what's happening? What hotel you at?" He answered my question with a question. Before I could speak he said, "I need you to come to where I am. I'm at this broad's house."

Something in his voice didn't sound right. It came across as low and scratchy.

The type of voice men have when they've been using. At that point, my instincts kicked in, and I said, "I don't have a car, Dana. I thought you would be able to get to me."

He said, "I can't right now." Then, out of nowhere he said, "You know I need some money, right?"

That floored me. I couldn't believe it. First of all, he didn't ask me. He told me, like I was one of his women. Reality sunk in, and I knew he was back using. Whatever went on at his location, I knew I didn't care to be a part of it. He went on to tell me why he needed the money, but I barely listened because of his dishonesty. I told him we would have to get together on another day, and I hung up.

I thought to myself, "Damn, Dana. You are headed down the wrong path. You've come so far and you've done so well." After shedding a few tears over him, then realizing I could do nothing to help him, I called Tricie and told her what happened. She said he had asked her for some money, too.

The time arrived when I needed to compartmentalize. I had an important meeting that week, and I couldn't afford to let Dana's drama distract me. The meeting went well. Once again, I demonstrated my leadership and value in a few exercises, and I am sure my detached feelings toward the process prompted me to say some things that others would have thought to be too controversial to say at the time. Those others still lived in the "better-to-be-seen-and-not-heard" mode, otherwise known as fear, in my book.

With the meeting completed, we all headed to the airport. Even though the meeting ended on a high note, the number of District Managers in Florida would still be cut by 30% or more. That saddened me already, but the harder part of determining who those individuals would be was yet to come. So far, we had only determined the number of positions needed.

I never got the chance to see Dana. I decided to touch base with Tricie from the airport. When I called her, she said she tried to call me, which I didn't doubt because I kept my phone on silent most of the week. She told me Dana went to jail for armed robbery. It happened the day I arrived in Dallas. Apparently, after

Dana and I talked, he went up to KFC, stuck his finger in his coat pocket and robbed them. He didn't even have a gun! To make matters worse, he walked back to the girl's apartment that could be seen directly from KFC. How crazy was that?!

That did it for Dana. He just got his third strike, *and* he now resided in Texas. Everybody knows Texas don't play. With him being in a different state and with no connections or support, prison would be a whole different ballgame for him. His gang affiliations probably wouldn't be as strong or mean much in Texas, since gangs aren't as prevalent there. While I was talking to Tricie, Dan, the new State Director for our Florida region walked up. He would be determining whether I stayed or left. I told Tricie I'd call her back.

Dan and I spoke for a minute, summing up the meeting. He then put his hand on my shoulder and said, "Get some sleep this weekend." He gave me that look that revealed I was "in," but I knew he couldn't say it. I smiled. I told him to have a safe flight and that I looked forward to working with him. I also told him he wouldn't be disappointed. Remember, closing is what I do.

As I handed the gate agent my boarding pass and walked onto my flight, I thought about the paradox of drugs in my life. The jail door slammed on Dana that week because of drugs. That saddened me deeply. I'd lost him again, just like everyone else close to me who chose drugs as their path. But, I couldn't help but smile as I thought about the contradiction of my opportunity. I would continue to run a half billion-dollar drug operation.

A month later, I was featured in our company's annual report. There I sat, humbly, on top of the world in the drug game.

My Savior Continues

Lisa gave birth to our third daughter, Nadya. I guess you could say that I am truly the king of my castle. I have five women catering to me (I say that with great love, mind you). I live with my wife, Lisa, and our three beautiful daughters—Iman, Zhara and Nadya, and then there's CoCo Chanel, our female Shih Tzu. Moving to Atlanta profited us greatly in terms of home buying.

We live in a 10,000 square foot home in a gated community. Some of our neighbors include rappers Yung Joc & Rick Ross, R&B singer, Donell Jones, and Gospel singer, Dottie Peoples. As a child living in the projects, I remember having to walk up and down five flights of stairs due to a constantly broken elevator. Now, I have an elevator taking me up and down the four flights in our home, and it works all the time.

My fortieth birthday party meant more than just recognizing a certain number I achieved along my biological range. Although I always love bringing people together for a good time, my celebration meant more. My fortieth birthday celebration had great purpose and resolve.

First of all, that celebration presented an opportunity to pay respect to my brother, Anthony Holloway, who never made it to age forty.

Secondly, that celebration spiritually connected me with my mother, in remembrance of our tradition of celebrating our birthdays together. Her birthday was three days after mine. It is because of her I know how to love unconditionally, weep unashamedly, and give without looking for anything in return.

Last, but certainly not least, that celebration honored my father, the man who made me who I am today. It is because of every book he challenged me to read, every word of wisdom that he shared, and every time that he told me to find a way (because there was nothing to go back to) that my father would be proud to see how successful I had become from selling drugs, the legal way.

We partied for three full days! Friends and family from all across the country came to join in the festivities. It was a real testament to those I love and who love me. I often questioned all that love because sometimes I could be a pretty tough friend to keep. Not because I made it a point to be difficult or anything like that, but because I kept so many different circles of friends. I have friends from the many different schools I attended, friends from the many different jobs I held, and friends from the many different cities and neighborhoods I have lived in.

With the constant changes in my childhood, sometimes I hesitated before opening up to new friends because in the back of my mind, I knew I would be torn apart from them just like times before with other people. So, why build up something only to experience more pain and disappointment due to separation? Additionally, with so many friendships developed over the years, a very busy work life, and the time I needed to spend with my growing family of girls, it became hard to return calls, visit, or generally keep up with everyone. Moreover, some part of me has always been a loner; more often than not, I turned off my phones so that I could read, study, assess my life, and figure out what I needed to do to continue to move forward.

So, to show my gratitude to all my friends, I set it out for the entire weekend. If Friday alone had been my only celebration, I would have felt it highlighted only a small portion of the best moments of my life. Friday evening we laughed, danced, ate, and drank on the rooftop of the Lucky Lounge in Atlanta until five o'clock Saturday morning.

Then came Saturday with a party catered for several hundred people at my home. Several chefs cooked lobster, crab, steak, sushi, fried fish, vegetables and, of course, we had unlimited liquor. We had one of Atlanta's hottest bands, Indigo Blue, play for three hours. I looked at my watch at seven-thirty that evening and observed hundreds of my closest family and friends in a splendid frenzy, grooving to the band and celebrating life—my life. I am so grateful that I was alive to see it, and I don't ever take that for granted. I almost missed that fortieth year too many times, but as my dad often told me, there was always more planned for me in this lifetime.

Saturday night, Norris, my best friend from college and an Ups N Downs partner, DJ'd the party. He and I had grown even closer over the past few years because he lives in Atlanta, too. Besides all that, he's just a damn good DJ. I asked him to hit a set for all the music that shaped my life, i.e., house, stepping, bass, crunk/snap, hip hop, and more. He truly kept people dancing non-stop from eight o'clock in the evening until they were hardly standing at five o'clock Sunday morning. It was truly amazing.

Rounding up the event on Sunday, we enjoyed a fish fry, crab boil, and once again dancing into the wee hours of the morning. Three incredible days were put aside to celebrate my love and appreciation for everyone. I spared no expense to make it fun. Money did not stand in the way of my expression of love for everyone. That party exemplified what legal drug dealing can afford a person.

Throughout *my* journey of drug dealing, I wasn't concerned about enemies trying to kill me, police trying to arrest me, workers trying to cheat me, or people trying to steal from me. I did not have any of those every day feelings of anxiety and malaise that drug dealers on the street experience. I was giving and receiving love in an unconditional way and celebrating in love and peace, not fear. I was cursed so often by illegal drugs and the devastating impact they had my life. Ironically, from that curse, I learned some valuable lessons that saved my life. So, even the curse was a savior.

Being exposed to the meetings and the recovering addicts I saw early on with my mother, and then later with my father and brother, taught me how devastating illegal drugs could be to a person's life. My father shared with me the principles he learned in recovery, and he passed on to me his insatiable study of spiritual truths. He served them to me one lesson at a time. Had he not suffered so greatly, his flair for and appreciation of life may not have been so fervent. In turn, he might not have ever learned some of the powerful principles I was then exposed to and carried forward as the foundation of all my learning and practicing.

The legal drug sales that became my career increased my capacity to want to help people live healthier, happier lives. This coincided nicely with my spiritual foundation, but it also exposed me to skills and tools that would allow me to teach and coach others to be the best they can be. While I acquired more information and experienced more learning, growing, and thriving from legal drug sales, illegal drugs were still ravaging and sometimes overwhelming my life. They were even putting me in situations that could have ended my life because of my connections to them.

What I have witnessed throughout my life has made me think very seriously about the prevalence of drugs in our society along both of these paths of access. As human beings, we are all looking for comfort for what ails us, both mentally and physically. In many cases, those who are fortunate enough to be served by our health care system can afford the legal access, but can become addicted to drug usage just as easily as those who have little access to health care and may simply be looking for a "fix" that may only be available through illegal channels. Each and every individual may not readily have the same choices, but are often trying to fill the same needs.

To me, all of my life experiences prepared me for this moment. Compared to all of my family and friends who may have collectively sold a few thousand dollars worth of drugs on the streets, I've sold a few billion dollars worth— off the streets. Our chosen professions are absurdly similar in description, yet diametrically opposed in consequences.

Ultimately, the choices I have made have produced a greater, more powerful and lasting impact for my own life and the many lives I've touched so far along on my journey. Yet, it is still those obstacles that prepared me for those choices I've made that I continue to ponder the most. I have seen how choices when accompanied by transcendent blessings, a bit of luck, and an abundance of love and faith, have not only allowed me to live an extraordinary life, but to consider drugs equally my curse and my savior.

Appreciation

Most of us come into this world with what some would define as a "curse." If we didn't come here with one, perhaps one or two curses attached themselves to us along the way. I hope that this book has given others the inspiration to realize that sometimes your curse can be your savior. Adopting principles such as love of self and of others, forgiveness, visualizing, decision making, hard work and, yes, a little luck can help just about anyone overcome anything.

As you have read, there have been numerous people in my life supporting me along the way. So, I would like to use this section to thank a few people, some who were already mentioned in the book, but equally important, many who were not. I left out many other stories of interconnecting events throughout my life to spare my readers from a 500-page autobiography.

In memory, I want to again mention three people who meant the world to me...

First and foremost, my father, Sam Gibson: I could never have survived without his unconditional love toward me. It was his goal to make me the most well-rounded man I could be—from my intellect, physique, health, domestic abilities, and financial status to, most importantly, my role as a loving human being. Well, Dad, your dream for me came true; I am all that you wanted me to be. No words can express my love for you—I've tried to find them, but they don't exist.

With no less appreciation, my dearest mother, Evelyn Farmer: Her love for me proved so limitless. I am ever so grateful for her perseverance with trying to better herself for the benefit of my brother, my sister, and me. She never ever gave up.

Last, but certainly not least, my older brother, Anthony Holloway. Ant did his best to protect me from the streets—and he succeeded. What I'll always remember most about him is that he believed in me, no matter what.

Now, introducing those who are still around, loving me and encouraging me...

To my daughters Iman, Zhara and Nadya: You give me reason to love and reason to live. I love you all more than you will ever know.

To my wife, Lisa: You have been by my side through many of my most tragic moments and my greatest triumphs. Thank you for loving me and supporting me as I followed dream after dream.

To my baby sister, Eboni: You will always be my "Shugah Bum." I love you as if you are my own daughter. It's just us now, so let's make the best of it.

To my nieces and nephews, Keshya, Tocki, Anthony Jr. (AJ), Marvell, Markell, Chris Jr (CJ), and Destinee Lyn: I love you all. May you also "find a way" to a better life.

To all the others who raised me: Grandma (Dorothy Holloway, deceased), Aunt Bob & Uncle Larry, Aunt Betty, Aunt Freddie, Enner & Wright, and Ms. Olivia. I thank you all, from the bottom of my heart, for taking me into your homes. You treated me like your own child, even when times were difficult for you. I will forever be grateful.

To Pint—or as my girls affectionately call you, "Grandma Pint": I am not sure where to begin or how to end with my expressions of love and gratitude toward you. The impact you had on my dad, my girls, and me has been/is one of the most beautiful and genuine expressions of unconditional love. You are a real ANGEL.

To all my other aunts and uncles: Aunt Hannah, Aunt Arlene, Aunt Aida, Uncle Dobie, Uncle Charles, Uncle Bill and Uncle Eddie (deceased). I love you very much. So much love to all the Gibsons, Wilsons, Holloways, Lanes, Collins, & Farmers.

To my in-laws: Much love to The Twittys, McBradys, & Broaduses in Indianapolis. James and Mychael (BoBo), I am proud of you; keep it movin!!

To my adopted families: the Linwoods in Peoria; the Atwaters in St. Petersburg; and the Lees in Chicago, thank you for accepting me and never making me feel like an outsider.

To my Whitney Young Dolphins, Florida A&M Rattlers, Pershing Rifles and Beta Nu Alphas: Lawd, THANK YOU!! There was something special about you and our generation. I know, without a doubt, your achieving nature and loving ways were critical to my growth and development.

To my "Pharma Family": Thank you, thank you, thank you! Thank you for letting a little drug-born, project-raised boy—struggling to avoid a statistical outcome—into one of the noblest professions in the world. Helping others live healthier, happier lives has brought so much joy to me and has allowed me to do so much for my own family. A special thanks to Hank Allen, Glover Johnson, Clint Lewis, Cheryl James, Art Thurnauer, Michelle Keefe, Forrest Harper, Lasonja Chapple, Booker Wright, Monica Sturgis, Mark Mosely, Jim Horsey, Crescenda Bramlett, Fred Dillick, Jerry Burnfield, Dave Szamborski, Michelle Taylor, Monica Danielly Green, Doug Alexy, Mary Mischler, Mike Umbles, Mark Gorris, Maya Manning, Mahendra Sahadeo, Darryl Davis, Jay Dooley, Al Valentine, Tonecia Browder, Ken "Kwap" Kwapesheski, Jihad Rizkallah, Ron Borgmier, Darren Yoakum, Rachelle "Clark", Andrea Clark, Mark Whalen, Jamie Scott, John Hooten, Chris Ogle, Kevin Cooper, David Reed, Shana Johnson, Michelle Nash, Elaine Willis, Tom Kilker, Ron Wilson, Al Lustig, Michael Romano, Tim Holick, John McCarthy, Jeff Harshfield, Chris Thompson, Terri Harris, James Jean-Pierre, Eric Hudson, Lenard Everette, Marvin Spears, Sean Griffith, Tracy Powell, Charisse Smith, Pamela Bargeron, De Cavanuagh, Debi Baker, Ken & Lynn Shareef, Tonya Gaston, Johnny Howard, Cathy Buhring, Janee Goraum, Amy Covell, Sterling Wilson, Erika St. Jean, and Rodney Gillespie. I could go on and on listing names of colleagues who were/are a part of my past/present career—these are just a few. Please forgive me if you're a colleague not mentioned by name. Just know that in my heart I appreciate everyone who has provided me with so much opportunity to learn from them professionally.

To all the teams of which I've been a member and leader: The Tribe, Commandos, Pioneers, Storm and A-team. Without naming names, you all know who you are. Thank you for leading me, following me, but most importantly, standing beside me.

To my first editor and proofreader, as well as loving friend, Maeve Duffey: Thank you for not just cleaning up a very raw manuscript, but for helping me to shape some of my thoughts and feelings, and finally for ensuring a much more readable text. The fact that you provided this "gift from your heart" is a testament to your warm, loving nature. It is really cool that your talent has helped both Dad and me creatively express ourselves to the world.

To my second editor, Terri Liggins: Thank you for helping me bring alive something so personal, so painful and yet so joyful. You have an incredible gift and I am so appreciative of your input and insight.

To Norris Sumrall, Damali Hill, Rachel Webb, and to a few others who've asked to remain anonymous: Many thanks for your careful reviews and generous feedback.

To Les Brown, I am forever indebted for you lending your voice, your legacy to this book, and your inspiration to me!

I truly wish I could name ALL the friends and family who have played a role in my life, but that would mean many more pages, as well. So, to anyone I've come in contact with, you know my spirit and you know my love…

One love…

Jemal

Index

1 Ellsworth, Scott. <http://www.tulsareparations.org/TulsaRiot.htm>

2 "Chicago Housing Authority," The Electronic Encyclopedia of Chicago, 2005, 18 Oct. 2010 <http://encyclopedia.chicagohistory.org/pages/253.htm>.

3 Jones, J. (1981). "Bad blood: the Tuskegee syphilis experiment; a tragedy of race and medicine. NY: The Free Press

4 "Subculture," MSN Encarta, 7 Jun. 2010 <http://encarta.msn.com/encnet/features/dictionary/dictionaryhome.aspx>.

5 Glaze, Lauren E, "Probation and Parole in the United States, 2002," Bureau of Justice Statistics, 17 Aug. 2003, 7 Jun. 2010 <http://bjs.ojp.usdoj.gov/index.cfm?ty=pbdetail&iid=1110>.

6 Glaze, 4.

7 Conyers, John, ""Drug Laws and Policies: The Need for Reforms and Creative Solutions," Drug Policy Alliance, 7 Aug. 2004, 13 Jun. 2010 <http://www.drugpolicy.org/library/08_ 14_ 04conyers.cfm>.

8 U.S. Department of Justice, "Violent Crime: National Crime Victimization Survey," Apr. 1994, 13 Jun. 2010 <http://www.druglibrary.org/schaffer/govpubs/violent.txt>.

9 School Evaluation Services, "Gold Medal Schools," U.S. News and World Report, 12 Dec. 2007, 15 May 2010 <http://www.usnews.com/articles/education/high-schools/2007/11/29/gold-medal-schools.html>.

10 "About The University," Florida Agriculture and Mechanical University, 15 May 2010 <http://www.famu.edu/index.cfm?UniversityHistory>.

11 "Prominent Members of Alpha," Alpha Phi Alpha Fraternity, 25 Jun. 2010 <http://www.alpha-phi-alpha.com/Page.php?id=139>.

12 "Ranger School," Wikipedia, 25 Jun. 2010 <http://en.wikipedia.org/wiki/Ranger_ School>.

13 "Jet (magazine)," Wikipedia, 6 Aug. 2010 <http://en.wikipedia.org/wiki/Jet_ %28magazine%29>.

14 About the Museum," DuSable Museum of African American History, 6 Aug. 2010 <http://www.dusablemuseum.org/about>.

15 "HIV/AIDS FACT Sheet," The Henry J. Kaiser Family Foundation, Jul. 2007, 28 Jun. 2010 <http://kff.org/hivaids/upload/6089-04.pdf>, 1.

16 "Remembering Rosewood" <http://www.displaysforschools.com/history.html>

About the Author

Jemal Omar Gibson is a Regional Sales Director for AstraZeneca. He also served as an Officer in the U.S. Army as an Airborne Ranger. For years, he has actively worked toward many educational and mind-empowering initiatives both corporately and privately as a community leader and motivational speaker. He now hopes to inspire us all as a first time author. Jemal resides in the Atlanta, Georgia area with his wife, Lisa, and three daughters—Iman, Zhara, and Nadya.

To learn more, go to www.jemalgibson.com

Made in the USA
Charleston, SC
29 July 2011